THE ART OF
DELIBERATE
SUCCESS

To Alen,

With Best Wishes

to you.

David Keane

Praise for The Art of Deliberate Success

This excellent book reminds us of one of the most important facts in achieving success: that it happens as the result of deliberate choices and actions. If you want to make your approach to genuine achievement more rigorous and reliable, read it.

Tom Butler-Bowdon — author of *50 Success Classics* and *Never Too Late To Be Great*

In The Art of Deliberate Success, David Keane offers a guide for gaining true alignment as one of the few sustainable advantages in a relentlessly competitive environment. I would recommend it highly for the leaders and managers of any ambitious organisation.

Brad Jackson — Professor, The University of Auckland Business School

David is an astute observer of what's really going on! A prolific author and, dare I say it, a Thought Leader on the power of intention — being deliberate about what you want to create in your professional and personal world. He is a voice of reason in a world of confusion. His message is a calm call to remember what's true and what really matters.

Matt Church — founder of Thought Leaders Global and co-author of *Thought Leaders*

Dr Keane brilliantly tackles the issues of achieving success while at the same time dealing with the struggles of living a balanced life today. He lays out a game plan for success that anyone can understand and adapt to their circumstances, to increase their personal effectiveness, and turn intention into meaningful purpose and action.

Robyn Mackay — Manager of Learning and Development, Deloitte

Many development programs fall short as they fail to take into account the complexity of life. David Keane's work and book delivers on all counts. The depth and scope of the book is commendable and will prove to be a powerful and transformational experience for all readers.

Michael Henderson — corporate anthropologist

THE ART OF
DELIBERATE
SUCCESS

The 10 Behaviours of
Successful People

DAVID KEANE

JOSSEY-BASS
A Wiley Imprint
www.wiley.com

First published in 2013 by Jossey-Bass
an imprint of John Wiley & Sons Australia, Ltd
www.josseybass.com

42 McDougall St, Milton Qld 4064
Office also in Melbourne

Typeset in Garamond Regular 11.96/14.35

National Library of Australia Cataloguing-in-Publication data:

Author:	Keane, David
Title:	The Art of Deliberate Success: The 10 Behaviours of Successful People/David Keane.
ISBN:	9781118487648 (pbk.)
	9781118487754 (hbk.)
Notes:	Includes index.
Subjects:	Conduct of life.
	Success in business.
Dewey Number:	158.1

Cover design by Michael Freeland
Cover image: © Jupiter Images/F1 ONLINE
Internal design by Peter Reardon, pipelinedesign.com.au
'Slow Dance' by David L. Weatherford
'Management Time: Who's Got the Monkey?' by William Oncken Jr., Donald L. Wass and Stephen R. Covey, Harvard Business Review, November 1999
'Begin' by Brendan Kennelly, *The Essential Brendan Kennelly: Selected Poems with Live CD* (Bloodaxe Books, 2011)

Printed in Singapore by C.O.S Printers Pte Ltd
10 9 8 7 6 5 4 3

Limit of liability/Disclaimer of warranty:

To Carmel and Sinéad:
We are all in this one together.

And to the 860 workshop and coaching clients
who have taught me so much.

Contents

Contents

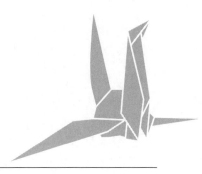

About the author

David Keane is an internationally renowned authority on human achievement and success. Through his keynote speeches, workshops, mentoring, writing and consulting he has transformed the lives of thousands of people.

His team of certified trainers deliver high-impact workshops and coaching programs to business, government and not-for-profit organisations throughout the world.

Dr Keane believes that all success, be it personal, professional or organisational, begins with individuals first taking 100 per cent responsibility for their own development. This 'inner-work' approach can initially seem daunting, but it is also incredibly empowering.

Clients include Accenture, ASB Bank, BP, Citigroup, Commonwealth Bank, Dell, Deloitte, Heinz, Hewlett-Packard, Kiwibank, McDonald's, Microsoft, the New Zealand Government, PricewaterhouseCoopers, Red Cross, Shell, Telstra and Westpac.

For more information, please visit the book and workshop website www.artofdeliberatesuccess.com or Dr Keane's own website www.drdavidkeane.com.

Prologue — living by choice,
not by chance

An unexamined life is not worth living.

— SOCRATES

Some years ago, a friend of mine, David Dier, died after a short illness. David was 37 and had a beautiful wife and a young family. At the time, his passing had a profound impact on me. On one level, I felt the obvious sadness of losing a good friend and the tragedy of his loss to his family. On another level, I really began to think about my own life and, in particular, the work I was doing coaching and working with people who wanted to achieve more success in their professional and personal lives.

I began to think more deeply about what it truly meant to be successful. For David Dier, being successful meant living every moment as if there was no tomorrow. David was full of life and energy. He loved to act on impulse and wasn't too concerned with what other people thought or said. At the same time, he was a careful planner, and was very deliberate in his professional life and with the work that he accomplished. Looking back on it now, I believe David certainly lived life to the full and I am sure he would have no regrets and no wishes to have done things differently. To me, David Dier is one of the most successful people I have ever known.

Following David's death, I wondered if all the research I had completed into the patterns and behaviours of successful leaders and managers might have a more general application to everyday life. This eventually led to the creation of a workshop and coaching program where, over the following five years, I worked intensively with more than 860 people from all walks of life. The people I worked with included artists and architects, business owners and bureaucrats, factory workers and firefighters, homemakers and health professionals, professors and pastors, scientists and songwriters, waiters and writers, and people who were so independently wealthy that their time was their own.

During the many workshops and, in particular, at many of the follow-up one on one coaching sessions, I began to see clear patterns emerging. People who were successful had achieved their success through conscious and deliberate choices or ways of being. In contrast, people who were less successful tended to live their lives in a more haphazard or indiscriminate way. In short, successful people lived their lives by choice, not by chance.

To complement my practical experience, I also embarked on a comprehensive study of the 'success' literature. I read several hundred books from the diverse fields of self-help, life coaching, time management, personal productivity, personal mastery, the psychology of achievement, spirituality and practical philosophy.

The book you are holding is my report to you of how successful people approach their lives. It represents my synthesis of what it really takes to be successful and is based on extensive study and research, combined with direct experience of what works in practice. It is also based on my journey as I attempt to live my life along the lines described between the covers of this book. If you would like to know more about me, my life and what I have done, you can read 'My story' at the back of the book.

It is my sincere wish that you take time to read this book carefully, reflect deeply on the ideas as they apply to you, and then take *action* to put in place any necessary changes to the way you live. It is also my wish that you share these ideas with those close to you. This is not only helpful for those you teach, but it also enables you to better appreciate the ideas for yourself. There is certainly truth in the saying that 'we learn best what we teach'.

What is success?

At my workshops, one of the first things I ask participants to do is to write down their definition of success. Before you read any further, please take one or two minutes to also do this. Thinking about your life in general, write down what it means for you to be successful.

If you're like most people, your definition of success may have included some elements from the following list:

- Achieving my goals.

- Being the mum or dad I am proud to be.

- Creating fulfilling relationships, especially within my family and close friends.

- Engaging in challenging and rewarding work.

- Enjoying a comfortable lifestyle.

- Enjoying work-life balance.

- Experiencing an exciting life where I am not afraid of taking risks.

- Experiencing intellectual stimulation and satisfaction.

- Feeling a sense of happiness.

- Gaining financial freedom and becoming free to make my own choices.

- Feeling content with who I am.

- Gaining the respect of my colleagues.

- Having security and stability.

- Leading or being at the top of my profession.

- Living an energetic and fun life.

- Living a healthy, fit and long life.

- Living a passionate life that is in alignment with my principles.

- Making a difference in the lives of others.

- Providing for my family.

Every time I do this exercise in workshops I am amazed by two things: first, how easily and quickly people are able to write down their ideas and, second, the vast range of responses that the exercise generates. These common aspects show that what it means to be successful is one of the most important questions on people's minds and also that how people answer that question is unique and meaningful to them. How you define success — consciously or unconsciously — has a profound impact on your day-to-day decision making, your priorities, and ultimately how your life unfolds.

One of my favourite stories illustrating the importance of defining success is the tale of the businessman who is walking along a beach at about 11 am. As he walks, he comes across a fisherman sitting on the sand enjoying the sunshine. He asks the fisherman what he is doing resting so early in the morning when clearly the weather is beautiful for fishing and his boat is just sitting there idle. The fisherman tells him that he was out early that morning, the fishing was good, and he caught enough to support himself and the needs of his family. And now, with his work done, he can simply sit down and enjoy the sunshine.

The businessman tells the fisherman that he is nowhere near fulfilling his potential and he should put more effort in, fish for longer, and then within no time he could have enough cash to buy a second and third boat, which would triple his income. The fisherman asks why he should do that, and the businessman tells him that with the strong cash flow, he could invest his money in a much bigger fleet of boats or, if he wanted to, he could horizontally integrate into fish processing or other businesses. And then within a few years, he could take his enterprise and potentially list it on the stock exchange, which would provide even greater capital for future investments.

Somewhat bemused, the fisherman asks the businessman, 'And then what would I do?'

'Well,' says the businessman, 'that's the best part — you would be so rich that you could spend your day sitting on the beach!'

What is REAL success?

Success is not to be pursued; it is to be attracted by the person you become.

— JIM ROHN

As the story about the fisherman illustrates, it is very important that you carefully define success in a way that makes sense for you. It really matters. Your definition governs every aspect of your behaviour, ranging from what you do for a living to your choice of life partner. It even influences how you spend your time and money. Only *you* can define the real meaning of success for you. Comparing yourself to other people is an absolutely pointless exercise.

Several of the definitions of success listed in the preceding section involve the 'achievement' of some goal or other. For many people, success is achieving financial independence, or arriving at a point in their lives where they have ultimate freedom in what they do and how they spend their time. I believe that the pursuit of this 'achievement' is one of the greatest causes of stress and unhappiness in our society today. It sets people up to be happy only when the goal is achieved. It seems that the time and effort leading up to the achievement is the price to pay for some future state of bliss. And, of course, we know what happens when we achieve a goal—yes, something else takes its place and the cycle begins again.

To overcome these problems, I suggest that real success can be defined simply as:

> *Being on the pathway to the achievement of worthwhile dreams—whatever these dreams may be.*

When you define success in this way—what I call *real success*—it provides several advantages. First, it allows you to make success personal—you use your dreams and choose what success means to you. Some people see success as having reached a certain level of accomplishment (for example, monetary wealth, a certain position within an organisation, power and influence, status or, indeed, fame). Others decide that success is achieving a work-life balance, reaching one's potential or engaging in work that makes a positive contribution to their local community. Still others have radically different ideas about what success means. The key here is to actively choose what success means *to you* and thereby escape the problem of living someone else's dream.

The second advantage of this definition is that success is now not something that is scarce or restricted to a few. Real success is possible for everyone because we all have different dreams and therefore are not competing with each other for some limited resource. When we look at it this way, we can be genuinely happy for the success of others as they move closer to what is important to them.

The third, and in my view most important, advantage of the above definition is the way it incorporates the idea of being on a pathway.

In my coaching work, I have noted that many people feel considerable frustration because they cannot see a connection between what they are doing each day and their larger goals. They live lives of 'quiet desperation' as they await states of happiness and fulfilment that are always around the next corner: the attainment of a promotion, fully grown kids, more leisure hours or some other future scenario. The problem with this approach is your ideal future never really comes — there is always something else you desire — and in the meantime you are bound to be dissatisfied.

By thinking about success as a pathway, you immediately feel more satisfaction in your life because you can enjoy the feeling of knowing that what you are doing right now is moving you to where you want to be.

The idea of the pathway takes on profound significance when the time comes for you to die. If your life happens to be long, you can look back from your deathbed knowing that you travelled some worthwhile paths and perhaps even achieved some worthwhile dreams. If, on the other hand, like David Dier your life is unexpectedly cut short, it would be satisfying to know that at least you were on the way to worthwhile dreams and had even made some progress on these pathways.

It is therefore very important that you consciously identify what your dreams are and live every day knowing that you are on that pathway. To do so is to create your unique meaning of success — one that resonates with you and is relevant to your life and circumstances. As you shall see as you read through this book, it is vitally important to know what success really means so that you can live a truly fulfilling life, without regret. You can begin to live your life by choice, not by chance.

The power of purpose

The three components of happiness are something to do, someone to love, and something to look forward to.

— GORDON LIVINGSTON

When you know what you mean by real success, you have a real sense of purpose in your life. And with this purpose in mind, you can work on yourself every day to ensure that you move further along the pathway.

I have noticed that successful people work first and foremost on themselves — they see their development as an 'inside job', as I like to put it. Instead of blaming circumstances, or the situations in which they find themselves, for them not achieving their goals, they work on improving their own skills so that, over time, they get better and better. As business philosopher Jim Rohn says, 'Don't wish it was easier, wish you were better'.

I have also observed that some smart organisations are recognising the importance of aligning the personal goals and aspirations of employees with what their organisations are trying to achieve. With more and more high-skill, knowledge-based workplaces, many workers now choose their place of employment based on the accuracy of this fit. One human resources director I worked with has asserted that 'in the war for talent, alignment is key'. When you feel a strong sense of alignment with your work, you develop an eagerness to learn more and to apply what you are learning. You also become highly energised because you know in your heart that what you are doing today is contributing to your tomorrow.

Before giving you an overview of the chapters to come, and some advice about their practical application, I want to draw your attention to three myths that have a big impact on our lives. These are the myths of the stressfulness of life, the goal of happiness, and the notion that busy is best.

Myth 1: life is stressful

In survey after survey, 'stress' is identified as one of the most pressing problems of our age. Indeed, for organisations, 'stress' has major implications as it is the prime contributor to absenteeism, workplace conflict, low productivity and low morale. It is also behind the reported phenomenon of 'presenteeism', a situation where employees are physically present but their minds are not on the job. One study conducted by researchers at Tufts-New England Medical Center in Boston and reported in the *Harvard Business Review* found that presenteeism was costing employers far more than absenteeism.

During my workshops, I ask participants to identify the causes of stress in their lives. All can easily generate a long list of factors, such as financial woes, relationships, childcare, ageing parents, work-life imbalance, unclear expectations at work, or too much to do with too little time. I then ask the participants to examine these factors one by one, with the aim of isolating the underlying reason each factor causes them stress. In 100 per cent of cases, it is not the factor itself that is stressful but the participants' *reaction* to the factor that causes them stress. This is a very important point. Once recognised, it can fundamentally change your life. In simple terms, it means that you can choose to be stressed or not.

Now, in putting forward this argument, I am aware that some stress — which I prefer to call pressure — is actually healthy and useful. It helps us to get out of bed in the morning and raises our energy levels when there is a task to be done. The interesting question is at what point does stress turn from being healthy to unhelpful and potentially destructive?

I believe that you already know the answer to this question. If you look at situations where you were in the unhealthy zone, you will notice telltale aspects of your behaviour. For example, some people become very quiet and introverted; some develop a short fuse and become irritable; while others develop excessive behaviours such as eating, drinking or even sleeping too much. I know one person who knows she is stressed when a rash appears on the inside of her left wrist!

The key point here is for you to develop an awareness of the signals that indicate you are moving from feeling healthy pressure to unhealthy stress. When you become sensitive to stress in this way, you can take action and make decisions that dramatically reduce the problems of stress in your life. This, then, is one of the most important steps towards becoming successful. It is becoming so self-aware that you can actually use stress to your advantage.

Myth 2: happiness is the goal

If your goal in life is to be happy, I can guarantee that you never will be. Now that is a strong statement, but I wanted to make it clearly so that you would be shocked and perhaps look at the idea of happiness again.

In the exercise I outline at the start of the prologue, many people write down that being happy is what they really mean by being successful. The trouble with happiness is that it is a feeling that gains a momentary foothold, but then is replaced by other feelings. It's a bit like the sun on your face: wonderful while it lasts, but after some time the clouds come.

If we set up our lives seeking happiness, we are assured of disappointment. In my coaching work, I have seen that people who are driven by the search of happiness are never really successful because their mental state is highly volatile and unreliable. The quality of their lives is determined by what happened yesterday (or five minutes ago), and they are constantly seeking the next 'high' to make them happy. This self-perpetuating state of dissatisfaction explains why, for some people, spending money, eating and drinking, or even working hard can become such addictive activities.

In my experience, it is far better to see happiness not so much as a goal or something to be achieved, but rather as a result or by-product of doing something else. And the best way I know of doing that is to make 'living a life of purpose' your primary motivation. When you know what your purpose is, and live every day moving closer and closer to what is important, happiness is what you get. Happiness, therefore, is not something you go after. It comes to you.

Myth 3: busy is best

How often have you been asked if you are busy? It's a most interesting question because behind it lurk some fundamental assumptions that colour how you might answer—irrespective of the truth. Perhaps the most significant assumption is that being busy is a good thing. And, conversely, not being busy—being idle—is undesirable. For some reason, people assume that to be busy is to be productive and, by extension, content.

Now you may think I am harping on a technicality here, but I am convinced that this one question has a profound influence on how we live and the results we get in our lives. To test this, the next time you are asked the question, 'Are you busy?' simply say 'no' or 'not really' and see what kind of reaction you get. You may hear, 'Oh dear, what's wrong?', 'It will come right' or, my personal favourite, 'Lucky for some'—in other words, 'I am busy and you should be too'. If you are feeling really adventurous, you could try it with your boss and see what happens. The most likely outcome is that you are given more work to do!

The problem is that this mistaken logic is so ingrained in our culture that we don't even notice it. For example, people who are seen to be the busiest are more sought after and more highly rewarded in organisations.

And, if you are a parent, there is thought to be something wrong with you unless you are constantly ferrying your kids from one sporting activity to the next. The implication here is that being busy is socially acceptable and normal, while not being busy is abnormal. This leads people to generate busyness in their lives for the sake of being busy.

It is far better to be busy with the things that really matter and to ignore the things that are not that important. In this way, you can really focus and do your best on things that are moving you closer to real success. Incidentally, my answer to the question 'Are you busy?' is, 'I am as busy as I choose to be!'

On being DELIBERATE

The purpose of this book is to help you uncover your own version of what it means to be really successful and then give you a practical framework, along with tools and techniques, to help you on your way. I use the word 'uncover' because many people live life without reference to what it means to them to be successful. In effect, their definition of real success is cloaked over or even wholly unexplored, resulting in a life of considerable frustration. In my experience, successful people make very deliberate choices about how to organise their lives and, moreover, have a clear idea about their priorities each day.

To help explain the various patterns and behaviours of real success, I contend that successful people live DELIBERATE lives. A deliberate life is one where the person actively chooses certain ways of thinking and acting. This is in contrast to a passive life, where the person feels like a victim of circumstance without any real choice or control over what happens to him or her. To further explain Deliberate Success and give a structure to this book, I have taken the 10 letters of the word D·E·L·I·B·E·R·A·T·E, aligned a key element of what a really successful life looks like to each letter and then written a corresponding chapter. The following is an overview of these chapters.

D: Decide

Almost without exception, successful people take the time to articulate exactly what they want their lives to be about. For them, success is no accident, nor is it a result of being 'lucky'—in contrast, they are focused on exactly what it is they want to achieve.

While successful people are realistic enough to know that things never work out exactly as planned, they understand that it is better to be moving in some direction rather than simply living day-to-day, opportunistic lives. They know that deciding on a direction means they are more likely to identify and seize opportunities that move them closer to what matters most.

In chapter 1, I help you look at these fundamental issues and provide you with practical tools that you can use every day of your life. More specifically, I help you to develop your Unique Life Purpose (ULP) statement and a set of campaigns that will provide you with a mental compass for your daily living.

E: Eliminate

For many of us, our lives are far too complex. Successful people know that less is indeed more. By removing all kinds of clutter and excess from their lives, successful people are able to concentrate on what is truly important. Clutter can take many forms, including too many material possessions and untidy work environments. A common cause of clutter can be not knowing what to eliminate and what to keep.

Another form of excess may be the relationships in your life. Successful people are masters of managing their network of friends, colleagues and associates and ensuring that their relationships are closely aligned to their goals and aspirations. This may involve actively eliminating some relationships and fostering others.

Chapter 2, therefore, takes you on a journey where you have an opportunity to systematically 'audit' the different aspects of your life. The key word in this chapter is *simplify*. You may be surprised by how cluttered your life actually is!

L: Language

We can tell so much about people by the words and language they use. If you carefully listen to successful people, you will notice that they use positive language and 'can do' words. In fact, they realise that by seeing the glass as half-full, they will attract other positive people into their lives. Positive people help us achieve our goals far more quickly than negative people do.

Successful people have also developed the habit of using positive language in their self-talk. By doing so, they effectively program themselves to continually move towards what is important despite apparent setbacks or problems. In contrast, less successful people, because of their negative internal language, are easily discouraged and give up far too quickly.

Chapter 3 gives you definite ideas to help ensure that the language you use—both externally and internally—moves your life in a positive direction.

I: Information

Every person has a unique way of working with information. For example, some of us prefer to read and reflect, while others like to discuss, debate and decide quickly. Others still are highly visual and think in pictures. While our unique style is not important, what matters is that we know our preferences and organise our lives to reflect what works best for us.

By being deliberate about how we work with information, we can organise our lives and use technology appropriately. This affects how we use email, how well our filing systems serve us, how well we organise our computer data and, ultimately, how effective we are at identifying key issues and acting on what is most important.

Chapter 4, then, helps you to develop a way of working with information that best matches your unique circumstances. Again, I predict that you will be surprised by what you find out about yourself.

B: Beliefs

When we take the time and care to deliberately articulate what we believe in, we greatly simplify our daily living. You will notice that successful people have an inner stability and calmness that comes from knowing what they are truly about. As a result, they are less influenced by temporary setbacks. They know that setbacks will occur, but they see these as starting blocks, not stumbling blocks.

In contrast, less successful people tend to be driven by what other people think of them and, as a result, make decisions that reflect their need for external approval. Such uncertainty leads to fickle behaviour, unreliability and, ultimately, a life without direction.

The beliefs you hold are of critical importance and, accordingly, the purpose of chapter 5 is to review what you believe and what you don't. When you are really clear about your beliefs, the quality of your life is greatly enhanced.

E: Energy

Being able to effectively manage our energy levels is critical. Without energy, we simply do not have the strength to perform what needs to be done. Successful people deliberately manage their energy in four key areas: body, mind, emotions and spirit.

Taking good care of your body is the first step towards effectively managing your energy levels. With a plan of care covering nutrition, regular and appropriate exercise, and proper rest you lay the foundation for having sufficient energy.

As well as excellent physical self-care, you also need to take care of your mind. Through learning various exercises and techniques, it is possible to expand your mental capacity enormously and to hone your powers of attention.

While physical and mental wellness is foundational to increasing our energy levels, actively managing our emotions is equally critical. With practice, you can develop the skill of managing your emotions so that you are not controlled by your feelings. The successful people I have worked with have mastered this skill and, as a result, they handle pressure better and are much more adept at dealing with stress.

At the end of the day, it is having a strong spirit that gives meaning to our lives. When people have spirit, they feel a connection between what they are doing and what they consider to be the purpose of their life. Without this connection, life is just a series of disconnected events that do not contribute to the bigger picture of who we want to be.

Chapter 6, therefore, explores several ways of enhancing your energy by providing you with a series of tools and suggestions that you can put into practice right away. You will also identify your greatest energy sappers and learn ways of avoiding them.

R: Responsibility

Successful people accept 100 per cent responsibility for their lives. They clearly see that the situation they find themselves in is not an accident, but the result of choices that they have made in the past. For many people, this is hard medicine to take. Many of us live our lives blaming others (or our organisation or the government) and regarding ourselves as victims of circumstance.

When you deliberately choose to accept total responsibility, your life begins to change in a fundamental way. By realising that your current life is the result of past decisions, it follows that the shape of your future will be determined by the decisions of today. It is, therefore, logical to conclude that choice is always available to you, and that it is the consequences of your choices — not the actions of others — that determine your future.

The purpose of chapter 7 is to shock you. My experience in workshops is that people sometimes need to be stopped in their tracks and made to look in the mirror. Amazingly, once you take full responsibility for your life and begin to live accordingly, you dramatically reduce the amount of unwanted stress in your life.

A: Action

Without action, nothing happens. The successful people I have worked with are experts at directing their energy to where it is most needed. They know that all the planning and goal-setting in the world is wasted without action. Effective action begins with making a direct connection between what needs to be done and your unique purpose and goals. If that connection is crystal clear, procrastination is easily overcome, motivation is high and energy flows to get the task done.

Successful people can maintain 100 per cent focus on the task in front of them without the distraction of other priorities. In my experience, this is a skill that can be learned and chapter 8 shows you how.

T: Time

We do not manage time — we manage the use of our time. Because each of us has exactly the same amount of time available — 168 hours per week — the choices we make about the use of these hours is what determines the outcomes we generate in our life. Successful people have worked out ways of planning the use of their time so that their energies are directed to what matters most to them. They work in a focused way so as to make the time available really count — and then they stop when it's time to stop.

Chapter 9 gives you the very best advice about using your time well. You will learn a range of techniques and tips that will ensure that you get the best out of every hour. Paradoxically, being deliberate about your time involves doing *less*—by being less busy, you actually achieve more.

E: Evaluate

By deliberately putting in place ways of evaluating your performance you can accurately measure your progress towards what is important to you. This feedback is critical in maintaining your energy and in making sure that your goals continue to reflect what you truly want. Successful people seek out feedback because they are constantly looking for ways of improving their performance. In this final chapter, I show you how to measure what matters and to learn from your experiences.

In essence, if you are being DELIBERATE, you can build the life you want by focusing on these 10 different aspects of your life. You will notice that the power of this approach comes not only from the care and attention you give to each of the elements, but from the *integration* between the parts. This book not only provides you with individual good ideas, but it also gives you something far more significant: a coherent framework for living your best life.

How to get the most from this book

It is my sincere wish that you find this book to be of practical value. You will notice that, beyond this prologue, there are 10 chapters, each focusing on a different aspect of being DELIBERATE. Each chapter is further divided into 10 areas that require your attention. The epilogue deals with keeping your motivation high and learning to live with greater success in your life. Along the way, you'll encounter many insights, quotations and gems of wisdom from those who have journeyed before you.

To help increase the practical value of the book, I have devised a simple self-assessment quiz that measures the amount of deliberateness in your life. The Deliberate Quotient (DQ)® Quiz contains 100 questions and is designed to focus your attention on a range of issues and, ultimately, to prompt you into making targeted changes. The DQ Quiz follows this prologue and can also be taken online at www.artofdeliberatesuccess.com.

If you want, you can score the quiz online, email the results to yourself, and save them for future reference. (Your code for accessing the online quiz is provided at the start of the DQ Quiz in this book.)

The DQ Quiz is not a scientific or precise instrument but rather is a simple self-assessment tool for heightening your awareness of the level of deliberateness in your life. Likewise, your DQ score is only of value to you and it does not make sense to compare your score with other people, who will undoubtedly score themselves differently from you.

One approach to getting the most out of this book is to quickly scan each of the chapters and then take the entire DQ Quiz before reading the individual chapters in detail—some of which you may choose to prioritise over others, depending on your results. If you do decide to complete the quiz before a full reading of each chapter, you may find that in the initial reading of the quiz you wonder about the meaning or intent of some of the questions. This is normal so do not be discouraged—remember you have not read the book yet! If you are unsure of the meaning, simply give yourself a '5' and move on to the next question.

Following this initial taking of the quiz, I recommend that you read, understand and *apply* the ideas from each of the 10 chapters, and a good way to do this is to focus on one chapter each week for 10 weeks. In particular, I encourage you to do the application exercises at the end of the chapters. Then, at the end of each week, retake just that section of the DQ Quiz. This allows you to experience and apply the ideas for real and then come to a realistic assessment of how deliberate you are in each of the areas. At the end of the 10 weeks, you can total your revised scores, divide by 10, and arrive at your 'new' DQ percentage.

Of course, the real power of the DQ approach is that it allows you to quickly identify those areas of your life that require the most attention and work. My advice is to focus on just one or two areas at a time. When you feel that you have done enough work in that area, you can move to the next area for improvement. From time to time, you can retake the entire quiz (every three months is good) to get an updated measure of your DQ score. Hopefully, your score increases over time!

I further recommend that January and July are good months in which to take the quiz—January is a time of new beginnings, while July is half-time—in this way you can remind yourself of the key concepts while finetuning what is already working well for you. Re-reading the book every year—perhaps at Christmas time—is also a good idea.

You may also find it helpful to involve your partner, friends or work colleagues in the DQ Quiz by asking them to try it for themselves. As well as helping others in their lives, you get the benefit of their ongoing support and encouragement as you go about making changes to your life for the better.

As you read each chapter, I encourage you to read with an open mind and to think about what will work for you in your unique life situation. I wish you well as you begin to live your life by choice and not just by chance.

There are only two ways to live your life. One is as though nothing is a miracle. The other is as though everything is a miracle.

—ALBERT EINSTEIN

The Deliberate Quotient (DQ)® Quiz

Register online for your free subscription

The online version of the quiz at www.artofdeliberatesuccess. com calculates your DQ results automatically and displays them graphically. Use this code to register on the website and take the quiz:

A13PB-5HY76-KY863

The quiz is designed to help you formally review various aspects of your professional and personal life so you can identify your strengths along with opportunities for improvement. It takes about 20 minutes to complete.

There are 100 questions in the quiz — 10 for each of the 10 aspects of being DELIBERATE. The idea is to look at each question and then score yourself on a scale of 0 to 10. You are scoring yourself on the basis of your *current behaviour*, not what you aspire to. It's best not to think about the answers for too long. Go with your initial intuition.

Each question is prompted by the phrase 'To what extent do I…'. Register your level of agreement as follows:

10 Fully agree; 100 per cent; every time; certain
5 Sometimes agree; likely, but not always; I'm not sure
0 Disagree; no way; cannot see it happening; never

Score yourself any number between 0 and 10 for each question.

If you have difficulty with any of the questions, reading the relevant section of the book will help you.

When you have responded to all the questions, go back and add up your score for each of the 10 aspects and then enter your totals on the results page.

 Decide

Be black and white about what's important to you.

DECIDE — what's important	Score (0–10)
To what extent do I...	
1 Have clarity about what I value most (and least)	
2 Know what I want to have, do and be	
3 Know what 'enough' means for me	
4 Have a well-crafted Unique Life Purpose (ULP)	
5 Choose my campaigns so that I know what is important to me and can plan accordingly	
6 Discuss my ULP and campaigns with my partner, selected family and selected friends	
7 Have specific time-limited goals defined for particular campaigns	
8 See a clear connection between what is important to me and the work that I do	
9 Carry a written statement of who I am, my values and what I'm aiming towards	
10 Set triggers in my life to automatically reinforce my ULP as I go about my day	
Total for *Decide*	

✳ Eliminate

Stop the things in your life that don't
really matter.

ELIMINATE — focusing on the important	Score (0–10)
To what extent do I …	
11 Acknowledge that the fulfilment of my desires influences my life	
12 Keep an accurate list of everything I own	
13 Review what I own in the light of my ULP, values and goals	
14 Take steps to remove items from my life that are no longer relevant	
15 Remove clutter from my workspace	
16 Honestly review my relationships with family, friends and associates	
17 Terminate or reduce relationships that are not offering me value	
18 Identify relationships I want to build/foster	
19 Eliminate all unnecessary responsibilities or tasks that belong to someone else	
20 Continuously strive to simplify my life and reduce unnecessary complexity	
Total for *Eliminate*	

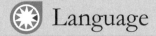 Language

*Your internal voice creates you—make it soothing like
the sound of the aqua ocean.*

LANGUAGE — your internal soundtrack	Score (0–10)
To what extent do I...	
21 Notice my language and the words I use	
22 Study other successful people and the words they use	
23 Actively work to expand my vocabulary	
24 Recognise reactive language and avoid using it (for example, must, if only, have to, but)	
25 Frequently give thanks for what I have	
26 Cultivate an abundance mentality within myself and others	
27 Observe how my inner voice influences my performance	
28 Consciously choose the inner talk or soundtrack that plays within my head	
29 Seek out people who are vibrant and speak positively	
30 Read books and listen to audio that I find uplifting	
Total for *Language*	

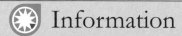

Information

The colour of newsprint reminds us to be discerning in an information-soaked word.

INFORMATION — managing inward and outward flows	Score (0–10)
To what extent do I…	
31 Understand my unique information management patterns	
32 Know the advantages and disadvantages of different modes of communication	
33 Take care to adjust my mode of communication to suit particular circumstances	
34 Have strategies in place for handling and storing incoming information	
35 Develop skills of effective information handling such as speed reading, key issue identification and creativity	
36 Know my limits and avoid information overload	
37 Make my electronic files easily accessible thanks to a logical filing system	
38 Regularly maintain my computer to ensure efficient performance and data security	
39 Continue to upskill myself in the use of various technologies	
40 Feel in control of the technology I use	
Total for *Information*	

✺ Beliefs

We believe that the sky is blue when, in fact, it's mostly pink.
Where else are we mistaken?

BELIEFS — guiding your behaviour	Score (0–10)
To what extent do I...	
41 Know my own beliefs and what is important to me	
42 Feel calm and authentic when I recall my beliefs	
43 Bounce back from setbacks or 'failures'	
44 Live my life according to my beliefs and not other people's	
45 Understand that how busy I am is independent of how successful I am	
46 Reject the idea that other people are more deserving of success than I am	
47 Believe that all the resources I need to be successful will become available to me	
48 Believe that my current situation can be changed in all respects	
49 Regularly recall my list of affirmations	
50 Continually review my beliefs so that they are in alignment with my ULP	
Total for *Beliefs*	

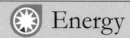 Energy

Oranges are a source of energy and vitality. How many such sources
do you have in your life?

ENERGY — synchronising your body and mind	Score (0–10)
To what extent do I...	
51 Know what times of day I work most productively and take advantage of these	
52 Eat well and get appropriate exercise	
53 Get proper and sufficient sleep	
54 Nurture and care for my mind so it can be the best it can be	
55 Use the power of attention to focus my mind and banish distraction	
56 Control my emotions so that they don't control me	
57 Actively manage my greatest energy sappers	
58 Regularly get outdoors to experience the vastness and magnificence of the world I live in	
59 See a connection between the life I am living and my ULP	
60 Still my mind through the practice of some form of meditation	
Total for *Energy*	

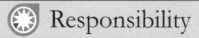 Responsibility

When you happily accept complete responsibility for your life
you see things in a new way.

RESPONSIBILITY — accepting and taking ownership	Score (0–10)
To what extent do I…	
61 Accept responsibility for my life and what happens to me	
62 Acknowledge that my current circumstances are a result of my prior decisions	
63 Believe that the future can be different from the past	
64 Believe that choice is always available	
65 Acknowledge in advance that not everything will work out as planned when I make decisions	
66 Learn from failure and move on	
67 Say 'sorry' quickly, when I need to	
68 Say 'no' to responsibilities that are not mine	
69 Take personal responsibility for the level of stress in my life	
70 Provide an example to family, friends and associates of someone who accepts responsibility	
Total for *Responsibility*	

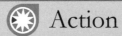 Action

Go and take action in ways that bring out
the best in you.

ACTION – getting work done	Score (0–10)
To what extent do I…	
71 Make a conscious link between the task in front of me and my ULP before I begin working	
72 Overcome procrastination and get on with what needs to be done	
73 Operate 'in the zone' so that I am really absorbed by the task in front of me	
74 Have no attachment to the work or the outcome, but simply attend to what needs to be done	
75 Reconnect with sensory awareness (sight, touch, smell, hearing and taste) if my mind wanders while performing tasks	
76 Work calmly and efficiently	
77 Keep focused without getting distracted by other less important tasks	
78 Take short pauses between different tasks or activities	
79 Avoid 'multi-tasking' where possible	
80 Stop when it's time to stop	
Total for *Action*	

 Time

*Purple is the colour of royalty. Be the king or queen of
your most important resource—time.*

TIME — achieving your priorities	Score (0–10)
To what extent do I...	
81 Schedule time for planning the week ahead	
82 Assess which tasks are most important and prioritise them	
83 Bear in mind my unique energy cycle in planning my days	
84 Think about my campaigns when planning my week	
85 Chunk my time so that I can focus on important tasks without distraction for certain periods of time	
86 Know, in dollar terms, how much my time is worth per hour	
87 Say 'no' to things that are not important	
88 Identify and avoid my biggest time wasters	
89 Live by choice and not by chance	
90 Maintain flexibility so that I can seize unexpected opportunities when they arise	
Total for *Time*	

✳ Evaluate

*Regularly get your blue pen out and formally review
how you're going.*

EVALUATE — managing your overall performance	Score (0–10)
To what extent do I…	
91 Seek to learn from my past with the intention of improving for the future	
92 Know what I want to measure and track within my life	
93 Have systems in place to collect information about my performance	
94 Regularly review my progress in various performance areas	
95 Evaluate myself according my own goals rather than comparing myself to others	
96 Celebrate what has worked well	
97 Identify, plan and document areas of strength and weakness for improvement	
98 Ask for help when I need it	
99 Refuse to be discouraged and maintain a positive attitude	
100 Remember that REAL Success is being on the pathway towards achieving my dreams, not having achieved them	
Total for *Evaluate*	

✹ DQ results page

1   Transfer the scores from each of the 10 sections and add them up to find your overall total:

ASPECT	Total score
Decide	
Eliminate	
Language	
Information	
Beliefs	
Energy	
Responsibility	
Action	
Time	
Evaluate	
Overall total	

Divide the overall total by 10 to calculate your DQ percentage:

My DQ percentage is: x per cent

2   Looking at the total scores above, my two highest scoring aspects are:

Strength 1: _____

Strength 2: _____

3   Looking at the total scores above, my two lowest scoring aspects are:

Weakness 1: _____

Weakness 2: _____

4   Now work on a plan to develop your strengths and tackle your weaknesses. Begin by (re-)reading the relevant chapters of this book.

Decide — what's important

The purpose of life is to live a life of purpose.

— RICHARD LEIDER

As I begin to write this chapter, I am looking up at the framed quotation on the wall over my desk. The quotation reads:

When you are inspired by some great purpose, some extraordinary project, all your thoughts break their bonds; your mind transcends limitations, your consciousness expands in every direction, and you find yourself in a new, great and wonderful world. Dormant forces, faculties and talents become alive and you discover yourself to be a greater person by far than you ever dreamed yourself to be.

— PATANJALI

As far as we know, Patanjali lived almost 2500 years ago in India where he led a simple life as a mystic and philosopher. I really like this quotation because, for me, it shows the great power in having a clear purpose to your life. Just imagine your consciousness expanding in every direction and dormant forces becoming alive in you. It's wonderfully motivating and inspiring.

Now here is the most amazing — and tragic — thing: most people are unclear about their main purpose in life. They live what I call 'lives of drift', where they simply go from one day to the next, doing the same old thing in the same old way, and then wondering why their lives are so boring or why they never make any progress towards what they really want to do. Some may even have dreams of their future, but generally these dreams are so vague or unrealistic that they cause people to be disheartened even before they begin to make progress. The purpose of this chapter, therefore, is to help you become crystal clear about what is important to you. But before we begin this process, it is useful to consider why so many people do not take the time to clarify their real objectives in life.

Brian Tracy, who in the course of more than 30 years has helped more than four million people clarify their goals, estimates that only 2 per cent of people in the developed world have a clearly defined sense of purpose. Based on my own experience, I agree with Tracy's assessment. The interesting aspect to consider is why, and there are three basic reasons: lack of knowledge, lack of know-how, and fear.

The first of these, lack of knowledge, is to do with not understanding how a clearly defined purpose can affect every area of your life. When we are clear about what is important to us, we begin to notice new things. People and opportunities that we might not have noticed before suddenly become relevant and of interest to us. As a child, you may have played that game where you counted cars of a specific colour—say, yellow—as a way of passing the time on a journey. When playing that game, your attention was on yellow and even from afar you could identify that colour on cars or trucks coming out of side roads. Now the interesting point here is that after the game, if you were asked how many blue cars passed your way, you would have been stumped. It's the same way with your life: being clear about what you're looking for and what really matters focuses your attention on the *right* things and, moreover, prevents you from missing opportunities that may have been staring you in the face all along.

In other words, when you are clear about your purpose, your attention becomes focused in a way that allows you to identify opportunities as they emerge in your life. You can recognise these for what they are—fantastic chances to move closer to where you actually want to be. This phenomenon has been well documented for centuries, and some of the most successful people in history have applied this 'secret' to their lives. According to one classic book, *Think and Grow Rich* by Napoleon Hill (originally published in 1937), the key to success is 'definiteness of purpose'. As Hill so beautifully puts it, 'what the mind can conceive, and believe, it can achieve'.

In more recent times, Rhonda Byrne's book and movie *The Secret* has repackaged these fundamental ideas for the modern era. Byrne strongly makes the point that by being clear you invoke the Law of Attraction—'what you think about, you bring about'—and begin to make it work for rather than against you. While Byrne's book and movie have received a mixed response (some critics have argued that her approach is too simplistic and too materialistic) she has nonetheless awakened interest in the considerable power of merely *thinking* about what it is you are trying to achieve.

To be clear about your life purpose is to discover a solid point of reference for day-to-day decision making. That is, you have a way of assessing value as different opportunities and challenges come your way. Without this clarity, everything is equally unimportant and, therefore, being decisive is extremely challenging and stressful. With life purpose clarity, you have a mental compass to help and guide you.

The second reason why you may lack clarity about your life purpose is that you simply may not know how to arrive at that clarity. This chapter will change all that! In my experience, the task of clarifying is a process rather than an instantaneous event. It's not just a question of taking a few minutes to think about your life and then writing something that sounds good. As we'll see, it is a process that demands some deep thinking and perhaps even some sharp interrogation of the ideas you have lived with for a while. Many people 'think' they know what is important, but there is a big difference between vaguely thinking and really knowing.

The difficulty for most people is that they have not taken time away from their busy lives to honestly ask themselves the deep questions that are within all of us but seldom addressed consciously. Questions such as: What do I really value? What is important to me above all else? Given the choice, how would I decide between opportunities that may pull me in conflicting directions? Later in this chapter, I suggest a way you can take the time to really reflect on your life and uncover your answers to these questions.

The third impediment to establishing a clear life purpose can be summed up in one word: fear. It is the fear of discovering that your life up until now has been a lie. Sometimes in my workshops people get very emotional when they are given the opportunity to read out what they have written about their lives and what is now important to them. There can be tears of regret when they realise that they have been living their life unconsciously or without any real direction. At the same time, these tears can quickly become tears of joy as, perhaps for the first time in their lives, they can say who they really are and what is important now. It is literally the first day of the rest of their life.

So no matter how you have lived in the past, or how old you are, this book offers you a unique and wonderful opportunity to live more consciously and deliberately.

In the 10 sections that follow in this chapter, we'll explore different strategies for working out what is important to you. We'll begin with the idea that everything we do is governed by our values. Each of us has unique values and it is critical that you know what yours are. Then we'll move on to discover what you want to have, do and be in your life. This is where you chart your destination in life—a destination that is without limits and where everything is possible. Next, we'll look at the idea of 'enough'. Here you have the opportunity to say what enough is for you. There is no point in going after something if you already have it!

With all this preparation done, we will be at the exciting point of writing your Unique Life Purpose (ULP) statement. Your ULP is that mental compass we discussed earlier, which is designed to help you make good decisions. With your ULP in place, we will take a further step and create a set of 'campaigns' that reflect your ULP and allow you to take action to achieve real success.

Finally, the later sections of this chapter deal with finetuning your ULP and campaigns. They provide an indispensable toolkit for setting goals, aligning your personal and professional goals, and living every day deliberately—so it's important to get them right.

Note: In the sections that follow, you are invited to do some writing to help you clarify what is important to you. You may find it helpful to get a pen and a notepad now so you can record your thoughts. Alternatively, each of the tables from this chapter are available from the book website www.artofdeliberatesuccess.com. To access the tables on the website, you'll need the code provided at the start of the DQ Quiz in this book.

Let's get started.

Your values

Your values provide you with an opportunity to stamp your preferences all over your life.
—MICHAEL HENDERSON

At the core of your being is a set of values that govern every aspect of your life. For most of us, these values are hidden in such a way that we don't even notice them at work. And yet these values give your life meaning and direction in a most fundamental way. They are the reason you prefer one course of action over another, and know the difference between right and wrong. In other words, your values are beacons that guide you through life. They tend to be very stable and do not usually change dramatically. Indeed, our values are largely determined during our early childhood, through the influence of parents, teachers and the wider culture in which we are brought up. Certain values might be emphasised: achievement, courage, creativity, honesty or wealth, for example. There are, of course, many, many more.

While our values may not necessarily change, what can happen, over time, is that the *priority* we attach to our values might alter depending on our stage of life. For example, at 35, a person might emphasise the importance of wealth while at the same time valuing creativity. As that person ages, creativity might become the dominant value that gives most meaning to life. That's why it is so important to know your values and to recognise how and why you are prioritising them. So, what are your values? One good way to begin this discovery is not to think about yourself at all. Yes, you read that right!

To begin, think about two people you know well and who you really admire. They could be friends, colleagues, your boss, your partner or anyone who has had a positive influence on your life. The people you are thinking about don't need to be currently in your life — they could be from the past. Now, for each of these inspiring people, make a list as outlined in table 1.1 of the specific characteristics you admire in them.

Table 1.1: characteristics of people I admire

Person 1	Person 2
1 _____	1 _____
2 _____	2 _____
3 _____	3 _____
4 _____	4 _____
5 _____	5 _____
and so on...	

What you will notice about each of these people is they have characteristics that you yourself value. In other words, when we admire someone, it is not the person as such but rather what they represent that most attracts us to them. The values that you are attracted to are, in essence, your values—even if you think that a certain person embodies them more successfully than you do.

To go further with this, you could also do this exercise using people for whom you have little or no respect. Again, choose two people from your current or past life, and this time list the characteristics that most repulse you (as shown in table 1.2).

Table 1.2: characteristics of people I dislike

Person 1	Person 2
1 _____	1 _____
2 _____	2 _____
3 _____	3 _____
4 _____	4 _____
5 _____	5 _____
and so on...	

You will notice with this exercise that you have listed values that you either don't share or which you would be reluctant to acknowledge within yourself.

Now that you are getting a sense of what your core values may be, it is useful to broaden the scope of your search by systematically looking at other, perhaps less obvious, values that may be important to you. Table 1.3 is designed to prompt your thinking. The trick is to read through the entire list before beginning the next exercise.

Table 1.3: a list of values that may be important to you

Value description	Not important	Somewhat important	Very important
Achievement (results, tasks completed)			
Adventure (new experiences, challenges, excitement)			
Artistic expression (drama, painting, literature)			
Balance (proper attention to each area of life)			
Competition (desire to win, to take risks)			
Contribution (desire to make a difference, to give)			
Control (desire to be in charge, sense of order)			
Cooperation (teamwork, working with others)			
Creativity (new ideas, innovation, experimenting)			
Economic security (freedom from financial worries)			
Fairness (equal chance, equal hearing for all)			
Fame (desire to be well known, recognised)			
Family happiness (desire to get along, for respect and harmony)			
Friendship (intimacy, caring, support)			
Generosity (desire to give time or money readily)			
Health (physical fitness, energy, no disease)			
Independence (self-reliance, freedom from controls)			
Influence (desire to shape ideas, people, processes)			
Inner harmony (desire to be at peace with oneself)			
Integrity (honesty, sincerity, consistent values)			
Learning (growth, knowledge, understanding)			
Loyalty (duty, allegiance, respect)			
Nature (care for and appreciation of the environment)			
Order (organisation, conformity, stability)			

(continued)

Table 1.3 (cont'd): a list of values that may be important to you

Value description	Not important	Somewhat important	Very important
Personal development (improvement, reach potential)			
Pleasure (enjoyment, fun, happiness)			
Power (authority, influence over people or situations)			
Prestige (visible success, rank, status)			
Quality (excellence, high standards, minimal errors)			
Recognition (respect, acknowledgement, applause)			
Responsibility (desire to be accountable, trustworthy, mature)			
Security (desire to feel safe about things, surroundings)			
Service (desire to assist others, to improve society)			
Self-respect (pride in self, feeling worthy)			
Spirituality (belief or interest in a higher power or God)			
Stability (continuity, predictability)			
Tolerance (openness to others, their views and values)			
Tradition (treasuring the past, customs)			
Variety (diversity of activities and experiences)			
Wealth (material prosperity, affluence, abundance)			
Wisdom (desire to understand life, to exercise sound judgement)			
Other			
Other			
Other			

Table 1.4 outlines how you can note 10 values from the list (add others if you want to) that resonate most strongly with you. In doing this exercise, it is best to go with how you *feel* rather than trying to over-rationalise your selection, and to make your selections fairly quickly.

Table 1.4: my 10 most important values

1 _____

2 _____

3 _____

4 _____

5 _____

6 _____

7 _____

8 _____

9 _____

10 _____

Good—now for the next step (we are almost there!). Review your list of the values of those people you admire, and check if these values are somehow represented in your shortlist. If they are, great; if not, review your list as you think best. Finally, look at the 10 values you have listed, and highlight four that seem to 'jump out' at you as the most important of the set. These four, I suggest, are your most important values—the beacons that will guide you along the way. While you may have always known about your values, there is tremendous power in having them explicit in your mind. It means that the beacons guiding your life are now shining brightly.

Well done—you have taken a major leap towards living a deliberate life.

What do you want to have, do, be?

Making a living is necessary and often satisfying; eventually, making a difference becomes more important.

—DAVID CAMPBELL

You may be familiar with the saying that every journey begins with a first step. But there is also a little-known addendum to this saying: 'make sure that step is in the right direction'. If identifying your values is about creating beacons to guide the way, the next question is, 'To where?' That's what this section is about. What do you really want to achieve in your life? What will give you the most meaning and satisfaction? Many of us struggle to come up with answers to these questions. Sometimes we become so focused on our present situation or the achievement of short-terms goals that we forget about the ultimate destination.

I read an article that speculated on what it must have been like to be a passenger on one of the flights that crashed into the Twin Towers on 9/11. The article talked about the frantic phone calls made in those final few minutes. How many of those calls were to stockbrokers or bankers enquiring as to final balances? None—of course. Sometimes, it can take a tragic event, serious illness, redundancy or the death of a loved one for us to stop and think about what really matters. People I have worked with frequently say how events such as these, though devastating at the time, often turned out to be positive turning points in their lives. How good would it be to *create* such a turning point without going through a painful experience first? The key here is to think honestly about what you want to have, do and be.

Let's begin now: grab your notepad and pencil and go to a place—preferably somewhere outside—where you feel completely relaxed and alone and where you can take time to really reflect on your life and do some exploring. Here are some exercises to get you started:

- What gives you real satisfaction? What are you really good at, and what could you do all day long as though time was standing still? Look back on your life and bring to mind those occasions when you felt most proud and 'in your element'.

- If you knew that you could not fail, what would you most like to do?

- Imagine that you have just won the top prize in your national or state lottery. You are now a multimillionaire and can do anything you like. Once the initial euphoria has worn off — and you've taken all your dream vacations — how would you spend your time, and what would give you the most satisfaction?

- Now imagine that you are attending your own wake. All your friends are gathered and the eulogies are being read. The mood in the room is one of sadness, while at the same time there is a sense of celebration and gratitude for a life so well lived. What would you like to have read about you? Write it down.

These exercises are designed to alter your state of mind, allowing you to dissociate from pressing or immediate issues and start thinking about what really matters in the long term.

To complete this section, I invite you to get a sheet of blank paper and tear it up into eight pieces, roughly of equal size. On these bits of paper write down the eight things you most want to be, do or have in your life. ('Be', 'do' and 'have' are broadly defined — they can be anything you want, including relationships, accomplishments, experiences, contributions, satisfactions and material successes.) Some of these things may already exist in your life, which is fine (write them down anyway), while others are yet to be attained. Try to be as specific and as clear as you can.

When your notes are finished, review them, and put to one side any that don't seem to fit with the 10 values you wrote down earlier (as outlined in table 1.4 on p. 39). The task here is to get your Be, Do, Have list down to a small number — four or five is good. The priorities you finish up with should be truly significant and make you feel great when you think about them. Well done again — we're really making progress now.

What is 'enough' for you?

To the person who does not know where he wants to go there is no favourable wind.
— SENECA

A movie that I highly recommend to you is *The Shift*, featuring author and motivational speaker Wayne Dyer. This movie deals with the shift that occurs when we start growing in maturity, from what Dyer calls the 'morning' to the 'afternoon' of life. The morning of life is concerned with what we can accumulate and is primarily driven by the desires of our egos. In contrast, the afternoon is characterised by a softness and is more concerned with our purpose — what we can give rather than get—and our sense of contribution to the world. Dyer's main point is that the tactics that allowed you to be successful in the morning will simply not work for you in the afternoon. A different approach is required in the afternoon, one that is more focused on the things that give your life real meaning and significance. Importantly, this shift can occur at any time in one's life and needn't be determined by age.

Unless this shift happens, you may continue with tactics that were fine for the morning but become a burden in the afternoon. I see this frequently with people—mostly men—who have been working hard climbing the corporate ladder; when they get there, they feel 'empty' inside. As Stephen Covey puts it, 'You may spend your whole life climbing the ladder of success only to discover, when you get there, that the ladder has been leaning against the wrong wall'. Don't let that happen to you.

Now, don't get me wrong here, I am not saying that you should or should not be ambitious. What I am saying is that if you are ambitious for something, make sure it's what you really want and that you're doing it for the right reasons. How do you know where your ladder is taking you? One good way to find out is to ask a simple question: 'What is enough for me?' It's an odd but interesting question. It can be asked of all aspects of your life. For example:

- What is enough money?

- What is enough leisure?

- What is enough challenge?

- What is enough time?

- What is enough materialism?

- What is enough contribution?

- What is enough [ ]?

Answering these questions will help you to identify the 'wall' you are leaning against, how far up the ladder you are and, most importantly, how far up you *want* to go.

One area that can be very revealing is money: how much is enough for you? When I put the question to audiences, there is usually a vast range of opinion as to what it means to be 'financially wealthy'. For some, just paying off the mortgage on their current home is their definition of being rich. For others, being wealthy means generating enough cash from investments to maintain the lifestyle they want without needing a job at all. Generally, people estimate they would need between $1 million and $5 million to achieve such freedom. Others, of course, have a much higher estimate.

What figure represents financial freedom for you? How much is enough? Knowing the answer to this question means that you have a clear target and that in itself invokes the Law of Attraction. For example, if your number is $250 000, you will look for opportunities to get you closer to that amount. If, on the other hand, your number is $5 million, your approach will be entirely different. For a start, you will seek out bigger opportunities and be open to the risks that accompany them.

When you apply this logic to each of the other 'enough' questions, you'll begin to really understand what is important to you. You'll begin to weigh up the pros and cons of pursuing 'more' and perhaps conclude that 'more' is not necessarily better. This is particularly important when you need to find a balance between different aspects of your life. For example, the pursuit of more financial wealth can have a direct influence on how much leisure time you have available. As you do this exercise, you'll see all kinds of trade-offs to be made in your life.

You have now gained valuable insight into the things that motivate you in life, and the things you most want to prioritise in terms of being, doing and having. You also know what enough means to you. Now let's bring this all together.

Your Unique Life Purpose

Strong lives are motivated by dynamic purposes; lesser ones exist on wishes and inclinations.

— KENNETH HILDEBRAND

Your Unique Life Purpose (ULP — not to be confused with URL, although there are parallels!) is a short statement that brings together all the elements we have been talking about so far. In all the years I have been working with people, I have found the writing of a ULP to be by far the most profound and significant step someone can take in becoming more deliberate and in control of his or her life.

Before you write yours, let me examine what a ULP is and what it does for you. Here's what each word really means:

- *Unique.* You are unique; there is no-one else like you and there never will be. What you are today is a blend of your genes, your skills and talents, all your life experiences and the dreams that only you can dream. Because you are unique, it's important to know what makes you special and, therefore, live a life that only you can live. You want it to be your life, not someone else's life or someone else's opinion of what your life should be about.

- *Life.* When you come to die, you want to look back and be proud that you lived the life you had to the fullest. In my opinion, a full life is one where you gave your best in each area so that it was balanced and fulfilling, and you made a difference. All too often, people live such 'narrow' lives — overly focused on work, sport, leisure, or the accumulation of wealth or whatever — that they look back later in life with regret and a sense of missed opportunity.

- *Purpose.* At the end of the day, having a sense of purpose gives real meaning to our existence. A life of purpose is one where you wake up (most) mornings with a sense of excitement, a sense of passion and the energy to make things happen today. A good purpose will likely be focused on something more important than just yourself.

The great thing about your ULP is that it brings all that is important to you into one place. It's the ultimate point of reference for everything you do and for every decision you will ever make in your life. It's the creation of what I call your 'life compass'.

One good way to get started writing your ULP statement is to get your notepad and pencil again. Make sure you are nicely relaxed and that you feel good about yourself before you begin this exercise. Before you begin, you could quickly review all the writing you have done so far. In this exercise, your task is to write for 10 minutes continuously, and just see what emerges. Don't worry about your grammar, your spelling or anything else during this time — just write for 10 minutes without stopping.

Think about the values that are important to you, what gives you real satisfaction and how you want to be remembered. Begin with the words 'My unique life purpose is . . . ' and start writing.

Finished? Phew, that was exciting! What you have in front of you now is the basis of your ULP statement, written in your handwriting and in your words. When you feel ready, review what you have written and identify any themes that seem to be standing out as significant and important.

The final step is to take everything you have done and from it craft a ULP statement that is fairly short and memorable and that you feel really good about. Here are some examples of what others have come up with:

- 'My unique life purpose is to achieve quality relationships with those I care about, create harmony, comfort and joy in my life and environment, and enjoy a life-long commitment to learning, fulfilling occupations, creative expression, adventures, laughter and contentment. When my journey is complete, I will look back with satisfaction at a life lived to the full.'

- 'My unique life purpose is to maintain my health and fitness, enjoy and contribute to my personal relationships, obtain and sustain useful and satisfying employment, live an enjoyable and stress-free lifestyle and enjoy some travel and experiences outside my normal routine.'

- 'My unique life purpose is to be true to my values and defend the right of others to live according to theirs. Success is support without judgement, freedom without harm, recognition through contribution and fulfilment through knowledge.'

- 'My unique life purpose is to increase my joy through proactively and purposefully sucking the marrow out of life daily, at every opportunity—and by walking close to God.'

- 'My unique life purpose is to be a wonderful husband, father and friend who lives an exciting life while making a significant, positive contribution by inspiring and empowering people to achieve their full potential.' (This one is mine.)

All the examples above are meaningful and memorable for the individuals who wrote them. Now it's your turn—write down your ULP statement, again beginning with the words 'My unique life purpose is . . . '.

If you are not entirely happy with what you have done, don't worry—you can come back to it over the next few days and refine it some more. You will know that you've got a good ULP when it reads like the real and authentic you. As one workshop participant described it, 'It's like coming home'.

Congratulations on the writing of your draft ULP—you now have your life compass in your hand.

Your campaigns

It's never too late to be who you might have been.

—GEORGE ELIOT

While your ULP is an incredibly useful statement for all kinds of decision making, we need to go one step further if we are to confidently manage our time day to day and proactively plan for the future. That step is to derive a set of 'campaigns' from your ULP. A campaign is a short statement focusing on one particular aspect of your life that you want to 'advance' or move forward in some way. For example, based on my ULP listed in the preceding section, here is my set of campaigns:

- Look after myself.

- Be Carmel's 'partner of choice'.

- Be a Dad to Sinéad that she would be proud of.

- Be a supportive son and brother.

- Have friendships that are valued by me and by my friends.

- Engage in learning and educational activities throughout my life.

- Undertake work which is personally satisfying and meaningful, and which makes a positive contribution to the world.

- Have financial abundance and security until I die.

Together these campaigns represent what is truly important to me, and they give a reality to my ULP statement. As we'll see in chapter 9, your campaigns are a vital part of deciding where to put your attention and determining how to use your time. Before we get to work on *your* campaigns, let me make some comments on my list and show you what to look out for when you come to write yours:

- Each of the campaign statements is very practical. When you look at each statement, it should be possible to think of specific ideas or things you could do that would move the campaign forward in some way. For example, being a dad that my daughter would be proud of might involve me attending one of her sports events, or taking her and a friend to a movie that they both may enjoy. On the other hand, a campaign such as 'realise my potential' or 'to be happy' would not be as powerful because it is much more difficult to translate these general concepts into practical actions. General ambitions such as these need to be absorbed into the wording of your specific campaigns.

- A campaign is not a goal. Unlike a goal, which can be achieved, a campaign has a quality of never-endingness about it. This is important because you want to choose campaigns that are so significant that they will endure and remain important to you for a long time. I can, for example, imagine one day being the kind of grandfather that my daughter would appreciate in her dad. A campaign, therefore, is not only something that you can work on every day to inch it forward, but is also something that endures.

- You and your own self-care and development should be your first campaign. While the campaigns overall are not in any particular order of priority, I encourage you to make this exception for one simple reason: if you don't take good care of yourself, it is unlikely that you can be of service to others—be it your family, your community or your job. Think of the instructions you get on an aircraft during the safety briefing—'in the event of an emergency, put your own oxygen mask on first, even ahead of children and anyone else who may need your help'. Putting your own 'mask' on first is not a matter of being selfish; rather, it is the very thing that allows you to be of use and value to others. The philosopher and management thinker Charles Handy refers to such an approach as 'proper selfishness'.

- Your campaigns need to be in alignment with each other and operate together. Campaigns will tend to overlap slightly and complement each other, and this is a good thing — so that by working on one, you are inadvertently making progress on another!

- Choose your words carefully and feel happy with the phrasing you've chosen. You want to feel really energised when you read your campaigns every day.

To stimulate your thinking, here are some more campaigns that were written by others:

- Actively seek opportunities to learn, create, explore and experience.
- Create a home of warmth, order, beauty and nourishment.
- Do something beyond the 'call of duty' in my work every day.
- Empower others to be successful.
- Fulfil my hunger for creativity through music and writing.
- Learn something new every day.
- Practise gratitude.
- Practise simplicity.

Now it's your turn to write your campaigns, as outlined in table 1.5. Make them great.

Table 1.5: my campaigns

1	
2	
3	
4	
5	
and so on…	

Your campaign list, along with your ULP, represents what is truly important to you. We'll now consider how to put these great tools into practice in your life.

Discuss your ULP and campaigns

Great minds discuss ideas; average minds discuss events; small minds discuss people.
— ADMIRAL HYMAN RICKOVER

For many people, the exercises you have just completed in the preceding sections can have a powerful impact on how they see themselves and what they want their lives to be about. Perhaps for the first time they have real clarity about what they value, what they don't and what really matters in their life. If this describes you, it may be worthwhile to discuss what you have discovered with those people who are close to you. Experience shows that there are significant advantages to be gained from selectively discussing your ULP and campaigns with those people who matter in your life. Some people report that the very process of verbalising has really helped them to get extra clarity for themselves. I believe it was Yogi Bear who said something like, 'How do I know what I think, until I hear myself speak of it?'

If you are planning to talk to those close to you, be careful to only choose people who will be supportive of you and who will positively help you. You want to choose people who are able to look at things from your point of view — who are really willing to think about what's best for you without bringing their own interests and priorities into it. So, choose carefully.

When you have decided on your confidants, a good way to start is to ask the person to listen to, and not yet to comment on, your ULP and your full set of campaigns. Remember, your purpose is to voice your campaigns and to seek advice and constructive support from the person you are talking with. Importantly, your purpose is not to seek their approval or to be discouraged in any way. Of course, a supportive listener can also provide you with positive encouragement and even specific ideas that may be of assistance to you. Such a listener is likely to find what you say very illuminating. Phrases such as, 'I didn't know you cared about that', 'I'm glad you said that' and 'I would like to be/do that too' are all signs that you are on common ground and that your friend can actively support you.

If you are in a relationship, it can be very powerful to discuss your ULP and campaigns with your partner, and encourage your partner to think about his or hers. One of the greatest benefits is that you can develop a shared understanding of those things that truly matter to you as individuals and as a couple. I have recommended many times that a weekend away to discuss these issues is one of the best things you can do. Imagine the power of a couple who have individually crafted, but at the same time integrated, ULPs and campaigns.

In the same way, many people have found it constructive to discuss their ULP and campaigns with their boss or colleagues. This can be particularly helpful at the time of individual or team performance planning. Again, as in the case of personal relationships, it helps to clarify expectations and to identify people and resources that can assist you to achieve worthwhile dreams.

The role of goals

It is good to have an end to journey towards, but it is the journey that matters, in the end.
—URSULA LE GUIN

One of my favourite books is *Goal-Free Living* by Stephen Shapiro. In this book, Shapiro cautions against letting your goals take so much precedence in your life that you don't get to explore paths you never knew existed—paths that might lead to a more exciting, successful and rewarding life. Quoting Chuck Frey, Shapiro articulates the difference between 'goal people' and 'river people':

> Most of us are undoubtedly familiar with goal people. They are the individuals who write down their objectives and timetables for reaching them, and then focus on attaining them, one by one. By laying out a road map of future achievements in front of them, goal people give their creative minds a clear set of stimuli to work on. Their subconscious minds can then get to work incubating ideas and insights that will help them to reach their goals.
>
> River people, on the other hand, don't like to follow such a structured route to success. They are called river people because they are happiest and most fulfilled when they are wading in a rich river of interest—a subject or profession about which they are very passionate. While they may not have a concrete plan with measurable goals, river people are often successful because they are so passionate about their area of interest.

For me, this distinction between goal and river people is a crucial one because so often I have seen people who are so fixed on achieving some goal or other — in other words, so preoccupied with their destination — that they don't get to enjoy the journey or take advantage of the many valuable opportunities that emerge along the way. I believe a better approach is to set goals only where it makes sense to, and all the while be open to possibility — even to the possibility that your final 'destination' may alter.

When it comes to goal-setting, then, I encourage you to set some goals, but to do so carefully, and always in the light of your ULP and your campaigns. As I see it, goals only make sense when they are aligned with one of your specific campaigns, and when you are open to changing them as time unfolds. Goals simply help you along the way.

In my presentations I sometimes tell the story of a woman — let's call her Kate — who came to me for coaching because she and her husband were so uninspired in their lives. As I explored the background to the case, it emerged that the couple had been married for about 10 years, and that for most of that time they had had lots of energy and felt good about themselves. Each year, their main goal was to work hard and save enough money to take the month of December away from work and travel to Europe to visit family at Christmas. As Kate said, 'It was a struggle financially, but we were happy, and our lives had a purpose'. Then I asked what had happened to suddenly make their lives such misery.

They had won the national lottery! And it was millions of dollars. Now, Kate and her husband could go to Europe, stay in the best hotels, use top-of-the-range rental cars and take unpaid leave from their work at any time. 'But,' she said, 'our lives don't have any real buzz any more, it's all too easy; there's nothing to strive for'.

Of course, what had happened was the couple needed to update their goals to reflect their new financial situation. But first, they needed to craft ULPs and campaigns in order to identify what was truly important to them. The last I heard from Kate was that she and her husband had changed their jobs to work in an area which they were both passionate about — preserving the natural environment. They had found their 'buzz' again.

So what makes a good goal? Other than being associated with a specific campaign, a good goal is specific, measurable and time bound. Here are some examples, with a crucial phrase added at the end of each one:

- To weigh 85 kilograms by 31 May, or something better.

- To be debt free by 1 June, or something better.

- To have read 20 personal mastery books by 30 June, or something better.

- To have achieved the position of team leader by 31 December, or something better.

- To have opened three new stores by the end of the decade, or something better.

'Or something better' is an idea I learned from Jack Canfield, co-author of the *Chicken Soup for the Soul* series and author of the excellent *The Success Principles* book and audio program. By putting these words after each of your goal statements, you open yourself up to possibility. You can indeed be a river person while making the power of goal-setting work for you!

Because goals are time-bound, you will need to set and re-set them. I personally review my goals every quarter, in January, April, July and October. I find this approach keeps them fresh.

In summary, then, your goals are the specific, measurable and time-bound things that you want to achieve. The reason you want to achieve them is because they contribute to one or more of your campaigns, which, in turn, map onto your ULP. Your ULP is what gives your life direction and meaning and in this sense may be thought of as a life compass. It reflects your unique values, what you uniquely consider 'enough', and what you uniquely want to have, do and be. Visually, we could see it as shown in figure 1.1.

Figure 1.1: what your goals reflect

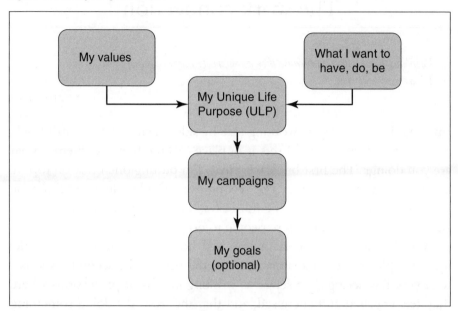

Now might be a good time to set yourself some goals. Remember: only set goals if you think they will be helpful in moving your campaigns forward. Some campaigns may have several goals, while others may not have any specific goals at this time. Table 1.6 outlines how to align your goals with your campaigns.

Table 1.6: my campaigns and specific goals

Campaign	Specific goals
1 _____	1 _____
2 _____	2 _____
3 _____	3 _____
4 _____	4 _____
5 _____	5 _____
and so on . . .	

The work connection

*People with goals succeed because they know where they are going.
It's as simple as that.*

— EARL NIGHTINGALE

Imagine three bricklayers working side by side. Each one picks up a brick, spreads it with mortar, and sets it in place. A little boy asks them, 'What are you doing?' The first bricklayer says, 'I'm putting one brick on top of another. Isn't that obvious?' The second says, 'I'm building a wall for the west side of a church'. And the third says, 'I'm building a cathedral. It will stand for centuries and inspire people to do great deeds'.

Which bricklayer represents you and how you relate to your work? Most people answer in a similar way to the first or the second response, with very few seeing themselves as working in jobs or professions where they feel engaged and energised, and that they're really doing something they feel passionate about. Research by the Harris Group, who surveyed 23 000 people from a range of industries and professions, backs this up, as follows:

- Only 20 per cent of respondents were enthusiastic about what their team or organisation was doing.

- Only 37 per cent said they had a clear understanding of what their organisation was trying to achieve and why.

- Only 50 per cent were satisfied with the work they had accomplished at the end of the week.

These statistics tell us that what people perceive to be important at a personal level is often at odds with the priorities of their organisations or the work they do. They are simply not engaged in a deep way with their work. But does it matter? My view is no. Let's go back to the bricklayers. After hours, the first bricklayer may well be a fabulous musician, spending every free moment of his time honing his craft as a master piano player and concert performer. To him, his passion is music, and bricklaying is a job that pays the bills while allowing plenty of time for music practice and performance. The second bricklayer may be a part-time community leader, who is passionate about making a substantial contribution to the lives of those she represents. She lays bricks during the day, saving her best energy for what happens outside of work.

The key here is that in each of the three cases, each of the individuals is passionate about something. Some people will get their passion from the work they do, while the majority will get it outside of their workplaces. The most significant point is to become really passionate about something.

If you are clear about what you are passionate about—and let's say it's not your work—you can then regard your day job as a means to an end. In my experience, this approach increases your work productivity enormously because you now have very clear expectations of your job and your organisation. You know why you work, and you are not distracted wishing you were somewhere else. You are deliberate. And that makes all the difference.

Now, just to be clear, I am not suggesting that the absence of passion in your work is to be tolerated or endured in some way—certainly not. Ideally, you want to find work that you can feel engaged with and that stimulates and energises you. Such an arrangement is ideal, but it is not necessarily the key to living a very successful life.

If you want a strong alignment between your work and larger life, you're searching for a nexus between three elements: what you are passionate about, what skills you have, and where there is a demand or need, as shown in figure 1.2 (overleaf).

Figure 1.2: the nexus between passion, skills, and demand or need

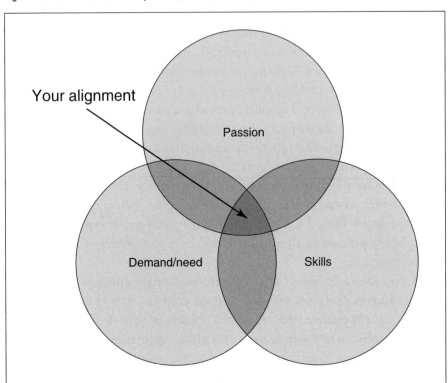

These three elements can be explained as follows:

- *Passion.* If you are doing what you are passionate about, chances are you'll do it really well. As Patanjali taught us, you'll release energies within yourself that will inspire you to think creative thoughts and that will drive you forward.

- *Skills.* You need to have, or be able to acquire, the necessary skills to make things happen. What are you good at? What are you willing and able to learn? Who else could you involve to complement your skills?

- *Demand/need.* You need to offer something that the world needs and values. There is no point in doing something that nobody cares about and nobody is willing to invest in. You need to offer value over the long term, so that you can continue to support yourself and your lifestyle.

When you think of your ideal job or profession, then, you are looking for a role that ticks all three boxes: passion, skills and demand. You will notice two or fewer ticks will only lead to problems for you. For example, I may be passionate about something, there may even be a strong need for it, but for whatever reason, I cannot develop a high enough skill level to make it work—with the result being frustration and anxiety. Or, I may have the passion and the skills, but there is no need or demand, which means that nobody is willing to pay me—with the result this time being loss of money and effort.

If you find yourself in a role that you would like to move from, identify which campaign it relates to, and perhaps set a goal to find another job or career. Depending on your situation, you might decide to move slowly or quickly, or to involve others at this point or not. The moment you get clarity and become decisive, you'll feel confident moving forward. As an aside, I sometimes tell clients who really want to move from their current situation to consider writing a future-dated letter of resignation (without sending it). It's amazing to see how this makes them feel, how it focuses their attention, and how it sensitises them to new opportunities.

In summary, I encourage you to find strong alignment between the work you do and your wider life. Ideally, you want to be living and working in the life of your dreams. Find something that you can become truly passionate about, use or develop the skills you need, and use them to deliver something that is really needed and valued by others. The more value you offer, the greater your reward. Remember, however, that finding this perfect job, while desirable, is not essential to living an amazingly successful life. The key is to be passionate about *something*.

Carry a written statement

A short pencil is better than a long memory when it comes to your dreams.

—JOHN DEMARTINI

Of all the things I've done over the years, encouraging people to take the time and effort to type up, print out and actually carry their ULP, campaigns and goals on their person has probably had the most impact.

When you carry these pieces of paper in your wallet or purse, something that I cannot fully explain happens. It almost has a magical quality about it. Because what you have written is so important, knowing that you always have it close seems to reinforce your resolve as you go about your day. Your point of reference for decision making is never far away. And, undoubtedly, the act of writing your priorities down makes them tangible and more real.

Over the years a number of workshop participants have sent me copies of the various things they have created to carry around with them: statements written in beautiful fonts, poems, drawings, paintings, key rings, business cards and symbols of various kinds. One person even made a jewellery piece that she always wears to remind her what is important in her life.

When I meet with successful people from all walks of life, and in all parts of the world, I am truly amazed by how many people carry such a statement on their person. I strongly encourage you to do the same. Lee Iacocca, the former chairman of Chrysler, had the same idea when he said, 'The discipline of writing something down is the first step toward making it happen'.

Set ULP triggers

In every block of marble I see a statue as plain as though it stood before me, shaped and perfect in attitude and action. I have only to hew away the rough walls that imprison the lovely apparition to reveal it to other eyes as mine see it.

— MICHELANGELO

When you reflect on your own day-to-day life, I'm sure you'll agree that it's very easy to let the ongoing events of your normal routine dominate your thinking. Everyday events such as work deadlines, meetings to attend and emails to answer all have the knack of keeping you busy and your attention focused. Likewise, outside of your work, you may have the daily pressures of children to care for, a house to manage or elderly relatives to support. Given all these demands, it can sometimes feel impossible to keep the bigger picture in mind.

This is where the power of your ULP comes in. One of the main benefits of doing all this work and going to the effort of carrying your statement around with you is that you can make deliberate, physical reference to it throughout your day. When you do this, you instantly connect with your greater purpose.

It is also a really good idea to learn your ULP so you can bring it to mind at any time. This is especially powerful if you find yourself in a difficult or stressful situation—you can simply recall your ULP and, before you know it, what was troubling you is suddenly put into perspective. You will feel much calmer and better able to deal with the situation you are facing.

I also recommend that you set specific 'triggers' in your daily life that remind you of your ULP at specific times. For example, when you put on your shoes to leave home, when you switch your computer on or off, when you are on your way to meetings, when you enter lifts, or when you put the key in your home or car door. It is best to choose specific events that you know are a regular feature of your day. With some experience, you'll come to look forward to these daily events happening because bringing your ULP to mind makes you feel good—it's akin to having several 'mental showers' throughout your day. I highly recommend this practice to you.

As we near the end of this chapter, I want to congratulate you on the work you have done so far. You have laid the foundation to live a more deliberate life and you have set yourself on a pathway that will guarantee real success in your life. You are crystal clear about who you really are and what's important to you. And you have developed some practical tools that you can draw on to make every day a great day. Welcome to the 2 per cent club—that exclusive club of people who actually write down what is important to them and so have a clearly defined sense of purpose.

Ideas for Action

- Watch Wayne Dyer's inspirational movie *The Shift*, which is all about making the transition from Ambition to Meaning.

- Type and print out your (draft) ULP statement, your campaigns and any goals you have set for yourself so far. If you need to, come back to these in a few days with fresh eyes. This process may take some time and some further refinement.

- Where appropriate, consider discussing your printed statement with a trusted friend, a loved one, a work colleague or even your boss. You're likely to be surprised how positive it is both for you and for them.

Destiny is not a matter of chance, but a matter of choice. It is not a thing to be waited for; it is a thing to be achieved.

—WILLIAM JENNINGS BRYANT

Eliminate — focusing on the important

Simplicity is the ultimate sophistication.

— LEONARDO DA VINCI

In the mid 1800s, American writer Henry David Thoreau decided to live alone for two years, two months and two days in a small log cabin in the woods near the shores of Walden Pond in Concord, Massachusetts. Why did Thoreau, a well-established man (he was friends with Ralph Waldo Emerson), decide to make such a dramatic change to his life? In his book, *Walden*, he tells us:

> *I went to the woods because I wished to live deliberately, to front only the essential facts of life, and see if I could not learn what it had to teach, and not, when I came to die, discover that I had not lived.*

What Thoreau learned from this experience was that most people enormously overcomplicate their lives (or, as he says, live lives of 'quiet desperation') when, in fact, by simplifying one's needs, a superior and more satisfying life is to be had. Simplicity is the key message from Thoreau. As an aside, following the publication of *Walden* in 1854, it is reported that Emerson wrote to his friend querying his 'simplify, simplify, simplify' statement on the grounds that two of those 'simplifys' were unnecessary!

Today, we can still learn from the experience of Thoreau in the woods. Although I am not advocating that we start living primitive lifestyles, we can make use of many of his fundamental lessons in our modern lives. I can certainly report from my own experience of attempting to live deliberately that looking for ways to simplify all aspects of my life has had a profound impact on the choices I make and the results I'm getting.

It sounds obvious to say, but the very best way to simplify your life is to eliminate those things that are unnecessary. When you eliminate the unnecessary, you put your attention on matters that are truly important. Your energy becomes directed, how you spend your time changes, and you work with a clarity that brings a refined quality to everything you do.

Before we start looking at each of the 10 areas in this chapter, I would like to tell you the story of a woman who attended one of my workshops. Anne, who was in her early 60s, was married to an older man who had recently been diagnosed with a terminal illness and was given, at best, three years to live. Following our workshop, Anne went home and, noticing that her house was full of clutter, decided to start eliminating 'stuff' that had accumulated over the years and was now no longer needed. As she worked she saw that many of the items belonged to her children, who had long since left home, and were unlikely to ever use them again. Within a couple of weeks, Anne had eliminated the clutter by giving things away to those in need, only keeping items that were truly useful or held special memories.

Anne told me this story and there were tears in her eyes when she said, 'Before our massive clean-up, every day at home was depressing, there were constant reminders of the past in every room we entered. But now, with less clutter, my husband and I can focus on what is truly important—the future. Although we only have a few more years together, we are now looking forward not backward. It's made all the difference. We're going to make them the best years ever'.

The purpose of this chapter, then, is to explore what areas of your life can be simplified. We'll begin our exploration by looking at the idea of desire itself, or the reasons we want what we want. When we begin to understand what drives our desires, we become much more self-aware and we make much better choices in all aspects of our lives. Next, we'll examine some strategies you can use to eliminate unnecessary items from your home and work environment. These strategies will help you to remove clutter, find better ways of organising things and generally feel good about your physical spaces. With our physical surroundings in good shape, we'll then move on to the more sensitive area of relationships and friendships. When you carefully look at who you associate with, you could well discover that adjustments need to be made so that who you spend your time with is in alignment with what you want your life to be about.

Let's begin with the idea of desire.

Desires and you

Manifest plainness, embrace simplicity, reduce selfishness, have few desires.

—LAO TZU

When you think about it, our lives are entirely concerned with satisfying some desire or other. Be it the impulse to scratch your head, the need to eat or the wish to impress your friend, we desire to satisfy our desires. For most of us, desires are such a constant feature of our lives that we don't even see them coming or going, and rarely think about the impact they have on our daily living.

Some desires form as a result of rational thought processes. Suppose I need to wash my hair and discover that I am out of shampoo. I now have a perfectly rational desire to go to the shop to satisfy my need for clean hair. It would be a mistake, however, to believe that all desires are formed in this manner. Many of our most profound desires are not rational, in the sense that we don't use rational thought processes to form them. Instead of us forming them, it would be more accurate to say that they form us. As William Irvine says in his book *On Desire*, 'They simply pop into our heads, uninvited and unannounced. While they reside there, they take control of our lives. A single rogue desire can trample the plans we had for our lives and thereby alter our destinies'.

These 'rogue' desires have a sneaky way of becoming part of our lives—they enter our house as a guest but soon become our master. They give us the illusion that their satisfaction will bring us happiness and peace. And because we are tricked, we mistakenly swing into action and begin working on achieving the desire, without any real pause for rational thought.

Where do these desires originate from? Some of them, no doubt, come from advertising, which has skilfully planted the seeds of desire within us. Why else do consumers, who were perfectly happy, suddenly find themselves wanting the latest SUV, electronic device or this year's 'must-have' colour clothing? Other desires emanate from our human need to impress others. Imagine what would happen if, instead of admiring our new SUV, our neighbours ridiculed or abused us for owning one. Soon our desire for such expensive accessories would disappear.

Now, just to be clear, I am not being anti-SUV (I have one myself!) and I am not suggesting that we stop striving to acquire material goods. The point I am making is that when we sleepily allow these desires to enter our minds, we can start down the road of attaining something that we don't really want. And that is where we begin to have problems — the effort involved in satisfying these desires can take us away from what we truly value or, worse still, we can move in a direction that is in conflict with our ULP.

So what, then, is the best way to manage our desires? The literature on this matter is very clear and consistent — the key is to be, as far as possible, content with what you have and awake to the role desire plays in your everyday life. While this may sound strange and almost impossible, there is strong evidence to suggest that being happy with what you have is fundamental if you are to lead a satisfying life. The mistake we make is to think that the attainment of whatever it is we desire will bring us contentment and happiness. This mistake is illustrated really well by Alan Carr, who has helped millions of people quit smoking.

Carr compares the smoker to a person who one day wakes up to discover that he has a pimple on his face. It's an ugly looking pimple, so he seeks the help of a friend, who gives him some of her special ointment to use. Sure enough the pimple disappears and everything is back to normal. A couple of days later, the pimple returns, but this time the pimple has brought two buddies that are even uglier and nastier. The magic ointment is applied again. All three pimples disappear, only this time, after just a day, he now has a crew of six pimples all busy doing their thing. And the ointment is applied again.

The mistake that is being made here is that instead of solving the problem, the ointment is, in fact, encouraging more pimples to come along. And, when you think about it, it's the same for us with the satisfaction of our desires. No matter how hard we try to satisfy these rogue desires, they simply give rise to newer and greater desires that scream out to be satisfied. It's a never-ending cycle.

The need to satisfy our desires not only consumes much of our time and energy, but can also influence our performance in a negative way. We can get so attached to the outcome of what we are trying to achieve that there is no smoothness or consistency in the work we are doing. This attachment to a desired outcome is described by Anthony de Mello in his book *Awareness*:

> *When the archer shoots for no particular prize, he has all his skills. When he shoots to win a brass buckle he is already nervous. When he shoots for a gold prize, he goes blind, sees two targets and is out of his mind. His skill has not changed, but the prize divides him, he cares. He thinks more of winning the prize, and the need to win drains him of power.*

Like the expert archer, when you are deliberate about your desires by actively managing them, you begin to be alert to the ongoing creation of new desires in your consciousness. This alertness gives you the mental space to judge whether the desire in question is useful or not. Awareness of the internal process by which your desires are generated and fuelled gives you tremendous power and mastery over your life.

Success and contentment, then, is not the complete absence of desire, but rather the proper management of it.

List the things you own

Maintaining a complicated life is a great way to avoid changing it.

— ELAINE ST JAMES

Interestingly, the first step in better managing your unwanted desires is to begin with your existing stuff — those items in your everyday living space that you come into contact with on a regular, or not so regular, basis. Through my coaching I have learned that our immediate living environment has a profound impact on all aspects of our lives. From the moment we wake in the morning, our mood is influenced by what we see and the things we habitually make use of. In my experience, most people greatly underestimate the impact their physical surroundings have on the quality of their daily lives. I would estimate that more than 50 per cent of people believe they have too much stuff. Yet for many, the thought of decluttering their homes is a significant source of stress and anxiety. You will hear people say that they 'don't know where to begin' or that they lack 'the time or energy' to sort through their belongings.

While there are several books available with clever ideas to help you declutter, I believe the problem goes much deeper than this. For many people, their stuff is a reflection of who they are, and it represents all sorts of emotional ties to their past experiences. One of the very best ways you can begin the process of decluttering is to undertake an audit of what you already own. This involves making a list of literally everything that is in your space. Go into each room of your home — including storage areas — and list what you see. If you want, you could put an estimated replacement cost on each item. If you're like most people, you'll be surprised by what you discover and the patterns that you see forming. When I have encouraged clients to do this exercise, they typically comment on:

- How much of their stuff they never actually use. Think here about all the CDs you never listen to, the clothes that stay in your closet unworn from one season to the next, and all those handy electrical gadgets purchased on a whim.

- The number of duplicate items they keep for no apparent reason. This is especially an issue for couples who have combined their individual households.

- How much of their stuff is out of date. Culprits here include electronic equipment that belongs to a different era, clothes you have been keeping when they are clearly no longer your style or size, and bottles and jars that should have been weeded out of the pantry years ago.

When you go to the worthwhile effort of listing everything you own (I do mine on a spreadsheet), you begin to see your environment in a fresh way. You'll also notice how much time and money you spend cleaning, maintaining and caring for all these items—and also, perhaps, that your home insurance policy underestimates the replacement value of what you own.

On a deeper level, one of the advantages of going to this effort is that it raises your awareness of your physical environment. It is very likely you will find yourself questioning some aspects of how you have been going about your life.

Review what you own

There is no greatness where there is not simplicity, goodness and truth.

—— LEO TOLSTOY

With your comprehensive list of everything you own in hand, you are now well placed to review what you own within the context of what is important to you now and in the future. The list you are holding is historical in that it represents the choices you made in the past for the person you were in the past. It is likely that you remember the emotional high that was associated with particular purchases. Researchers at Emory University report that brain scans reveal how a chemical called dopamine gets released in waves as shoppers first see a product and then ponder buying it. Interestingly, it is only the anticipation of purchase, rather than the buying itself, that releases dopamine. Once you have made your purchase, the chemical high flattens out within minutes, which explains why you are often left with the sense of regret known as 'buyer's remorse'. Reviewing what you own heightens your awareness of how you make purchases and how many of these purchases actually lived up to their promises. As a result, you'll become much more attuned to (and suspicious of) marketing campaigns that offer you improbable lifestyle benefits.

In my own life, I find that I am now far less influenced by the antics of advertisers and their promises. The result is that I have greatly simplified my lifestyle and have far fewer things, while I also really value those things that I do own. Without question, less is more.

During this review, you will likely come across items that are of importance to you in some way. These might be old photos, items that have a special meaning or indeed family heirlooms that you are keeping for the next generation to enjoy. I recommend that you carefully identify these items, noting their importance to you. This will help you sort through other less important items more decisively.

Because of the work you have done in chapter 1, you will have a crystal clear vision of who and what you are becoming—primarily articulated by your new ULP, campaigns and any specific goals you may have set for yourself. You can now look at what you own through the sharpened lens of these values and priorities.

Remove irrelevant personal items

Perfection is not when there is no more to add, but no more to take away.
— ANTOINE DE SAINT-EXUPÉRY

With the hard work done, you are now ready to go ahead and remove unwanted items from your space. For many people this process has a therapeutic effect in that it feels like the start of new beginnings and brings with it a sense of excitement and anticipation.

If you have a lot of stuff to sort, it is important to have a plan of attack so that you can make steady progress over time and keep the momentum going. If the decluttering exercise is a particularly challenging one for you, you may benefit from reading Judi Culbertson's book *The Clutter Cure*, which gives sound practical advice on identifying clutter, assessing worth and taking action. Depending on your situation, you might also consider getting help from a friend or even enlisting the help of a professional organiser.

In my experience, the following advice seems to work well:

- Begin with your bedroom. Because it's where we start and end our day, having a well-organised and inspiring bedroom makes a huge difference to your state of mind.

- Work from room to room. By concentrating your effort in specific areas, you'll see real progress as you finish one room and go to the next.

- Give to those in need (rather than sell). Many items that you no longer require will be of great value to someone else, and this consideration can really motivate you to part with things.

For many people, including Anne who we met at the start of this chapter, the process of eliminating unnecessary stuff from their living environments changes their lives. Because it is so visible, and the impact so personal, it literally changes how you see the world and your place in it. It is essential, therefore, that you are continually aware of your purchase decisions and ensure the things you buy are aligned to what is truly important to you. In his excellent book *Enough*, John Naish has helpfully identified key questions, which I have modified, to ask yourself before you buy something:

1   Do I *need* it, or just *want* it? Needs have a purpose, wants are more emotional.

2   How has my desire for this thing been created? Be cautious if it has been created by marketing or 'special offers'.

3   Why do I really want it? Is it because I want to be more 'hip', more attractive, smarter or just better off in some indescribable way? If so, be alert.

4   Can I achieve what I'm trying to achieve in some other way? Does more always seem better? Perhaps there are other options.

5   What will this really cost me? Given how much I make per hour, is it really worth that effort? What else could I be doing with my time?

6   Do I already have something that will do the same job? Perhaps what you have is good enough.

7   How much effort is it going to take to maintain this thing? Does it require maintenance, insurance and other forms of care and attention? Maybe the long-term implications are more of a problem than the short-term gain.

8   What's wrong with the one I have already? If broken, repair may be a better option, or just put up with the one you have.

9   If you conclude that you do really need it, can you borrow one for a while? Do your friends have one? Can you swap something or trade in some way?

10 Is it possible to rent it, rather than buy? These days, you may be surprised to know what you can rent or rent-to-own.

If, at the end of this interrogation, you want to go ahead and buy, at least you'll know that you really want it. Of course, you might decide to be less logical, and just buy it anyway! Either way, you are being deliberate.

Declutter your workspace

Simplicity allows the senses to rest from stimulation.

— GUNILLA NORRIS

Eliminating clutter from your work area is one of the most productive things you can do. I learned this lesson years ago when working with a consulting firm that had a 'clean desk' policy, which meant that office cleaners were instructed to 'trash' anything left on our desks or work surfaces overnight. As a junior consultant, I could not see the logic in such a stringent policy, but now, looking back, I see that I actually learned a great lesson.

A clean desk policy does more than ensure a tidy work area. It's really about creating a work environment that is without visual distraction, so that your focus is concentrated on what matters most. A cluttered work area creates temptations that are hard to resist and are likely to divert your attention as you work. In simple terms, a clean, clutter-free environment enables you to really focus on your work. I, therefore, highly recommend that you put some time aside to review where you work and, if you need to, plan a project to clean up your space. Your goal should be to have a functional work area that is devoid of potentially distracting items such as papers, notes, old reminders, stationery and excessive knick-knacks. You want to create a space for yourself — and your colleagues — that helps you to feel good about your work and is calm and refreshing. Here is some advice that may help:

- Think carefully about which storage options best match the nature of your work. Do you need files, folders or boxes for your various projects or clients? Is there a requirement to store materials in some kind of date order or in some other sequence?

- How much paper do you really need to store and for how long? Do the people who send documents to you keep a copy that you can access later if you need to?

- What facilities do you have in place for longer term archiving?

As well as your physical work area, the same ideas can be applied to your computer set-up. Do you have an organised way of storing your electronic documents and files? And do you have a system for managing multiple editions of the same document, so that you always know which is the most up-to-date version? (In chapter 4 we look at managing incoming information, including emails, and how to keep this under control.) If you are working in a team environment, where perhaps many people use the same work area, I would encourage you to take a leadership role in reviewing where you work and how you work together as a team. You may be surprised to find that many people prefer order over chaos, and that a decluttered environment can make people feel much more upbeat about their work.

David Allen, in his book *Getting Things Done*, says that you should set yourself up so that everything is allocated a particular place. This way you won't waste valuable time looking for lost information or trying to figure out where to store things. In essence, you want to be as deliberate as possible about the systems that make your workplace run smoothly.

List your relationships

The most important things in life aren't things.

— ANTHONY J. D'ANGELO

Of all the topics we discuss during our workshops, reviewing relationships is perhaps the most controversial and emotional for many participants. The idea here is that we systematically and honestly review all the important relationships in our lives, with a view to better understanding whether these relationships are helping us to become the people we want to be. I agree with George Bernard Shaw's assertion that between now and five years' time, the person you become will be influenced by two things: the people you meet and the books you read. In chapter 3 we'll discuss the books you plan to read, but for now let's focus on the people in your life.

Many of us only maintain regular contact with a small group of people. These individuals can have a major influence on our life, either because we spend a lot of time with them, or because their opinions matter so much to us that their feelings and expectations influence the decisions we make. These could be called close friendships and are likely to include your partner if you have one, your children, your siblings, and/or your close friends. Outside that close circle is what I call your network of associates — the people who are in your life for one reason or another but are clearly less significant than your close friends. Frequently, you will have built your network of associates through your life experiences — your school days, your professional affiliations, your leisure interests and your children.

The first step in becoming more deliberate about your relationships is to simply list the various people in your life, noting where the relationship began and why. In your notepad, create a table with two columns, as shown in table 2.1.

Table 2.1: my relationships with the people in my life

Person	Relationship nature and origin
1	
2	
3	
4	
5	
and so on...	

A good way to begin this table is to review your day today, and identify all the significant people with whom you have spent time, either in person, on the phone or by other means. You may then find it helpful to review your calendar for the past year or so. At this stage, there is no need to evaluate the relationship in any way — we'll do that next.

As you prepare this list you may already begin to see some patterns emerging. Some common ones include the following:

- Many of your relationships go back a long way — perhaps to your school days — with few newly formed relationships or friendships.

- A small number of key individuals in your life have been responsible for introducing you to other people.

- Many of your relationships are developed through your work.

- Your interest in a particular hobby or personal pursuit is responsible for a large part of your network.

- The number of people in your network is much smaller (or bigger) than you originally thought.

As you prepare this list, you'll become much more aware of your relationships, and hopefully more open to thinking about their role in your future.

Manage your relationships

Any fool can make things bigger, more complex and more violent. It takes a touch of genius—and a lot of courage—to move in the opposite direction.

—ALBERT EINSTEIN

When we did the relationship-listing exercise in a recent workshop, one of the participants noticed that many of the people in her network were 'past their use-by dates'. In other words, her network was stale and not serving her well. Perhaps that has happened to you too. If so, you now have a wonderful opportunity to refresh your relationships and begin moving in a direction that you can feel good about.

Before we get to looking at your list, it's important to be realistic enough to know that sometimes it's necessary to be with people who are not your ideal colleagues or even friends. For one reason or another, you may find yourself in circumstances that are difficult to alter—perhaps because of the role you have at work, or your social connections and obligations. Nevertheless, by systematically reviewing your list, you can better understand why you feel the way you do about people, and perhaps take steps to reduce your involvement where appropriate.

I believe that each of the people you've identified on your list will fall into one of two categories: to put it bluntly, these are 'to cull', or 'to cultivate'. People to cull are those who you actively want to reduce your involvement with. The key point is that these people are what I call 'toxic' to your overall health and wellbeing. They sap your energy and leave you wondering why you continue to have them in your life. You will notice that toxic people leave you feeling down and it typically takes some time before your enthusiasm for life is restored.

Many of your toxic relationships were likely formed when the circumstances of your life were different from your life today. Perhaps, years ago, you had common interests or were going through a similar stage of life. Or maybe your friendship began as you both supported each other in difficult or challenging situations. The trouble is that, over time, each of you has grown in different directions, and what originally held you together is no longer important. Sometimes, it is merely habit or tradition that keeps you involved in a relationship that is not healthy for you. It is also likely that the other person feels the same way about you!

In relationships such as these, the right thing to do is to reduce the relationship to a level that makes sense. Depending on the circumstances, this can be done quickly or over a longer period of time. You might, for example, decide to gradually spend less time with the person, and communicate with him or her more infrequently. Either way, I encourage you to reduce the number of toxic people in your life. You'll be glad you did.

People to cultivate, on the other hand, are those who encourage and support you, and who are in turn encouraged and supported by you. There is mutual benefit in the relationship. You will notice that time invested in these relationships is enjoyable and energising. You'll enjoy each other's company because you have a genuine care for one another, share the same interests and can offer mutual support. You will likely energise each other in a way that leaves you feeling more positive at the end of a conversation than you felt at the start. Moreover, the relationship will be enduring because *both* of you will want to strengthen and develop it.

Before you formally review your list of relationships, I recommend that you refer to your ULP, your campaigns, and any goals that you identified while reading chapter 1. This will provide you with a context in which to review each of your relationships. A good question to ask is, 'Is my continued involvement with this relationship helping me to live the life I want?' As you ask this question, I invite you to consider cultivating or culling as you think best. Remember, what you are doing is honest and honourable, both for you and for those in your life.

Identify relationships you want to foster

Things do not change — we change.

— HENRY DAVID THOREAU

One of the main advantages of going through the process of cultivating and culling your relationships is that you'll begin to see gaps between where you are now and where you want to be. You'll notice that many people in your existing network helped you become the person you are now, but to get where you're *going* you may need to foster new people in your life. To me, this is a really exciting idea, because you can develop new relationships in a way that is deliberate and purposeful, rather than aimlessly falling into associations that are just not right for you.

Many of my coaching clients have told me about how motivated they feel when they know what they are looking for in a relationship. When they find themselves in business or social situations, they feel much stronger and more confident when meeting new people, and also more assertive when it comes to beginning and ending conversations. Because your ULP, your campaigns and your goals are now so clear, the building of your new network should be an exciting and enjoyable experience for you.

Research shows that your friends and associates have a significant impact on the success you achieve. In one classic study begun in the early 20th century, Napoleon Hill spent almost two decades systematically researching the most successful people at that time (and published his findings in his book *Think and Grow Rich*). Hill found that high achievers tended to surround themselves with like-minded individuals who formed what he called their 'mastermind' group.

I would recommend, therefore, that you consider formally creating your own 'mastermind' group of people who you intend to make contact with on a regular basis. The aim of the group is to support each other's endeavours, to offer constructive ideas and to be a source of inspiration for all involved.

Eliminate unnecessary responsibilities

I define 'clutter' as any obsolete object, space, commitment or behavior that weighs you down, distracts you, or depletes your energy.

—JULIE MORGENSTERN

Over time, as we get involved in new things, patterns start to form in our attitudes and behaviour, and before we know it these patterns come to seem normal and expected. Along with these expectations, we can find ourselves with some extra responsibilities that take up our time, attention and energy. What was once novel has become routine. When you look at your life through the lens of your responsibilities, you may be surprised by what you find. You may discover that many of the things you are involved with are simply unnecessary. Perhaps they don't need to be done or, more likely, they don't need to be done by *you*.

Systematically reviewing your responsibilities in all aspects of your life is foundational to living a more deliberate life. As you examine each area of your life, you'll begin to clearly identify those responsibilities that rightly belong to you, and those that don't. In the workplace, knowing and concentrating on your responsibilities can make an enormous difference to your productivity and the contribution you can make to your organisation. It enables you to become 'expert' in what you are doing and to do it with a focus and reliability that engenders high trust among your colleagues and clients. In contrast, people who are unclear about their responsibilities tend to have difficulty focusing on what truly matters and, as a result, miss deadlines and produce work that is of questionable quality.

As you review your responsibilities in your work life, you may find that many of the things you currently do are 'accidents of history'. They are accidents to the extent that you may have inherited a task, a role or a responsibility that started as a one-off request and then just became routine and expected. For example, one person I know continues to receive copies of invoices even though her colleague only arranged this as an interim measure while her colleague went on vacation two years ago! Another common source of unwanted responsibility is captured in the phrase, 'But we've always done it this way'.

Become a master, then, of asking the right questions and isolating what it is you're uniquely responsible for in your work life. You'll be surprised at what can be eliminated, especially if you can find creative ways of getting work done through other people. This is not passing the buck; rather, it is a process of encouraging everybody to use their unique skills and talents to create a workplace that brings out the best in its people every day.

Outside of work, you're likely to find many opportunities to eliminate responsibilities that are not properly yours. Again, accidents of history can feature here: some things you're currently doing will reflect the continuation of old patterns that are no longer relevant to your future. Examples might be involvement in clubs or associations, schools, childcare centres, sports clubs, or charities that are no longer relevant or of interest to you. And in the home, I would encourage you to look at what you do and creatively ask: 'Does it need to be done and, if it does, does it need to be done by me?' In particular, I find this a significant issue for working mothers who tend to do a disproportionate share of cleaning and other domestic tasks in the home. Frequently, I recommend that working parents, after thinking what does need to be done around the house to keep it running smoothly, consider getting some paid help with chores such as cleaning, laundry, gardening and home maintenance. It can be well worth the extra cost because it gives you additional time to do what is truly important to you.

To help you review your responsibilities, you may find it helpful to get your pen and paper out again and use table 2.2 to list all the responsibilities in your life. Review each responsibility and, where appropriate, note possibilities for future changes in this area.

Table 2.2: my responsibilities and possible future actions

Responsibility	Review/action
1	
2	
3	
4	
5	
and so on...	

Based on my experience both in coaching and in my personal life, I can assure you that eliminating unnecessary responsibilities can have a profound impact on your day-to-day life. It enables you to enjoy a new sense of space in your life, which can be allotted to the things that really matter.

Strive for simplicity

One does not accumulate but eliminate. It is not daily increase but daily decrease. The height of cultivation always runs to simplicity.

— BRUCE LEE

An important idea from the management literature is the Japanese notion of Kaizen (*kai* meaning change and *zen* meaning good), which is about continually looking for ways to improve your performance, irrespective of how well you are doing now. It challenges us to be ever vigilant in looking for new ideas and in introducing small changes that, over time, make a significant difference in the results we get.

I'm a firm believer in simplicity. The more I study it and its application to daily life, the more I am convinced that finding ways to simplify what you do is a high-value, lifelong endeavour. When you start looking for ways of simplifying your life, you'll notice opportunities everywhere. The essence of simplification is to be found in two core ideas. The first is to identify and focus on the essential, and the second is to eliminate or drop things that are not essential. With practice, you'll develop a 'simplicity mindset', which will prompt you to regularly ask, 'What is essential here and what needs to happen next?' This question can be applied in any number of situations and circumstances. It is also the fundamental question behind great management and great leadership.

I, therefore, invite you to think about the different aspects of your life, actively look for what is essential in what you are trying to achieve and then come up with creative ideas for making things simpler. Remember, less is more.

In this chapter we have identified Elimination as a key tool if you are to become more deliberate in your life. We saw that before taking steps to eliminate various things from your life, it is important to spend some time thinking about how your desires first take root and how they influence your behaviour. When you 'wake up' to your desires, especially the rogue ones, you'll be much more discerning about the things, people and influences you *actually* want to seek out and foster in your life.

Beginning with your physical surroundings, you'll see your world in a new and refreshing way. You'll become an expert at isolating what is really important and this will help you to remove clutter and organise your home environment. With your home in good order, you can then direct your attention to your work life. Working with your colleagues, you might explore ways to remove clutter from your collective space in order to promote positivity and focus.

The next, and potentially most significant, step is to carefully review your key relationships and your network of associates. You may be surprised by what you find, and indeed motivated to reduce your involvement with people who are not aligned with what is important to you. As you engage with this process, you are encouraged to actively extend your network by forming new and purposeful relationships.

In all of this work, you'll notice that the key is simplicity. Simplicity is a powerful idea that is becoming increasingly relevant as our society gets more complicated and the pace of life quickens. More than 150 years ago, Thoreau surely got it right:

> *Simplicity, simplicity, simplicity! I say, let your affairs be as two or three, and not a hundred or a thousand; instead of a million count half a dozen, and keep your accounts on your thumbnail.*

Ideas for Action

- If you're in need of extra motivation or inspiration to get started on your decluttering, read one of the many books on the subject that are available from your local bookstore or public library. I especially recommend *The Clutter Cure* by Judi Culbertson and *Enough Already!* by Peter Walsh.

- After you have begun the process of elimination, periodically review the tables you have completed and any notes you have taken during this chapter, noting how far you have come. Is your life now more closely aligned with your ULP, your campaigns and your goals?

- Celebrate. Well done for coming this far—you're well on your way to being deliberate, and truly successful, in your life. Why not treat yourself in a special way to celebrate the work you have done? You may even include some of your new friends!

Do not wait; the time will never be 'just right.' Start where you stand, and work with whatever tools you may have at your command, and better tools will be found as you go along.

—NAPOLEON HILL

Language—your internal soundtrack

Do not speak—unless it improves on silence.

—BUDDHIST SAYING

Your language defines you. From the moment you accept this truth, your life changes. You become acutely conscious of your language, deliberate about the thoughts you think and careful about what you say. In my experience, when people realise the significance of their words it's almost like they are 'waking up' to a new and wonderful world.

Behind our words and the language we use to describe things are our thoughts. Every day we have thousands of thoughts, some of which we consciously bring to mind, while others—perhaps the majority—enter our consciousness for no apparent reason. Many of our thoughts come to us uninvited and many are the same unwanted guests that were with us yesterday, last week or last year. Our thoughts and the words we use to express them are vitally important because together they influence how we feel. How we feel to a large extent governs our performance, which in turn determines the results we get in life. Our lives are shaped by endless cycles of thoughts, words, feelings, actions and consequences or results (see figure 3.1, overleaf).

Figure 3.1: the thoughts to results cycle

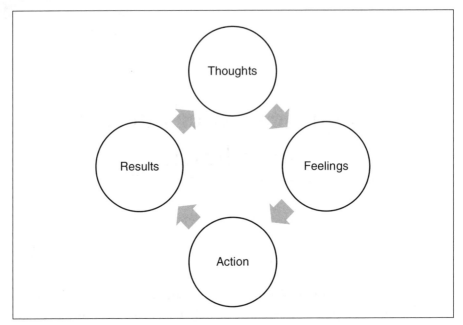

For me, the words we use are like the soundtrack of a movie. You may have noticed that a carefully crafted soundtrack can make or break a movie and, to a large extent, it is the soundtrack, not what's on the screen, that triggers our emotions as we journey from scene to scene. It's the same with every aspect of our lives. The language and the words we use are a reflection of our thoughts and have a direct influence on how we feel and how we go about our daily living.

Perhaps one of the most empowering discoveries you can make on your journey to achieving real success is that you can *choose your thoughts*. Yes, you heard me right. It does not matter what your current situation is, what major challenges are on your horizon or what your upbringing was like; you can *choose* what to think. You can change the soundtrack at any time and you can turn the volume up and down as you wish.

In his book *As a Man Thinketh* (originally published in 1902), James Allen gives a beautiful account of how we can become active in cultivating our thoughts:

> *A man's mind may be likened to a garden, which may be intelligently*
> *cultivated or allowed to run wild; but whether cultivated or neglected, it must,*

and will, bring forth. If no useful seeds are put into it, then an abundance of useless weed-seeds will fall thereon, and will continue to produce their kind.

Just as a gardener cultivates his plot, keeping it free from weeds, and growing the flowers and fruits which he requires, so may a man tend the garden of his mind, weeding out all wrong, useless, and impure thoughts, and cultivating towards perfection the flowers and fruits of right, useful, and pure thoughts. By pursuing this process, a man sooner or later discovers that he is the master-gardener of his soul, the director of his life.

He also reveals, within himself, the laws of thought, and understands, with ever increasing accuracy, how the thought-forces and mind-elements operate in the shaping of his character, circumstances, and destiny.

The purpose of this chapter, then, is to show you how you can become the gardener of your own mind by deliberately choosing your language and your words. We'll explore 10 different aspects of this skill, ranging from modelling the linguistic choices of highly successful people to identifying what is most useful to think about. Together we will identify unique affirmations that are closely aligned with your ULP and your campaigns.

Watch your language

Evidence is conclusive that your self-talk has a direct bearing on your performance.

— ZIG ZIGLAR

When you become aware of the words you use in your daily life, you may be surprised. Our language gives us a strong indication of how we look at things, with each of us having a unique lens, or way of viewing the world, that tends to be quite consistent throughout all aspects of our lives. For example, are you a person who habitually sees possibilities? Or are you someone who sees restrictions and obstacles everywhere you turn? Do you see the glass as half full or half empty? Are you mostly positive or negative?

If you really want to find out how your thoughts are influencing your life, I suggest you start by closely observing and listening to yourself. Simply observe your current behaviour. A useful way to do this is to imagine that you have a miniature version of yourself perched on your own shoulder.

Quietly and without comment, become an observer of your life and your world. You might consider doing this for up to a week, recording any interesting observations as they arise.

If you're like most people, you'll be both shocked and excited by what you discover. The shock comes from uncovering certain recurring patterns. You may, for example, become aware of yourself putting up barriers to success even before you begin or, indeed, your language may indicate thoughts of low self-worth, defeat or self-sabotage. Of course, you may also be pleasantly surprised to note the positive nature of your outlook—although almost all of us will be able to identify at least some areas in which we are being held back by our internal soundtrack. This is where the excitement comes in. For many people, this exercise is empowering because they begin to understand that their thoughts and words can be changed at any time. Your language can reflect conscious and deliberate decisions. When you get to this crucial point, your life will never be the same.

The language of success

Our life is what our thoughts make it.

—MARCUS AURELIUS

One of the very best ways to discover the power of language is to listen to the way other people speak. Just by listening carefully, without comment or judgement, you'll learn to become attuned to the power of language.

You can begin your study with those close to you: your family, friends, work colleagues and the people you encounter in everyday life. Further afield, television and radio interviews, speeches, autobiographies and communications of all kinds can also help you to appreciate the mindsets of different people and how their thinking contributes to the results they are getting in their lives. One of my favourite activities is to listen in on conversations in public places—trains, buses and airports are ideal locations—and notice how people use words to create their worlds.

Some of the most interesting observations I have made include the following:

- You can quickly tell if someone has accepted responsibility for a situation or if he or she has a victim mentality and is seeking to blame others. Generally, the person who is clearer about personal responsibility is far more positive and thinks more about solutions than problems.

- Those who are constant complainers drain the life, energy and enthusiasm from the people around them.

- People who use forward-looking 'can-do' words find it much easier to get agreement and support for what they are doing. They tend to energise those around them.

As you develop your awareness of language, especially the language of people you admire, you'll begin to notice certain patterns of speech that you can learn from and emulate. You'll become very aware of your own words and the impact they have on your life. In essence, you'll become deliberate about your language.

Expand your vocabulary

Don't be afraid to take a big step if one is indicated. You can't cross a chasm in two small jumps.

— DAVID LLOYD GEORGE

Experts estimate that William Shakespeare, a master linguist, used only about 20 000 words out of the 700 000 available in the language. Most of us will apparently use only between 4000 and 5000 words in our lifetime. When you become more self-conscious about the words you choose, you will inevitably want to expand the range available to you. You'll become aware of new words, seek out their exact meaning and find opportunities to use them in your verbal and written communication. I know several people who record new words in a notebook and then later look up their meaning in a dictionary, or who use a thesaurus to find alternate ways of expressing similar ideas.

The act of writing down new words and their meaning is an excellent way of expanding your existing vocabulary. And the benefit of doing so is that instead of relying on the same old set of words, you develop resources to become precise and nuanced in your self-expression. So instead of being lazy with language, I would strongly encourage you to take an active interest in words and their meanings. In no time, you'll not only become a more skilled communicator, but you'll also find yourself choosing your words more carefully and deliberately.

Recognise and avoid reactive language

We are disturbed not by what happens to us, but by our thoughts about what happens.
— EPICTETUS

In *The 7 Habits of Highly Effective People*, Stephen Covey makes the point that personal effectiveness is largely influenced by individuals making the decision to become proactive (Habit 1). When people are proactive, they take responsibility for their own lives and the choices that they make. They become an active participant in their lives, rather than waiting for events outside their control to turn in their favour. The key to really understanding what it means to be proactive is to see choices everywhere. When you think about it, we always have choices, and each of the choices we make has different consequences and implications.

As you work to become more deliberate about your language, you'll notice that proactive people use proactive language. You'll recognise proactive language because it always indicates that choices were indeed available and that, from the possible alternatives, a certain course of action was actively selected. In contrast, people who are not proactive — let's call them reactive — tend to use language that suggests they have little or no choice in their lives.

Table 3.1 shows some phrases to look out for.

Table 3.1: reactive versus proactive language

Reactive language	Proactive language
I must...	I will...
I have to...	I choose to...
I should...	I can...
If only...	We are where we are...
There's no choice here...	There's always another way...

You will notice that all the phrases on the right have a much more positive energy associated with them. If you're like me, you will find yourself gravitating towards people who speak in this way.

To demonstrate that different words have different energies, I sometimes ask audiences to make a list of the things that they need or have to accomplish over the next month or so. This could be work that has to be done, various tasks that are outstanding and all the errands at home waiting to be done. Alongside each item, I ask participants to write down the emotion that comes to mind for each of the need-to/have-to tasks. Invariably, people have negative comments such as, 'Why me?', 'I've been putting this off for so long' or 'I wish this or that was done'. Thirty or so minutes later, I then ask the same audience to make a list of the things they would *choose* to do over the following month. Again the list is quickly generated, but this time there is a sense of 'looking forward' when I ask for the emotion associated to each item. Clearly, people feel much more positive about the things they would *choose* to do. The most interesting part of this exercise comes when I ask the audience to compare the two lists. Very often, people are dismayed to find that many of the items on the first list also feature on the second list!

When you do things because you choose to, you're far more likely to follow through with your intentions — and to take pleasure in doing so. Truly successful people know this secret and work hard to always see choices and possibilities in their day-to-day lives. Most importantly, their speech habits reflect this.

Develop an attitude of gratitude

There is a calmness to a life lived in gratitude, a quiet joy.

—RALPH BLUM

Through studying and working with successful people, I have learned that an absolute key to attracting more success into your life is to be grateful for what you already have. Most people take the opposite approach. They dismiss or take for granted the many good things in their lives and, instead, focus on what they are lacking or have yet to attain. This is a fundamental error.

There are at least three reasons why developing an 'attitude of gratitude' is a good idea. First, when you pay attention to what you are already grateful for, you'll instantly bring to mind positive feelings. It does not matter if your current situation is not absolutely ideal; for example, you might be affected by ill-health, financial pressures, work challenges or relationship difficulties. But it is always possible to find things to be thankful for. You can train yourself to recognise—and regularly bring to mind—some of the many positives that are always there but somehow tend to get overlooked. Once you learn to look at your life in this way, you're likely to be surprised by just how many good things you begin to see.

As you do this, you will cease to be preoccupied with your perceived shortcomings and, instead, feel filled with joy and happiness for all that you do have. When I help clients to look at their lives in this way, and so think more positively, I am always amazed at the rapid effectiveness of this process. As the motivational author Wayne Dyer puts it, 'When you change the way you look at things, the things you look at change'. So right!

The second reason for fostering an attitude of gratitude is equally compelling. When you isolate and deliberately name what you are grateful for, your attention—and your subconscious mind—instantly goes to work generating more of those things that are positive. Equally, focusing on what's lacking encourages your mind to develop negative, self-perpetuating habits of perception. Very simply, an attitude of gratitude transforms your attention into a potent force for good.

While the two reasons I have already outlined should be convincing enough, the third advantage has tremendous practical application because it directly affects everybody around us. When we have gratitude in our hearts, our first response is to be thankful for the people in our lives and what they do for us. You'll notice that when you are genuinely thankful for other people — and let them know — they will react in a very positive way to you. Feeling appreciated is a deep human need, and by expressing your thanks you are connecting with others in a way that is meaningful and encouraging.

In my own life, I go out of my way to acknowledge and thank those people close to me. People are genuinely surprised by simple gestures such as handwritten cards and thankyou notes, small gifts and other novel ways of simply saying 'thank you'. I especially like to engage with people doing routine (and often trying) customer service jobs to let them know that I appreciate the work they do and the service they have given me. In my experience, this can have a powerful impact on both them and me. Try this for yourself and just see what happens!

So, what is the best way to live with an attitude of gratitude? In his brilliant books *The Gratitude Effect* and *Count Your Blessings*, John Demartini gives us many practical suggestions and exercises, which I would encourage you to study and start applying in your life. I agree with Demartini that practising gratitude is less about specific practices and more about evolving a way of looking at the world in which 'thank you' is your first reflex.

In my experience, it is very important that you cultivate an attitude of gratitude every day. Among the most practical suggestions for doing this are the following:

- As you awaken, and before you go to sleep, bring to mind specific things that you are grateful for — if you like, you could note these in a journal near your bed. These don't need to be big or profound, but may be simple things like the clean air you breathe, the friends you have, or the many small opportunities you have to experience joy or satisfaction. I find that when I do this at night, I sleep better; when I do it in the morning, before my day starts, I feel upbeat even before my feet touch the ground.

- Carry something that reminds you to be thankful for the many good things in your life. I carry a small pebble and, throughout the day, as I touch or feel the pebble, I quickly bring to mind something to be grateful for. This simple reminder always puts me in a positive state of mind.

Once you get into the habit of gratitude you'll never want to give it up, because it makes you feel really good inside. And when you feel good inside, your language will change to create a perfect alignment between your inner and outer worlds.

Adopt a mindset of abundance

We don't see things as they are; we see them as we are.

—ANAÏS NIN

Closely associated with an attitude of gratitude, and equally important, is what I call an abundance mentality. Again, this is a mindset that will naturally find expression in your thinking, your language and your actions. A good way to understand this idea is to think of its opposite: a small-minded and restricted outlook, where the focus is very much on short-term gain and 'what's in it for me'. I am sure that we all know someone who is characterised by this world view. Now consider the difference between a person who wants to get the biggest slice of the pie and a person who wants to make the pie bigger so that everyone can have enough for their needs. Your approach to 'pie management' will reflect your attitude towards abundance.

People with an abundance mentality go about their lives in a particular way. For a start, they are genuinely interested in the welfare of others and they really want other people to have success, good fortune and prosperity. They take this approach because they know that the success of others does not diminish their own success in any way. If you take this truth to heart, your actions will be geared to helping others achieve their goals and aspirations, knowing that providing this support is in perfect alignment with your own values and ULP. Your success really is my success.

People who believe in abundance believe that there is more than enough for everyone. They take the view that if there is shortage at the moment, we can work together to expand what is possible and to satisfy all our needs. They do not take short-term advantage of people; instead, they prefer to nurture long-term, mutually advantageous relationships. According to Stephen Covey, they think 'win-win'. Win-win thinking can only come from faith in abundance.

When you reflect on the advantages of fostering an abundance mentality, you'll never want to take any other approach. It will influence many aspects of your life, especially your work and relationships. In your work, you'll think in terms of cooperation rather than competition, and actively seek out ways of doing business that is beneficial to both you and your business partners. In my own business, for example, my workshops and seminars are promoted and marketed through my carefully selected partners, who I know share my 'pie management' philosophy. I have turned down many opportunities to work with organisations and people who I believe are only interested in short-term gain or making a quick profit. In your relationships, belief in abundance will lead to higher quality, more enjoyable and more enduring ways of being together. With genuine care, love and respect, the people in your life will not only feel better, but they will respond in kind, and treat you in the same way.

Listen to your inner voice

Your vision will become clear only when you look into your heart. Who looks outside, dreams. Who looks inside, awakens.

—CARL JUNG

As you become aware of your language, you'll come to understand that your thoughts give rise to an inner voice, which, in turn, drives your behaviour. With just a little practice, you can develop the skill of tuning into your inner voice and start to see that you are not your thoughts; rather, you are the *observer* of your thoughts.

Whether we like it or not, our inner voice is always talking to us. It may be quietly encouraging us, telling us that we are on the right track, or motivating us to keep going despite the setbacks or apparent problems. On the other hand, that inner voice can be our worst critic with its snide negative comments about the value of what we are doing. The most important thing is to become aware of that voice and know that it can have a dramatic impact on your performance and the results you get in your life.

In my seminars, I sometimes demonstrate this crucial point by asking an audience volunteer to take part in an exercise with me. This exercise, which I learned from Wayne Dyer, involves the volunteer standing at the front of the room facing away from the audience, just focusing on me. I ask the volunteer to bring to mind—without telling me—a time when he or she felt really proud of an accomplishment. With that picture in mind, I ask the volunteer to outstretch his or her stronger arm and really resist me as I put downward pressure on the arm. As I start to apply the pressure and the volunteer continues to think positive thoughts, I struggle to move the arm down—it's really strong.

Next I ask the volunteer to think—again without telling us what it is—of a time when the volunteer felt ashamed or let down in his or her own behaviour. I apply the same pressure to the arm again, and this time, no matter how hard the volunteer tries, I can easily move the outstretched arm down. I then ask the person to come back to the original positive thought, and strength instantly returns to the arm. The lesson is this: simply by choosing a different thought, we can dramatically influence the results we get in our lives.

One of my favourite books, *The Inner Game of Work* by Tim Gallwey, applies this idea to the workplace. Using concepts that he originally discovered while coaching professional tennis players, Gallwey puts forward the idea that all too often we interfere with our natural abilities by over-thinking and over-instructing ourselves. Gallwey succinctly describes this phenomenon of 'self-interference':

> *When I was playing at my best, I wasn't trying to control my shots with self-instruction and evaluation. It was a much simpler process than that. I saw the ball clearly, chose where I wanted to hit it, and let it happen. Surprisingly, the shots were more controlled when I didn't try to control them.*

In essence, then, what you think about really matters. It affects your performance in every aspect of your life. As you become aware of your thoughts and the language you dress them in, you'll automatically want to reach for better thoughts because you know that better quality thoughts lead to a better experience of life.

Choose your soundtrack

Just take the first step in faith. You don't have to see the whole staircase. Just take the first step.

—MARTIN LUTHER KING JR

Deliberately reaching for better quality thoughts is by far the quickest way to change what's playing on your internal soundtrack. As with everything else we have discussed in this book, it's a matter of first becoming conscious of what's happening, then being proactive.

Two of the very best — and proven — ways to modify your soundtrack are positive affirmation and visualisation. The technique of positive affirmation was first developed by motivational author Louise Hay and involves consciously choosing words either to help eliminate something from your life or to create something new. For example, we may have got into a negative pattern of thinking that influences how we view our workplace and perhaps the contributions we make. Our internal voice might be whispering to us, 'Nobody ever sees my value', 'My job is too stressful' or 'I'll never be successful'. All these negative comments will undoubtedly make you feel down and prevent you from living to your full potential, thereby instigating a self-fulfilling prophecy.

If we deliberately choose to replace these negative whispers with more positive ones, we'll immediately feel better about ourselves. In place of the phrases above, we might say, 'Everybody at work appreciates me', 'I am always relaxed at work' and 'Everything I touch is a success'. The point here is to choose language that makes sense to you and sounds like you, even though you may not entirely believe it to be true — yet. As you repeat these positive affirmations to yourself, your subconscious mind will set to work making them come true.

In her books *You Can Heal Your Life* and *Experience Your Good Now!*, Hay suggests that you write your affirmations down, learn them, carry them with you and repeat them often out loud to yourself as you go about your day. In little time, according to Hay, you'll see seedlings of success and, as you do, any beginner's doubt will vanish as you discover a powerful new tool for making positive things happen in your life.

In the course of reading numerous business autobiographies, I have discovered that many highly successful people have adopted this technique.

Entrepreneur Bill Cullen (author of *It's a Long Way from Penny Apples*) describes how every morning he stands in front of a large mirror and tells himself how wonderful he is, and that today is going to be a great day. Funny as this may sound, Cullen started out with scant education, selling apples on the back streets of Dublin, yet is now one of Europe's leading dealer agents for Renault and Opel automobiles. Very similarly, Siimon Reynolds, one of Australia's top advertising executives, begins and ends each day by reciting his affirmations.

The most important thing about affirmations is to make them — you guessed it — *affirmative*. That is to say, focus on what you want to bring about, not on what you are trying to reduce or eliminate. It's just like a mother telling her child, 'Stay on the pavement' rather than, 'Don't run on the road'. Staying on the pavement is clear to me, while running on the road has given me an idea!

To get you started with creating your own list of positive affirmations, here are some to consider:

- My life is a success.

- I take responsibility for my own life. I am free.

- I am inspired. I am enthused. I am powerful.

- I let neither an up nor a down interfere with my dreams.

- Out of this situation, only good can come.

- I love to be of service, for it fulfils me and inspires others.

- I am grateful for my balanced life.

- The more I am grateful, the more I have to be grateful for.

- The more blessings I count, the more obstacles I mount.

- I am filled with energy and enthusiasm.

- I trust that all my needs will be taken care of.

- I love serving my clients, and my work is fulfilling and inspiring.

- I turn every experience into an opportunity.

- I am capable, competent and in the perfect place.

- My job and my dreams are mutually aligned.

- New doors are opening all the time.

- My age is perfect, and I enjoy each new moment.

I encourage you to take some time now to write your own affirmations, and to practise them out loud every day. You'll be glad you did.

The second powerful tool for altering your internal soundtrack is creative visualisation, a theory pioneered by Shakti Gawain in her book *Creative Visualization*. Whereas affirmations are language based, the power of visualisation is that it taps directly into your imagination. The idea is to deliberately use your imagination to create a clear image, idea or even feeling that you want to bring into being. By focusing on the goal regularly, you'll begin to believe it's possible, and this will help you bring it into reality. Quite literally, it's a case of making your dreams come true.

In my experience, when you practise both positive affirmations and creative visualisation, you are saying to your mind, 'I am deliberately taking charge here and here is where we're going — let's go together'.

Seek out positive people

A mind once stretched by a new idea never regains its original dimensions.
— OLIVER WENDELL

Not so long ago, through a most unusual sequence of events, I had the opportunity to coach a patched gang member. Trev — not his real name — had just turned 40 and almost half of his adult life had been spent in prison for robbery and drug-related crimes. When I met him, he really wanted what he called a more 'normal' life. Having missed out on seeing his own six children growing up, he was determined to be there for his grandkids. However, since being released from prison five years earlier, he had continued to battle with drug addiction and, despite rehab, was unable to go clean and found himself getting back into trouble. When I coached him, he himself came to the conclusion that it was his friends and the company he kept that was his greatest problem. Even with the best of intentions, Trev saw temptation all around him, and he found it very hard to resist doing what he knew was wrong.

Many of us are like Trev in our own ways. The friends we have and the company we keep have a major influence on us. Put simply, they can either help or hinder us as we try to make progress towards what is important to us. In chapter 2 I mentioned Napoleon Hill's recommendation that people who have identified their 'major definite purpose' should go about creating a 'mastermind' group of like-minded friends with whom they can share experiences and encouragement. More recently, motivational speaker and author Earl Nightingale also concluded that the friends you keep are probably the single biggest influence on what you consider to be achievable. Again, the lesson is simple: be mindful of the company you keep because it will influence your thinking in a big way.

What I am recommending, then, is that you deliberately select your friends based on your ULP statement and your campaigns. You will have the satisfaction of knowing that you are helping, and being helped by, others on similar journeys to you. As the saying goes, 'It's what you learn after you know it all that counts'.

Study books and audio

The highest reward for a person's toil is not what they get for it but what they become by it.
—JOHN RUSKIN

If you want to become expert in any subject, it makes sense to study it closely and to learn as much as you can from those who have gone before you. You can pick up on their language and ways of thinking. Otherwise, if we journey on our own, our learning is slowed because we only have our own experience from which to learn. Deliberately tapping into others' accumulated knowledge is a smart strategy.

Surprisingly, very few people go to the trouble of making a serious study of personal success literature. Sometimes, they have a fleeting interest and perhaps pick up a random self-help book at an airport, read it for a while, and then leave it somewhere gathering dust. Others, while having a desire to improve their lives, simply do not want to put the work and effort into serious reading and study. When you think about it, however, it's really not that hard to become an expert in any subject. If you are willing to put some effort in, you'll be surprised by how much you can read and learn in a single year. Author Brian Tracy makes the point that if you were to read a book a week, within a year you would have read more than 50 books. In five years, more than 250 books read would put you in the top 1 per cent of experts in your chosen area of study.

Reading a book a week sounds daunting, but when you know how it's no trouble at all. When most people think of reading, they imagine themselves in their most comfy seat, with long stretches of uninterrupted time (that is, with no kids, or partners) in which to really get into what they are reading. If you're like me, and lots of other people, this is just not a practical reality. Instead, it is far better to think of reading as something you do 'between' other things as you go about your daily life. How often have you found yourself with five or 10 minutes to spare, perhaps waiting for someone or something? It is in these moments that you can make progress on your reading.

Of course, the key to getting the most out of these times is to always be prepared by having your current book nearby as you go about your day. I always carry a book in my bag and will not leave home without taking my bag with me. I and many others I have coached have been surprised by how much it's possible to read, even between delayed trains or when standing by the stove as dinner cooks.

While it's desirable for you to begin your own collection of personal mastery books, there are other ways of getting started. If you visit your local public library, you'll find rows and rows of relevant books that you can borrow and enjoy. In my experience, most libraries have extensive up-to-date collections just waiting to be borrowed.

If you are in a position to start your own collection, however, you'll be able to re-read your favourite books and also share them with friends and family. In his audio program *The Art of Exceptional Living*, business philosopher Jim Rohn stresses that the building of a personal library is one of the greatest legacies you can leave to the next generation.

As well as books, I also encourage you to explore the audio versions of books that are available nowadays. There is something special about an author reading his or her book to you, and it can provide a deeper level of understanding beyond the text itself. Sometimes I make the comment that I have learned more from listening to audio books in my car than in my 11 years of university study! It's also a good idea to put audio books on your iPod or MP3 player so you can listen as you travel or commute to and from work.

As you will have guessed by now, I am a big fan of reading about and learning as much as possible from others' journeys. To make it really work for you, however, you need to carefully select the books that will be most helpful for you and then look for opportunities every day—between things—to get your reading done. As you become more deliberate about your reading, you'll notice your language changing, and you'll be on your way to becoming an expert in the most important subject of all: your own life.

In this chapter we have acknowledged the power of language to influence all aspects of our lives. We have seen that there is a strong connection between our language, our thoughts, how we feel and the actions we take. I hope you now feel confident about your ability to intervene positively in this cycle, and to develop your own vocabulary for growth and change.

Ideas for Action

- Without trying to make any changes, simply observe your own language—both internal and spoken—for the coming week. You may find it useful to record what you discover in your journal. What patterns are you seeing? What is surprising to you?

- Look back on the 'Choose your soundtrack' section of this chapter, review the sample affirmations and then create some of your own. Write them down on a piece of paper and practise saying them aloud in the morning and at night, and also throughout the day. What are you noticing?

- Depending on what you find most interesting, make a shortlist of three books that you would like to read over the next month or so—you might want to review the 'Recommended reading' section on p. 267 for ideas. Once you have your list, source these books at your local bookstore or library.

All serious daring starts from within.

—EUDORA WELTY

Information — managing inward and outward flows

To go in the dark with a light is to know the light.
To know the dark, go dark.

— WENDELL BERRY

'The most powerful commodity I know of,' said Gordon Gekko, the character played by Michael Douglas in the movie *Wall Street* (1987), 'is information'. Although we may not agree with other aspects of Gekko's lifestyle or moral standards, there is, nonetheless, truth in what he says. Information, or lack of it, can make all the difference to how you live your life and what you can achieve.

When you start thinking about the role of information in your everyday life, you'll discover that it has a profound impact on how you feel. Experts estimate that the average person living in a westernised society is exposed to between 3000 and 5000 different 'messages' throughout the day. These messages come from obvious sources such as advertising billboards, television and radio, road signs, and the many other forms of coercion and instruction we come across every day. Less obvious are the 'peripheral' messages that pop up in your web browser or are overheard in conversation, or which you inadvertently absorb from junk mail in the seconds before it is binned.

Sometimes, then, your exposure to information can be somewhat random and trivial. Nonetheless, at other times exposure to information can fundamentally alter what's on your mind and how you behave on any given day. For example, you may have had the experience of waking up in a positive frame of mind only to have your equilibrium upset by a chance meeting, overheard comment or unsolicited email. Whatever might have been said is then more or less with you all day, subtly (or not so subtly) influencing your mood and actions.

Modern technology has had an enormous effect on the volume, speed and intensity of our interactions with information of all kinds. Richard Saul Wurman, who describes himself as an information architect and philosopher, was one of the first persons to identify the now prevalent phenomenon of 'information anxiety'. In his book of the same title, he proposes that *The New York Times* now contains more information than the average 17th-century man or woman would have encountered in a lifetime. He goes on to say:

> *We are like a thirsty person who has been condemned to use a thimble to drink from a fire hydrant. The sheer volume of available information and the manner in which it is often delivered render much of it useless to us.*

What is striking about Wurman's comments is that they were made in 1987, well before the internet became a central feature in most people's lives.

One of the biggest problems of modern technologies is that they deliver their cargo of information to us whether we have requested it or not. Unlike previous generations, who had to go to considerable trouble, and even put themselves at risk, to find out what they wanted to know, our modern world is such that information seeks *us* out — whether we want it or not. As an example, think of all the time we spend reading unwelcome emails or dealing with pop-up windows as we go about our work. Research such as that compiled by Tim Ferriss, author of *The 4-Hour Workweek*, is showing us — and I can confirm this from my own coaching — that email and its effective management present huge challenges for many people. Consider the following statistics:

- 66 per cent of people read email seven days a week and expect to receive a response the same day.

- 61 per cent continue to check email while on vacation.

- 56 per cent experience anxiety if they can't access email.

- 41 per cent check email first thing in the morning.

- 18 per cent check email right after dinner.

- 14 per cent check email when they get home from work.

- 14 per cent check email right before they go to bed.

- 40 per cent have checked their email in the middle of the night.

In one fascinating study conducted by King's College in London, IQ tests were administered to three groups: the first did nothing but perform the IQ test, the second was distracted by email and ringing phones, and the third was stoned on marijuana. Not surprisingly, the first group did better than the other two by an average of 10 points. The emailers, on the other hand, did worse than the stoners by an average of six points! Another study, conducted by Rutgers University, found that millions of users of internet-enabled mobile phones are unable to go more than five minutes without checking email — they have become addicted to information.

The real problem here is that we have let these technologies creep up on us and, along the way, we have forgotten that we actually have a *choice* about the information we expose ourselves to. Unfortunately, many people do not exercise this choice and, as a consequence, their lives can be unduly shaped by what's in their inbox or, worse still, they can suffer from the severe stress of information overload.

In this chapter, we will take a step back in order to critically examine the nature of information, its role in our lives and how best we can make *deliberate* choices about its impact on us. Along the way, I'll offer practical suggestions that I hope you will find useful. Let's begin with the basics — identifying the sources of information that influence *your* life.

Your unique information management style

Before you try to change something, increase your awareness of it.

— TIM GALLWEY

Consider the last time you made a major purchase — let's say a washing machine, television, or even a house. How did you go about it? Did you extensively research what you required? Did you seek out product reviews and read them carefully? Or did you loosely define what you wanted and then trust the advice of the salesperson? Your answer may well reveal something interesting about your habitual mode of dealing with and processing information in order to make decisions in your daily life. The key point is that there is no right or wrong approach, but it is worthwhile assessing how you deal with information in various situations. When I work with clients, they tend to be unaware of their information preferences. It's just something that people don't consider in any formal sense. Yet developing such an awareness can allow you to organise your life in surprising new ways.

When you start paying attention to information, you'll begin to notice that, depending on the situation, your 'information processing style' can alter, based on the importance of what you are dealing with, the risks involved and the level of trust you have in your information providers. This in itself is an interesting insight and worth thinking about. At what point does your style alter? As you contemplate further, you'll inevitably begin to question what is actually meant by the rather broad term *information*. Is there good and bad information, or is it all down to interpretation? Without getting too philosophical about it, I believe it's helpful to look at information as something that in some way creates an inward impact on its recipient. Information, according to management theorist Peter Drucker, is 'data endowed with relevance and purpose'. As we'll see later in this chapter, most of us suffer not from information overload, but from data overload.

A good way to better understand your information preferences is to consider how you learn best, because learning and information are linked. While there are several approaches to profiling your learning style, one method that I have found particularly helpful is that adopted by Peter Honey and Alan Mumford in their book *The Manual of Learning Styles*. This involves answering 80 questions, self-scoring the results and then drawing a four-cornered kite that indicates your preferences for learning. People generally have a tendency to veer towards one of the four descriptions: Activists, Reflectors, Theorists and Pragmatists. As you read more about each in the following list, identify which one you think best describes the kind of person you are:

- *Activists* involve themselves fully and without bias in new experiences. They enjoy the 'here and now' and are happy to be dominated by immediate experiences. They are open-minded rather than sceptical, and this tends to make them enthusiastic about anything new. Their philosophy is 'I'll try anything once'. They tend to act first and consider the consequences afterwards. They tackle problems by brainstorming. Their days are filled with activity and as soon as the excitement from one activity has died down they are busy looking for the next. They tend to thrive on the challenge of new experiences but are bored with implementation and longer term consolidation. They are gregarious people constantly involving themselves with others but, in doing so, they seek to centre all activities on themselves.

- *Reflectors* like to stand back to ponder experiences and observe them from many different perspectives. They collect data, both firsthand and from others, and prefer to think about it thoroughly before coming to any conclusion. The thorough collection and analysis of data about experiences and events is what counts, so they tend to postpone reaching definitive conclusions for as long as possible. Their philosophy is to be cautious. They are thoughtful people who like to consider all possible angles and implications before making a move. They prefer to take a back seat in meetings and discussions. They enjoy observing other people in action. They listen to others and get the drift of the discussion before making their own points. They tend to adopt a low profile and have a slightly distant, tolerant and unruffled air about them. When they act it is generally with an awareness of the big picture, including the past as well as the present, and others' observations as well as their own.

- *Theorists* integrate observations and disparate facts into complex but logically sound theories. They think problems through in a step-by-step logical way. They tend to be perfectionists who won't rest easy until things are tidy and fit into a rational scheme. They like to analyse and synthesise. They are keen on basic assumptions drawn from principles, theories and models. Their philosophy prizes rationality and logic. Questions they frequently ask are, 'Does it make sense?', 'How does this fit with that?' and 'What are the basic assumptions?' They tend to be detached, analytical and dedicated to rational objectivity rather than anything subjective or ambiguous. Their approach to problems is consistently logical. This is their 'mental set' and they rigidly reject anything that doesn't fit with it. They prefer to maximise certainty and feel uncomfortable with subjective judgements, lateral thinking and anything flippant.

- *Pragmatists* are keen on trying out ideas, theories and techniques to see if they work in practice. They positively search out new ideas and take the first opportunity to experiment with application. They are the sort of people who return from management courses brimming with new ideas they want to try out. They like to get on with things and quickly and confidently act on ideas that attract them. They tend to be impatient with ruminating and open-ended discussions. They are essentially practical, down-to-earth people who like making decisions and solving problems. They respond to problems and new opportunities as 'challenges'. Their philosophy is, 'There is always a better way' and 'If it works, it's good'.

Your natural learning style will determine how you work with information, how you seek it out, how you process it and how you use it to make decisions. Accordingly, an awareness of your preferences will help you to better organise many aspects of your life. For example, if you are a reflector, you'll make sure that you have plenty of time in which to evaluate information and not put yourself in situations that demand immediate responses. Such awareness could help you to estimate how long you need to complete a certain task, or even to choose a career that makes sense for you.

Modes of communication: pros and cons

I suppose it is tempting, if the only tool you have is a hammer, to treat everything as if it were a nail.

—ABRAHAM MASLOW

Years ago, the communications philosopher Marshall McLuhan made the famous statement that 'the medium is the message'. In other words, the medium of communication selected can often influence the way the message is received. Today, for example, information received in a formal letter is likely to be treated with a different level of respect than, say, the same information conveyed by text or email. What McLuhan recognised was that different media are more appropriate for certain tasks than others.

Organisations now face the challenge of helping their staff to select the right media for the right purpose. More and more, we need to be encouraged to use the full range of information tools rather than just relying on what is easy or convenient. Some years ago now, Harold Geneen of ITT Corporation observed,

> *In New York, I might read a request and say no. But in Europe, I could see that person's face, hear their voice, understand the intensity of their conviction, and the answer to the same question might be yes … it became our policy to deal with important problems on the spot, face-to-face.*

As technology becomes increasingly sophisticated, it is helpful to assess the different capabilities of the tools available to us. According to researchers Daft and Lengal in their studies on information processing and organisational design, each medium — whether telephone, email, text, memo, online video, group work or face-to-face conversation — has a degree of 'richness' that is determined by a blend of the following four factors:

- *Feedback.* Immediate response (feedback) allows questions to be asked and corrections to be made without a delay.

- *Multiple cues.* A message may contain not only words, numbers and graphic symbols but also the sender's bodily gestures, facial expressions and vocal inflection.

- *Language variety.* This is the range of meanings that can be conveyed with language symbols. Numbers, for example, can convey greater precision of meaning than words, which are used to convey a broader set of concepts and ideas.

- *Personal focus.* A message will be conveyed more fully when personal feelings and emotions infuse the communication.

Within the Daft and Lengal framework, face-to-face communication is the richest form of information media, followed by audio-video, audio only and then written media. Face-to-face is the richest form because it provides immediate feedback, so that understanding can be checked and interpretations corrected, and also allows for the observation of extralinguistic cues (body language, facial expression) that can convey important information. The telephone is a somewhat weaker medium than face-to-face communication. Feedback is fast, but visual cues are not available. Written communication is weaker still. Feedback can be slow because cues are limited to words on a screen or, even slower, paper. Formal standard numeric documents such as computer reports are lowest in information richness because they provide no opportunity for visual observation, feedback or personalisation.

The Daft and Lengal framework, therefore, suggests that we select the medium appropriate to the nature of the communication. Rich media are good for complex situations, whereas more distanced options are suitable for more straightforward tasks. Personally speaking, thinking in terms of information richness has helped me to become much more deliberate in choosing the right information tools for whatever task I am faced with.

Communicate effectively

Dig the well before you are thirsty.

—CHINESE PROVERB

Because communication is such a large part of our lives, I encourage you to take some time out to actively reflect on the range of different media you use and their appropriateness for different situations in your life. You may be surprised to discover that your information management approach has simply 'evolved' over time and that there are, in fact, much better ways of doing things.

Some time ago, I worked with an organisation that, as a group, had lost their sense of team spirit—partly because they had become overly reliant on email as a way to communicate with each other. Members of this group had begun to 'hide' behind their emails, saying things to their colleagues that they would not dream of saying to their faces. As we got people away from their computer screens and into personal contact with each other, we noticed an immediate improvement in cooperation and trust between individuals.

In my view, therefore, one of the very best investments an organisation can make is to implement standards and policies outlining how their people should communicate with each other. The same can be usefully done in relation to outside stakeholders such as customers, suppliers and business partners. Here are the kinds of questions and issues that might be addressed in such a policy:

- When should we use email? When should we use the phone? When is face-to-face contact the most appropriate?

- What is the best use of email? Email should be responded to within a 24-hour period. It is not a medium of choice to set up an appointment in five minutes. With this time expectation established, email changes from an 'always on' medium to one of convenience for non-urgent matters.

- When should we use CC and when should we use 'Reply All' in our emails?

- What does the use of BCC (blind copy) in emails imply? Using BCC can lower trust between people and messages can be inadvertently forwarded beyond their intended audience.

- Who owns emails? All staff ought to be aware that emails are owned by the organisation, and may be audited at any time.

- What's the best use of the subject line? The subject of the message should accurately summarise the contents. Also, abbreviations in the subject line can be useful; for example, for your attention (FYA), for your reading (FYR) and for your information (FYI).

- How can emails be clear and effective? Where action is required of the recipient, this should be specified at the start of the email. Where meetings have been arranged, it is highly desirable for an agenda to be circulated in advance, and for there to be a chair and minute taker if appropriate.

The same ideas behind organisational policy making also apply at a personal level. In order to become a more effective communicator, you might ask yourself: at what point does a back and forth email discussion require a telephone call or face-to-face get together? Conversely, when is a phone call or personal visit unnecessary and potentially disruptive? How do you best deliver bad news to someone? These are perhaps obvious questions to ask, but in my opinion they are not asked often enough. Being clear about your information management preferences can help you to use the many tools at your disposal more effectively and with more sensitivity.

I acknowledged earlier that email management is a constant problem for many people. It seems that the sheer volume of emails that need to be read, filed, deleted or responded to (or a combination of these things!) every day can be very difficult to deal with efficiently. If this is true for you, I would hazard a guess that you lack a clearly defined system for dealing with incoming and outgoing mail.

The most important decision you can make about email is how frequently to check it. Amazingly, most people have an 'always on' approach, which in my view is a recipe for disaster in your life. I would encourage you to set specific times and to stick by them. In his brilliant book *The 4-Hour Workweek*, Tim Ferriss shows us that it is entirely possible to live a productive life while only checking email once a day, or even once a week, even in the corporate environment.

When you do check your email, having a pre-defined approach is vital. I recommend that you make it your goal to have an empty inbox. In order to realistically achieve this, you really need to engage with each email only once, and deal with it there and then. The system I use is 'the four Ds method' as suggested by Kerry Gleeson in his book *The Personal Efficiency Program*:

- *Do it now!* If it can be done now—say, within the next 10 minutes—do it and be done with it.

- *Delegate it.* Send it to the right person to get it done. You might also set a reminder in your calendar to follow it up if you don't hear back in a reasonable amount of time.

- *Designate it.* If it's an email that will take you some time to respond to—perhaps you need to do some more work, get supporting information from somewhere else or just think further about it—drag it to your task list, calendar or 'to do' folder. Set a reminder in your calendar so that you'll be sure to come back to it.

- *Discard it or file it.* Delete the email if you don't need to keep a copy. File it if you need it for your records.

Along with the four Ds, here are some other points and useful suggestions that have been generated in my workshops:

- Take email alert off. It's annoying, distracting and can tempt you to check your email outside your designated times.

- Be timely, but don't necessarily respond right away to email. It creates expectations of immediacy that you do not want to encourage.

- Use filters to direct emails to specific folders.

- When drafting an email, enter addresses last to avoid sending it before it's ready to go.

- Use paragraphs and proper grammar. Check the email with the spell checker before sending it.

- Be careful what you write — it may be forwarded to someone you didn't want to see it.

- Do not reply to an email when you are upset.

- Include in your email signature a message about how frequently you check your inbox, and how you can be contacted if the matter is urgent.

- Always pause and re-read before pushing send.

Being deliberate about your information management is yet another way of being deliberate about your life. This control is easily within the grasp of everyone and makes all the difference to how you live your life in and out of work.

Incoming information

The notes I handle no better than many pianists. But the pauses between the notes — ah, that is where the art resides!

— ARTUR SCHNABEL

I mention some of my favourite books in earlier chapters. Another is *Lila: An Inquiry into Morals* by Robert Pirsig. Pirsig, better known as the author of the 1970s classic *Zen and the Art of Motorcycle Maintenance*, describes in *Lila* the adventures of a man named Phaedrus as he travels by boat down the Hudson

River on his way from Kingston to Florida. The purpose of this journey is not really to get anywhere, but to allow Phaedrus some space and time to gather his thoughts so he can come to grips with what he really believes about his world and his place in it. In one scene, we have Phaedrus on the deck of his boat with a set of trays where his various thoughts are recorded on thousands of 3-inch × 5-inch index cards, which have been carefully arranged in a certain sequence. Phaedrus believes that the purpose of the cards is not to help him to remember anything but actually so he can forget—his mind can then be totally empty so he can think.

We too must find ways of not getting bogged down by the information that comes at us from all directions in our daily lives. The key task is to take time out to actively and deliberately consider how you are going to handle the information that you know is coming your way. For example, what relationship will you have with various sources of news? Is daily news important to you? If so, are you more interested in national or international events, science and technology, business and commerce, or the latest celebrity gossip? While your specific interests are not of concern here, the important point is that you have decided what your news intake priorities are.

When you apply this thinking to all information sources—email, social networking, blogs, magazines, trade and industry publications, radio and television, and even work gossip—you'll notice yourself becoming much more discerning about what you engage with. Suddenly, you will notice yourself saying 'no' to many activities that are time consuming but hold little value for you.

Managing incoming information is also about establishing placeholders or 'buckets' for storing relevant information. One of the very best approaches to structuring your life in this way is extensively described by David Allen in his book, *Getting Things Done* (*GTD*). The goal is to organise your life so that you don't have to 'remember' anything. With a blank mind, you're free (like Phaedrus!) to apply yourself to the tasks that are actually important to you, safe in the knowledge that whatever system you have in place will reliably store important information for future access.

In my coaching, I have often recommended to people that they manage their day-to-day professional lives from a single work journal that contains all their to-do lists, meeting notes and related ideas. With a single journal, you'll always know where you recorded something and, therefore, avoid the problem of constantly asking yourself, 'Where did I write that down?', which seems to be a big issue for many people. When your work journal gets full, you can date it and put it in storage until the information contained in it is no longer relevant. I especially recommend this approach for managers who have multiple people reporting to them. It's an excellent way to keep track of what you have delegated and to whom, and, because the journal is always with you, you can record ideas and plan future work to be delegated in the same place.

When you are deliberate about your processes for handling incoming information, you will remove a major source of (perhaps underestimated) stress from your life. You will be much more effective, because you know that as more information is coming your way, you have a way to deal with it. You're ready.

Practical tools for information management

To read without reflecting is like eating without digesting.

—EDMUND BURKE

In all my years of helping people become more successful, I have consistently maintained that improving your information management skills is one of the very best ways you can develop yourself professionally. With just a little effort, you can boost your productivity in three key areas: speed reading, mind mapping and creative thinking. The great news is not only that these skills are essential to achieving success in every career but also that they are easily learned. Unfortunately, many of us did not learn these skills when we were younger; personally speaking, I spent years struggling with information problems before I learned that there was a better way.

The first area to work on is speed reading or, more accurately, the acquisition of effective reading methods (it's not just about reading quickly). Many of us leave school with the idea that the only way to read a book is line by line, from beginning to end! As you mature in your information habits, you begin to realise that this is a crazy and outdated idea that is simply wrong. Recent research in the fields of learning and cognition is showing that the key to effective reading is effective comprehension, and that you can improve your comprehension or understanding by adopting different reading strategies, including the following:

- Before you begin, 'scope out' what you are about to read by closely looking at the structure of the information being presented, noting in particular the table of contents, section headings, conclusions, tables or illustrations, and any summary paragraphs.

- Scan the document to get a feeling for the overall flow and the approach taken by the author.

- When you read, read 'blocks' of words, rather than individual words.

If speed reading sounds like it would be of use for you, I recommend that you spend a day or two on a formal course, where you will learn more about these and other techniques for absorbing information efficiently.

Mind mapping is the second skill that I highly recommend. Developed by Tony Buzan, the technique is founded on the notion that our minds do not operate well with words or lists, but instead work best with images. The idea is well summed up in the old saying 'a picture is worth a thousand words'. Buzan discovered that our learning can be vastly improved when we present our brains with information in the form of colourful pictures, where concepts are more easily grasped and connections can be made between different ideas. Unlike text or long lists of information that are one-dimensional, mind maps have more flexibility and are much more memorable.

The basic idea is to begin with a blank page and, in the middle, draw a bubble containing one or two words that describe the concept under study. From there, draw branches radiating out from the bubble, representing different aspects of the main idea, and name each branch with one or two words along the line. Ancillary branches can then be added to show more and more detail. As the map develops, links can be drawn between different branches as appropriate.

Mind mapping can transform how you work with information of all kinds. As well as the paper method, which I have just described, you can get simple computer software that does the same job but also allows you to easily modify your maps and share them with others. Among the software available are iMindMap (the official Buzan version and the one I used to plan every chapter of this book) and MindManager, as well as many freeware products for both Mac and PC.

The third area to work on is your creativity. Creativity is a skill that can be learned—it is not just something for 'creative' types such as artists, poets, musicians or writers. All of us can use our creativity to generate new ideas and to solve problems. An essential way of fostering creativity is to break away from old patterns of thinking and to look at things afresh. According to Edward de Bono, the originator of the term 'lateral thinking', creativity is the key to almost all achievement; moreover, it is a skill that can be learned, developed and applied. A recurring idea in de Bono's books—for example, *Six Thinking Hats* and *Six Frames: For Thinking about Information*—is that having creative ideas is not about having flashes of inspiration, but is rather a deliberate process of altering 'how you think', which leads to what he calls *serious* creativity. For example, one of de Bono's techniques is to use random words to force you to look at an old situation through a new lens. Another technique is to imagine a problem from someone else's point of view—for example, that of William Shakespeare or the conductor of an orchestra. The idea here is that most of us are constrained in our creative thinking by deeply embedded patterns and a range of 'mental locks' that inhibit what we think is possible.

If we learn to rely less on linear and habitual thought processes, we give truly creative ideas a chance to blossom in our lives. Creativity, along with mind mapping and speed reading, offer you new opportunities to deliberately improve how you work with information. These techniques are easy to learn and they can be learned by you.

Information dieting

The will to win is not nearly as important as the will to prepare to win.
— BOBBY KNIGHT

As the technology of information becomes more and more sophisticated, we as a society find ourselves dealing with a new disease: information overload. The symptoms of this epidemic are increased stress levels, anxiety brought about by an inability to deal with large volumes of information, and the need to work longer and longer hours simply to meet the demands of our work. Sound familiar? If these are the symptoms, what then are the underlying causes?

To answer this question, and to offer sensible strategies to address the problem, we need to examine the patient more closely. Like any disease, correct diagnosis is crucial and, in this case, the problem we are dealing with is not information overload, but *data* overload.

You will recall that earlier in this chapter I defined information as data endowed with relevance and purpose. Interestingly, when I talk to people who are suffering from information overload, one of their constant challenges is sifting through vast quantities of stuff (data), in the hope of finding what's useful and relevant to them. For example, many of us spend hours surfing the internet in the hope of finding information that, one day, may prove useful. In the same way, we spend many hours per month keeping up with our professional reading, yet most of that time is spent sifting the wheat from the chaff, and reading things that are just not that relevant.

In his excellent book *Information Overload*, psychologist David Lewis presents us with the results of a worldwide study that he undertook with Reuters. In this study, thousands of managers from a variety of industries and sectors were questioned about their informational experiences and problems. Among the starkest findings were the following:

- Around one-third of study participants reported being swamped by 'enormous amounts' of unsolicited information. Those most at risk were in middle and senior management roles, and those with human resource management responsibilities.

- One-third of managers admitted that they 'collected as much information as possible' for use in decision making. They believed that they were forced into doing this by the unique pressures of their workplace and industry.

- One-fifth of participants believed that information was collected simply to keep up with colleagues. One-third of junior managers believed that information gathering was dictated by office politics rather than necessity.

- Two-fifths claimed to have wasted a significant amount of time locating information.

- Around half of respondents felt unable to keep up with the level of reading required by their jobs.

- More than half of managers said they often stayed at work late or took work home with them so as to cope with the demands of information overload.

- Two-fifths of participants described their working environment as extremely stressful. Decisions, deadlines, tension with colleagues, long hours and a volatile marketplace all combined to create mental and physical stress.

Writing in the conclusion to the Reuters report (aptly named 'Dying for Information?'), Lewis wrote:

> *What this ... makes crystal clear is that finding ways of dealing with the information burden is now one of the most urgent world-wide challenges facing business. For unless we discover ways of staying afloat amidst the surging torrents of information, we may end up drowning in them!*

In my experience, one of the very best ways to deal with the phenomenon of overload is to go on an information diet, where you perhaps spend three or four weeks with only restricted access to your usual information sources. This involves completely cutting out television, radio, newspapers and internet surfing, and processing your emails only at specified times. From time to time I have put myself on such a diet, and recorded my thoughts about the experience. Here are a few of my observations:

- Our need for up-to-date daily news reports is grossly overestimated. Most of the time what is reported in the news is not news but entertainment — and most of it is not relevant to us in any way. If you want to stay current with world events, it's much better to read quality weekly sources such as *TIME* magazine, *Business Week* or *The Economist*. A weekly perspective is much more helpful than the drip-feed of daily information doses.

- Most information, if it's important, will find you. You'll know about things that are truly important because they will come to your attention in the normal course of your day and in your interactions with people who matter.

- By temporarily absenting yourself from the 'information loop', you'll get the opportunity to ask questions of those around you. What's happening? What is your opinion on that? Are you sure it's true? You will be genuinely interested in the opinions of others and will become much more discerning about what is said, what you hear, and what you believe.

- Processing information can be incredibly time consuming. With the need for less information in your world, you regain control of your life and find yourself with so much more time to do the things that really matter to you.

This information dieting approach allows you to stop and connect with what is truly important to you, and is a critical first step to overcoming your information-overload problems. I predict you'll be surprised by what you discover about yourself, and with this insight you'll go on to design a new, more deliberate way of working with information.

A second strategy for overcoming information overload is to become more aware of when you have gathered enough information. Sometimes, spending effort collecting more data for analysis is simply not worth it. According to Barry Schwartz, author of *The Paradox of Choice*, too many of us mistakenly believe that more is better, when all that more information does is increase the choices available to us, resulting in greater confusion and anxiety. It's another case of less is more!

Your computer set-up

It's the little things that make the big things possible. Only close attention to the fine details of any operation makes the operation first class.

—J. WILLARD MARRIOTT

Winston Churchill said that he spent the first 25 years of his life wanting freedom, the next 25 years wanting order and the next 25 realising that order *is* freedom. In this spirit, something simple such as reorganising your electronic files is well worth your time and effort. An orderly life starts with getting the details right. While some organisations have policies regarding the structure of their electronic filing systems, many do not. Even for those that do, there still can be enough flexibility for you to create a personal system of your own. And then, of course, you need to organise your personal electronic files, such as any projects you may be working on, your financial records and your photographs.

The key to coming up with a good system is to think intuitively: what makes sense to you? Ideally, you won't have to think when you have new information to store or when you need to find something because you'll instantly know where to look. Whatever system you adopt, it's good to be consistent about it; where possible, for example, try to replicate the same basic structure for your paper files, your electronic files and your email folder.

A sensible file-naming convention for your files is absolutely vital. For example, when storing correspondence (say, letters or email drafts) are you going to embed the file name with a date at the start (yyyymmdd) so that they are in order on your screen? If you need to save different versions of the same document, how will you know which is the most recent one? For files that have become inactive or historical, how are you going to archive them?

Remember that the goal of developing a clear filing system is to feel good because you know that if you need to find a file or document, you can do so easily and with confidence that it's the right version. With an orderly set-up, you'll find it easy to keep a clean desktop, and you'll have direct access to your most frequently accessed documents. In essence, like our friend Phaedrus journeying down the Hudson River, you'll free yourself up to focus on what is truly important.

Computer maintenance and security

Motivation is what gets you started. Habit is what keeps you going.

— JIM ROHN

Many years ago, as a junior management consultant, I learned a lesson that has served me well ever since. On one of the first days of my working life, I was assigned to help a company build a financial model so they could more accurately put a cost to their products, which in turn would allow them to calculate a profit margin and price their products for sale. The complicated aspect of this assignment — and the reason they were enlisting the help of an expensive consulting firm — came down to the product in question: pigs. The trouble with pigs is that the meat can be cut in different ways and, depending on how it's done, the costs can alter widely because of the skill and time required to make the products.

As I arrived at the factory to begin work on the financial model, I was assigned a desk and computer in an office adjacent to the main factory. In preparation for my work, I decided to format a computer disk, which would allow me to save my work as I went. I keyed in the normal instruction (format a:) and waited for the green light over the disk to come on. I waited for several minutes, but no green light. Then to my utter horror, I saw a green light flashing on the hard disk of the computer itself! What had happened, in fact, was that someone had switched the names of the computer drives and I had inadvertently formatted and deleted the hard disk of the main computer.

In a state of panic I stopped the formatting process, but it was too late: all the important files had been lost. Within a few minutes, someone from the factory next door came to say that something was wrong and that the production line had just stopped. Not only was the computer I was working on for office use, but it also controlled the operation of the factory production line! I felt sick to my stomach and the nightmare turned worse when we discovered that there was no backup procedure in place for the computer, and all the files were lost. It took several weeks of working 24/7 to get things back to the way they had been and for the factory to operate as normal.

As you will appreciate, some lessons in life you learn the hard way and, for me, always having a reliable backup of computer files is never far from my mind. If you're like most people, this is one area that you need to look at closely. It amazes me to see some people's most important documents (and memories in the form of photographs) have not been securely backed up. As you consider how you can best secure your important information, here are some further points to bear in mind:

- Schedule your computer backup to occur regularly — at least once a month — and on a specific day, such as the first day of each month, so you have a definite reminder.

- Back up all your data files to an external data source that can be kept away from your computer, ideally in an off-site location. Many organisations have their own policies about backup frequency and locations for corporate data security.

- Consider using backup software, which speeds up the task by only copying files that have changed since last time.

- Test your backup routine by successfully restoring all your data files to another computer.

- Regularly defragment your computer's hard disk to optimise file opening and saving.

- Make sure your virus protection and firewall software is up to date and fully functioning.

Being deliberate with the safety of your most important electronic files is something you will never, ever regret. Trust me, I know!

Take opportunities to upskill

If you're walking down the right path and you're willing to keep walking, eventually you'll make progress.

— BARACK OBAMA

I live in New Zealand, and one of the nation's all-time heroes is Sir Peter Blake. Sir Peter was a yachtsman who led Team New Zealand in their boat NZL32 *Black Magic* to win the America's Cup in 1995, beating Dennis Connor 5–0 in a dramatic series of race-offs in San Diego. Five years later, Blake successfully defended the cup to become the first non-American to do so in the 150-year history of the event. In preparation for the races, Sir Peter famously asked a single question in response to each idea the team came up with: 'Will it make the boat go faster?' It's a good question. And it's a good question for you to ask in relation to the information technology you come in contact with. Does increasing my knowledge of this particular technology actually help with what's important to me?

Studies estimate that 95 per cent of Microsoft Office users rely on just 5 per cent of the features available. For those of us who have fairly basic needs, this is entirely okay and I would recommend continuing with this approach. For others, however, investing a little time and effort to learn about some of the more advanced features could really pay off. For example, learning to link several spreadsheets together or to use the Table of Contents features within your word processor can significantly increase your productivity.

You might also ask yourself, 'Can I use my voicemail or my phone better?' or, more broadly, 'Given advances in technology, am I still using the most appropriate tools?' Perhaps your information habits were formed many years ago, and have continued with you despite the availability of new tools that would serve you better. One approach to doing this is to review your work with the help of a knowledgeable colleague or IT consultant.

As an ongoing part of your professional development, take an active interest in emerging technologies, and be open to new ways of working. Remember, however, to continually ask Peter Blake's question, 'Does it make the boat go faster?'

Take charge of your technology

Everything popular is wrong.

— OSCAR WILDE

We have now taken a critical look at the role of information and information technology in our lives. There is no doubt that, compared to the generations before us, we indeed live in interesting times and that, properly used, today's numerous information sources can add richness and quality to our relationships, the work that we do, and even our understanding of the world.

Nevertheless, as we come to the close of this chapter, I want to remind you that, as a deliberate person, you are in control of your technology; it doesn't control you. All too often, our lives are governed by ringing phones, text messages and incoming emails. While all these technologies have undoubtedly made our lives easier and even more enjoyable, it is still important to think of them as tools that should assist, not dominate, us. As a society, we are in real danger of forgetting what's actually important to us — of mistakenly putting technology before human relationships. Don't let that happen to you.

Ideas for Action

- If you have not already done so, back up your computer now and store a copy of your most important files in a secure off-site location.

- Review your computer set-up so that it is well organised and serves you well. In particular, consider your folder and file structure and the naming conventions for your files. Do the same for your email inbox and your paper-based files.

- Learn how to use the powerful tool of mind mapping by downloading the trial software that is easily available on the internet. Many of these products are available for a limited time—usually two weeks—and they allow you to trial them for free.

- Find out something new about the technologies you use every day—what more can they do for you?

Nothing in life is to be feared. It is only to be understood.

—MARIE CURIE

Beliefs — guiding your behaviour

The gull sees furthest who flies highest.

—RICHARD BACH

Al Gore once remarked (quoting Mark Twain) that 'What gets us in trouble is not what we don't know — it's what we know for sure that just ain't so'. Indeed, sometimes we have to learn the hard way that our most cherished beliefs are in some way wrong or unhelpful to us. When you start living a deliberate life, you'll become more aware of the beliefs you hold, and how they influence the choices you make and the results you get. Many of us are not directly conscious of our beliefs, and seldom scrutinise our basic assumptions about ourselves and the world around us. Sometimes it is fear that prevents us from challenging ourselves in this way. Yet our beliefs are not fixed entities, genetically handed down or above interrogation — or at least they shouldn't be.

The purpose of this chapter is to challenge this kind of erroneous thinking. Together, we'll uncover the true nature of your beliefs, investigate where they come from and then subject them to some healthy cross-questioning. We'll also carefully examine some common beliefs in the same way. Who knows? Perhaps you'll change your mind about some ideas that have been with you for a long time.

Our beliefs might be described as the railway tracks of the mind in the way they act as a guiding mechanism: much as railway tracks govern the direction of a train, our beliefs determine the direction of our thinking, and what we consider to be possible, reasonable or true. When you think about it, the route outlined by railway tracks is the direct consequence of decisions made many years ago by a now unknown engineer.

Perhaps that engineer was working within certain constraints, had a limited budget, or was working with more basic tools to build bridges or cut through mountains. Nonetheless, the tracks are where they are and trains have taken that route ever since. The scenery has always been the same.

Recent scientific research is showing that our beliefs and the thoughts we think have the power to alter our body chemistry and even the structure of our DNA. In his fascinating book *The Biology of Belief*, scientist Bruce Lipton writes that our beliefs generate a field of invisible energy that influences the very structure and development of cells in our body. In other words, you can actually alter your genetic structure by modifying how you see yourself.

Furthermore, the beliefs we hold not only control what we think and how we behave, but they also have the power to influence the thoughts and behaviours of people around us. According to Richard Brodie, author of *Virus of the Mind*, 'A thought, belief, or attitude in your mind can spread to and from other people's minds'. Drawing on a field of study known as memetics, Brodie gives numerous examples showing how beliefs have the ability to spread quickly, duplicate and influence society as a whole. Of course, this is partly why we can speak about the development of distinctive 'cultures' in workplaces, institutions and even entire nations.

Our beliefs provide us with a stable context as we journey through life, and are often laid down during our formative years. They tell us what's possible and what's not, and alert us when we are going outside our comfort zones. But you need to ask yourself some key questions. Are they true? Are they fit for purpose? And do they bear a durable relation to your ULP?

Know your beliefs

Within you right now is the power to do things you never dreamed possible. This power becomes available to you just as soon as you can change your beliefs.

—MAXWELL MALTZ

A belief is any thought that you assume to be true. And the more you have that thought, the more it becomes true for you. So, what do you believe about yourself? Do you believe that you are capable, clever, attractive and lucky? Or are you unfortunate, undeserving and dumb? And how about your relationship with the outside world? Is the world out to trap you or is it there to support you and help you to live your best life? Depending on what you believe, your life will begin to take on a distinct shape. You'll start looking for evidence to support your beliefs and soon enough you'll start finding that evidence. Your beliefs will become stronger and more self-verifying as each day passes. And your life will come to reflect those beliefs like a mirror.

A great illustration of this important point is quoted by Robin Sieger in his book *You Can Change Your Life...Any Time You Want*:

There was a widowed farmer who had two sons who were five years apart in age. When the elder son got to the age of fifteen, the farmer, unable to give him any work on the farm, sent him away to find fame and fortune. As they parted at the farm gate, the farmer wished his son well and gave him one final instruction: 'Keep to yourself. Don't trust anybody, son, because everyone you meet will try to rob you. Look after yourself first and foremost.'

Five years later, it came the younger son's time to leave home, too. In the time that had passed, the father had remarried — this time to a soft and dreamy woman. The new wife really influenced the farmer and he became more mellow, forgiving and gentle. This time, as he said goodbye from the gate to his second son, his advice was somewhat different: 'The world is a beautiful and exciting place. Everyone you meet is fighting their own battles — they are doing their best. The best you can do is to help your fellow man — remember they will do the same for you.'

Many years later, the sons returned home for the very first time. Much older, the farmer asked, 'How did life go?' Each of the boys described their adventures and each found the world exactly as their father predicted all those years ago.

Where do our beliefs come from? We are born with no beliefs. To a very small child everything is possible; there are no limits, no preconceptions and no prejudices. As we grow, we gradually learn our beliefs from those around us — our parents, our wider family, and especially the friends we make in our early schooling. Several research studies have shown that around 80 per cent of our core beliefs have been formed by the age of eight. These early beliefs can be so ingrained in our thinking that they stay with us for the rest of our lives. This is partly because, as we get older, we cement our early beliefs by seeking out friendships with people who broadly share our perception of the world. Business philosopher Jim Rohn has proposed that we are amalgamations of the five people with whom we spend most time. Think about it; is this true for you?

But beliefs are not entirely passive things. They can be changed. Through careful and deliberate examination, it is possible to identify those beliefs that don't serve us well. To begin this process, it is useful to make a list of what you consider to be your most important beliefs. Go to a clean page in your journal and draw a line down the middle. On the left, write the belief itself; on the right, note when you first formed that belief. To get you started, complete the sentence 'I believe that…' 20 times, and try to touch upon all aspects of your life as honestly as possible.

Good. Simply identifying your most significant beliefs is the beginning of a vitally important mental audit. The head engineer has begun to reassess the placement and effectiveness of the tracks!

Question yourself

It is the mark of an educated mind to be able to entertain a thought without accepting it.
— ARISTOTLE

Before we get into your own beliefs, I want to list some of the more commonly held — and unhelpful — beliefs that I have collected while coaching clients over the years. If you share some of these beliefs yourself, add them to your list:

- It's not in my nature to…

- I can't afford it.

- I'm not smart enough.

- It will take too long.

- It's too late now.

- I'm too old (or too young).

- It will be too difficult.

- I'm not lucky.

- I don't deserve it.

- There is nobody to help me.

- It's going to be risky.

- I don't have the time/energy/stamina.

- I am too busy.

- Nobody in my family has done this before.

These beliefs, along with a thousand others, condition our thinking every day. Moreover, in the long term, they can shape our entire lives. So how do we go about examining these beliefs? A very good way was developed by author Byron Katie, in response to her own experience of living with beliefs that were causing her tremendous suffering and pain. When Katie put some of her beliefs under the microscope, she observed that many of them were untrue. The method she developed for examining beliefs is called 'The Work', and is composed of four short questions followed by what is known as a turnaround question.

Katie's four questions are:

1 Is it true?
2 Can you absolutely know that it's true?
3 How do you react when you believe that thought?
4 Who would you be without the thought?

The idea is to honestly ask yourself each of these four questions for each belief that you want to examine. To get the most out of the process, take your time over each question, wait in silence, and then just see what emerges for you. Once you've walked yourself through the four questions, turn the belief around by finding a statement that is the opposite of the original belief. Then try to find three genuine examples of how the opposite statement is true in your life.

Let's take an example. The belief 'I *have* to go to work' is one that many people claim to be true in their lives. In fact, it's a belief that many of us feel very negatively towards—most of us don't like *having* to do anything. Let's apply the first question—'Is it true?' Well, when you really look at it, nobody has to go to work. Sure, to attain a certain lifestyle or to maintain some kind of status in your community it might be desirable, but fundamentally nobody is standing over us whipping us on our way to work. There are many reasons going to work is a good idea, but it's not essential. When we apply the second question—'Can you absolutely know that it's true?'—we must, therefore, come to the conclusion that no, we cannot.

The third question ('How do you react?') helps us to identify the stressful thoughts that come our way when we think about our work as an obligation. We may resent the fact that our work limits our freedom or takes us away from what we really enjoy doing. Without the belief (which question four relates to), we may feel lighthearted and experience a level of freedom that is healthy and refreshing. We may even feel good about our work, knowing that it is something we are not obligated to do.

The final part of the process is to find a turnaround statement that expresses the opposite of our original belief. In our case it would be, 'I don't have to go to work' or, even better, 'I can choose to go to work or not'. Imagine the difference it makes to wake up in the morning and actively choose to go to work rather than believing that you 'have' to. You'll go willingly and in a much more positive frame of mind. As you begin to find evidence that the opposite statement is true, you'll feel better and better knowing that, in fact, work for you is a choice, and it's a choice you're genuinely making.

The benefit of questioning your beliefs is, in my view, beyond compare. Because your beliefs lurk in the background of your life, they infuse everything you do. They determine what you think, how you think and, ultimately, your behaviour and your relationships. As you now review your beliefs, you may be surprised by what you discover. You'll know you're on the right track when you feel an inner calm beginning to develop—a calm that says 'I'm in control', and which characterises your true and authentic self.

The 'failure' belief

Only one thing makes a dream impossible: the fear of failure.

—PAULO COELHO

By any standard, one of my friends, Matt Murray, is truly successful. Matt is one of the most positive people I know and is really good fun to be around. Over his lifetime, Matt has had a varied career as a professional banker, marketer, university professor and, finally, entrepreneur. Today, Matt is independently wealthy and spends his time doing things that he is truly passionate about, such as environmental projects and visiting remote parts of the world. One day, as I caught up with Matt in a café, I asked him what the secret to his amazing success was. He told me that, for him, real success begins with understanding the true nature of failure. To illustrate his point he told this story:

> *When I was young, Saturday night was the highlight of the week because that's when we went dancing at our local community hall. Soon after nine o'clock, the doors of the hall would open and the assembled crowd outside would make their way inside, where it was warm as the band began to play. The girls dressed in their finest clothes would be on the left side of the hall, where they would sit with their soft drinks chatting with their girlfriends. On the other side would be the boys, standing and likely having a beer with their friends.*
>
> *As the evening progressed, the boys would summon the courage to walk across the dance floor and ask their chosen girl for a dance. More often than not, the girl would look the boy up and down and, for whatever reason, reject the invitation and come up with some excuse such as 'I'm just with my girlfriends' or 'Not now, maybe later'. In other words — no way!*
>
> *At this, the boy would be left standing there — feeling dejected — and dreading the prospect of making the long walk back to the other side of the room with his friends looking on. For many boys, the embarrassment of the situation would leave them feeling down and the result was that they were unlikely to ask anyone else to dance that night.*
>
> *As I looked on at many of my friends going through the agony of failure, I began to look at the situation in a different way. Instead of being discouraged by a 'no', why not believe that 'no' was just one step closer to 'yes'?*

So with this belief, I would confidently make my way across the room, ask the girl to dance and, if she said no, simply turn to the next girl and ask her to dance, and so on, until I found someone to dance with me. Because my approach was different from all the other boys, soon enough girls would be impressed by my confidence, and actually want me to ask them to dance.

What I learned from that experience was that it's very important to see failure not as something final, but a step towards success. When we think of it this way, we don't have to put ourselves through the mental torture of 'walking back across the dance floor' but instead can focus on moving one step closer towards our goal.

Matt applied the lessons of the dance hall to his entire life — professional and personal. He actually welcomes 'failure' because, deep down, he knows that setbacks are gateways to future success. It's an approach that has worked really well for Matt, and I would encourage you to reflect on it as you examine your own beliefs about failure. How do you react to failure, rejection and setbacks?

For me, one of the major learning experiences of my life was discovering that the most successful people also have the most failures. When you study success literature, you'll find that people in all walks of life — business, politics, the arts, sports — have more down times than up times. And the reason for this is obvious: you learn more from your failures than from your successes. Donald Trump was once asked by a reporter how long it would take him to remake his fortune should he lose it overnight. He responded, 'Half as long and I would make twice as much, because I would now know what *not* to do!'

In a fascinating study of success and upward mobility conducted by Dr Edward Banfield of Harvard University, it was found that the single most important attribute of people who achieved great success in life was 'long time perspective'. Banfield, who carried out his study over 50 years, defined 'time perspective' as 'the amount of time an individual takes into consideration when determining their present actions'. In other words, the most successful people are those who make their decisions with the long term — not immediate gratification — in mind. This mental approach helps them to view their 'failures' in a wider context so that setbacks are not fatal to their overall success. As one athlete put it, stumbling blocks are really starting blocks.

In my own work with successful people, I have observed time and again that those who have achieved great success tend to have more stamina and self-discipline than others. Despite apparent failure, they keep at things longer and with a higher level of intensity. Very often this extra effort is the difference between failure and success. Someone once sent me a poem entitled 'Don't Quit' (author unknown) that perfectly captures the point I'm making here:

> *When things go wrong, as they sometimes will,*
> *When the road ahead seems all uphill.*
> *When the funds are low and the debts are high,*
> *And you want to smile, but you have to sigh.*
> *When care is pressing you down a bit,*
> *Rest if you must, but don't you quit.*
>
> *Life is strange with its twists and turns,*
> *As every one of us sometimes learns.*
> *And many a failure turns about,*
> *When you might have won had you stuck it out.*
> *Don't give up though the pace seems slow,*
> *You may succeed with another blow.*
>
> *Success is failure turned inside out,*
> *The silver tint of the clouds of doubt.*
> *And you can never tell how close you are,*
> *It may be near, when it seems so far.*
> *So stick to the fight when you are the hardest hit,*
> *It is when things seem worst that you must not quit!*

Our beliefs about failure are worth examining. If you can begin to see failure as your friend, teacher and guide, you'll soon discover that everything that happens to you happens for a reason; your job is to be an attentive student. Look towards the future knowing that what you experience today is paving the way to your tomorrow. And, please, don't quit.

What others think of you

What others think of you is none of your business.

—JACK CANFIELD

Of all the inhibiting thoughts that people have, the one that creates the biggest barrier to achieving real success is oversensitivity to what other people think of us. How often have we heard ourselves say, 'What would so-and-so say about that behaviour?' or even, 'So-and-so would turn in their grave if they knew that!' The reality is that no matter how hard you try, you will never fully meet everyone's expectations. There will *always* be someone, somewhere, who does not approve of or agree with you. The sooner you accept this fundamental truth, the better.

Now, just to be clear here, I am not saying that we should ignore the feelings, needs or expectations of others—these things should certainly enter into our thinking. But while it is good to be aware of others' wishes, this awareness should not be our sole point of reference when it comes to making decisions. The danger is that—and I have seen this many, many times—if you are not careful, you can end up living someone else's life by pandering to the whims of those around you. If you try to please everyone, you will satisfy nobody—least of all yourself.

For many of us, our beliefs about the opinions of others were formed in our early childhood and are deeply ingrained in our psyche. And because they are so deep within us, it takes a tremendous effort to learn to think otherwise. Perhaps the best way to examine the particular belief that others' opinions matter more than yours do is to ask, 'Where does this belief come from?' and 'Why is it a problem?' The idea that we should be sensitive to the opinions of others really comes from our desire (perhaps even evolutionary need) to fit in socially. Many of us crave the love and approval of others and will go to great lengths to achieve these things—even, sometimes, to the point of acting against our moral instincts.

In his book *The Four Agreements*, Don Miguel Ruiz advises that no matter what happens around you, 'don't take it personally'. Ruiz shows that many of our knee-jerk responses come from a mistaken assumption that 'everything is about me' when in truth this just isn't the case. When you take things personally, you put yourself centre stage, and then relate everything that happens around you back to yourself. For example, if someone you meet gives you an opinion and says, 'Hey, you annoy me', in truth that person is dealing with his or her own feelings and (no doubt) insecurities. The fact is that this person's opinion is totally independent of you. Of course, what is likely to happen is that the moment we hear the opinion we take it personally, and start analysing how it relates to us. We might think to ourselves, 'How dare they say that?', 'Am I really that kind of person?' or 'Do other people find me annoying too?' In reality, however, it was just someone else's opinion and because you took it personally, the comment came true for you. Opinion became truth.

The consequences of being highly sensitive to the opinions of others are significant and far-reaching. For a start, because people around us have different expectations and opinions, we'll be forever stretched by their competing demands. The consequences here are practical as well as emotional. For example, someone who tries to please everyone will often find themselves saying 'yes' to too many things and then struggling to deliver on what they promised — often pleasing no-one!

In our professional lives, too, we need to develop self-confidence in order to maintain a healthy detachment from the opinions of others. This is especially important when it comes to saying 'no' when this is the right answer. As you get better at being assertive in this way, your ability to deliver where it really matters improves enormously. As I like to say, when you say 'no', you are really saying 'yes' to something more important.

Interestingly, one research study found that people who rise to the top of the corporate ladder are not those who necessarily say 'yes' most often, but those who actually deliver on their promises. Reliability is more important than short-term popularity. I urge you, then, to carefully examine your beliefs and habits as regards the need to please. The best advice I can give you is to always do what *you* think is right — irrespective of the opinions of others.

Busyness and success

Everything is created twice — first mentally, then physically.

— GREG ANDERSON

You may recall that in the prologue I identified three Myths of Success—one of which was the idea that 'busy is best'. Behind this myth is the belief that the amount of activity in your life is a good measure of how successful you are. If we were to apply Byron Katie's first question ('Is that true?'), we may be surprised by what we find.

At the heart of this belief is the mistaken notion that activity leads to outcomes. In fact, it's not being busy that matters, but rather being occupied with the *right* kinds of activities. Many years ago, when I first became interested in success as an area of study, I spent two weeks each with 10 chief executive officers from large companies. One of these CEOs, David Bale, was one of the least busy people I have ever met. David ran a complex multimillion-dollar business that was a world leader in its field. Yet he never seemed hurried and had a calmness about him that permeated through his entire organisation.

As I studied David more closely, I noticed that despite the complexity of his business, he only focused his attention on a handful of important issues each day. He knew that full concentration on those four or five things, where he could make a unique contribution, was the very best way he could lead his company. Everything that fell outside his area of focus was either delegated or postponed. While we may not all be CEOs, we can nevertheless learn an important lesson from David Bale. If you can isolate those few things in your life that really matter and then focus your energy on them, you'll end up achieving far more with less stress.

You may well ask, 'If this is all so simple, how come we all don't do it?' Well, as you might expect, the answer is to be found deep within our shared cultural belief about being busy. There are two reasons we continue to mistakenly believe that busy is best. First is the circumstance that, as individuals, we derive a sense of meaning and self-importance from the things that we do. We get tied up in our own story and, before we know it, we've become the central character. Instead of looking at what needs to be done, we look at how we can be most involved in the doing of it. In other words, our ego takes over. For example, people new to team-leader roles sometimes struggle to 'let go' so that team members can get on with their work without the constant 'just checking' or 'helping' of their manager. If you are a team leader or manager, your role is to lead or manage—not do. In our personal lives, too, many of us occupy ourselves with things that we should not be doing at all. We forget that there are ways of getting the job done without our direct involvement. You might think here of DIY projects, household maintenance and community-based schemes that you can uniquely contribute to without overcommitting your time and energy.

The key is to clearly identify the outcome you are trying to achieve and then assess how your particular skills fit into the picture. When you do this, your own involvement in the story is not that important, your ego is in check, and you feel authentic. You are busy for the right reasons.

The second reason we believe that busy is best is social and cultural. People who are busy are seen to be industrious and successful, while those who are not are seen to be lazy. To get away from this false belief, you need to learn to accept that 'not doing' is an entirely worthwhile way to spend some of your time. In fact, becoming friendly with an element of relaxation in your life is highly desirable. One of my friends, Wayne Bailey, openly attributes his many successes in life to being a fundamentally relaxed and easy-going person. As Wayne puts it, 'Being relaxed has meant that I have had to become a better and more creative thinker. And that has made all the difference'. Indeed, Edward de Bono, who has written many wonderful books on creativity and lateral thinking, said that one of the biggest problems facing our society is that we don't value the development of thinking skills, preferring instead to reward doing and activity.

I, therefore, encourage you to take a step back, see what's really important, and examine how you can uniquely contribute to achieving outcomes that really matter. Along the way, see if becoming strategically 'lazy' helps you become less busy and more creative. I predict you'll discover a new side to yourself.

You deserve success

The harder you work, the luckier you get.

— GARY PLAYER

'When will I be found out?' 'Is my life a fraud?' You would be surprised by how frequently people I coach ask me one of these two questions. Behind both questions is a lurking belief that somehow we do not deserve success in our lives. Of all the beliefs we are examining in this chapter, this one *really* holds us back from achieving our full potential. When you start looking, you'll see that many people live with this false belief. Such individuals will justify their belief with such statements as:

- I'm not worthy of success.

- I'm not smart.

- I'm not lucky.

- I'm not qualified enough.

We've already looked at how our beliefs can have a significant influence on us, and this is certainly true for our beliefs about success. Further, we may discover that such thinking has been with us for a long time—perhaps even from early childhood. As we grew from children to young adults, we may have been programmed to have what is known as an 'inferiority complex'. For some reason, we took on the belief that we were not good enough or that other people were more deserving of success than ourselves.

When you examine this belief now, you will quickly come to the conclusion that you are a unique individual with unique talents and abilities. As we have already discovered, there is absolutely no point in comparing yourself to other people, and other people's opinions are of limited concern to you.

Another belief we may have is the notion that we are not smart enough and, therefore, others are more deserving of success than we are. Again, when we put this assumption to the test, we'll see that it is not true. The truth is that people are smart in different ways; your job is to discover the ways in which you are 'smart' and to build on those. One of the greatest developments of the past 25 years has been the theory of multiple intelligences, based on the work of Harvard psychologist Daniel Goleman. Finally, with more sophisticated ways of measuring different forms of intelligence (for example, emotional intelligence or EQ), we have moved away from the IQ test as the empirical measure of how smart we really are.

The idea that success is somehow associated with being 'lucky' is yet another belief we need to question. In my experience, persistence, discipline and hard work are much more important than luck. The notion of luck brings to mind a life lived based on the throwing of some kind of cosmic dice. In my view, it's much better to think of the numbers you get or the hand you are dealt as just the starting point in building a great life. How you play with the numbers or cards is what really matters.

In his intriguing study *The Luck Factor*, Max Gunther follows the lives of thousands of people, including Kirk Douglas and several professional gamblers, and concludes that your luck is something you can actually influence. Interestingly, people who are 'lucky' are much more *deliberate* in five key areas of their lives: how carefully they build their network of professional and personal contacts; how they tune into their 'hunches' of what is right and wrong; how they make 'bold' decisions when such decisions are needed; how they 'exit' from situations in order to minimise their losses; and, finally, how they have evolved a way of 'reality checking' the quality of their decisions.

What we are getting at here is that many of the excuses we use to justify the belief that success is not for us are simply untrue. Isn't it exciting to know that you don't have to believe everything you think!

Your beliefs about money

Happiness lies not in the mere possession of money; it lies in the joy of achievement, in the thrill of creative effort.

—FRANKLIN D. ROOSEVELT

Anthony J. F. O'Reilly, the former chairman and CEO of Heinz Company and former international rugby player, was once playing in a celebrity football game to raise money for charity. During the game, O'Reilly was tackled awkwardly and his injury required him to be taken to the local hospital for emergency surgery. As he waited somewhat anonymously in the waiting room of the hospital, a nurse came along with a clipboard and began asking him a series of questions. One of the questions was, 'Do you make more than $20 000?' O'Reilly famously answered, 'Some days I do, some days I don't!'

Beliefs about resources, and about money in particular, are really worth looking at. Many of us grow up thinking that money is scarce, difficult to come by, and even 'the root of all evil'. Many of my own early money beliefs were inherited directly from my parents because for them money was difficult, and indeed very scarce. But the reality is it does not have to be scarce for me.

It may surprise you to know that the vast majority of people who are millionaires today started with nothing. Through hard work, careful spending and saving, and the application of certain principles they were able to achieve a level of financial success that made them truly independent. I highly recommend that you make 'achieving financial independence' one of your goals—which is to say, that you include it in your list of campaigns and potentially make it part of your ULP statement. People who are financially independent have a level of freedom in their day-to-day lives because they don't have to think about money and, therefore, can focus their full attention on doing things that really matter to them. Major problems are caused when we hold distorted beliefs about money and the role that it plays in our lives. Perhaps not surprisingly, money troubles are a main reason marriages end in divorce.

The first inaccuracy is that we *earn* money. No, we don't. We get paid money for the *value* we contribute. Therefore, if you want to have more money, think of ways of contributing more value. This explains why some people get paid $15 per hour while others make $1000 in the same amount of time. The difference is in the value they offer. Once you accept this crucial point and reset your beliefs about earning money, you'll see money not so much as something to get but as a form of score-keeping for the value you are offering. Soon enough, your mind will actively start working on ways of increasing the value of what you are doing. One of the very best ways you can do this is to study the lives of people who have already achieved financial success. In his books *The Millionaire Next Door* and *The Millionaire Mind*, Thomas Stanley provides us with fascinating insights into the lives of financially independent people:

- About two-thirds are self-employed.

- Many are in businesses that could be classified as 'dull-normal' such as building, farming, accommodation or pest control.

- Most live in modestly priced homes with more than half occupying the same home for more than 20 years.

- Few received any inheritance.

- They generally live well below their means, wear inexpensive clothing and watches, and drive older cars.

- Many are interested in education and are skilled investors.

These books, along with other classics such as *Rich Dad, Poor Dad* by Robert Kiyosaki and *The Automatic Millionaire* by David Bach, provide revealing insights into the habits of financially independent people and the tactics they used to achieve what was important to them.

A second mistaken belief about money has to do with how money works to replicate itself. Albert Einstein referred to this as 'the miracle of compound interest' in reference to the incredible way that money increases in value, if properly invested. If most people in the developed world were, with a little discipline, to save and invest just 10 per cent of what they get paid from the time they begin work to when they are 65, on retirement they would be automatic millionaires. You can do the calculation for yourself.

The key to making this work in practice is to 'pay yourself first' — the wonderfully simple strategy outlined by George Samuel Clason in the story of *The Richest Man in Babylon*. When you 'pay yourself first' you save 10 per cent or more of your income first, and then live on the remaining 90 per cent. Most of us, unfortunately, pay ourselves last, and this is a crucial mistake — because when we get around to paying ourselves, the money is all gone.

So, no matter where you are now, begin to examine your beliefs about resources and, in particular, the role of money in your life. It's never too late to start on the right road.

There is always choice

Be yourself, everyone else is already taken.

— MIKE ROBBINS

As we'll see more extensively in chapter 7 (which focuses on Responsibility), an important belief to nurture is that you always have choices no matter what situation you find yourself in. Many of us, however, believe we are 'stuck' where we are and that nothing can change. People who feel this way will often cite the bills to pay, the children to take care of, the meetings to go to and the emails to be answered. This feeling can drag you down and, if you are not careful, zap your energy so you cannot move from where you are to where you want to be.

When you have an inner certainty that choices are *always* available, you'll be able to deal with your current reality in a way that allows you to confidently move forward into a different future. In my opinion, belief in choice is one of the true marks of a mature human being. When we believe we don't have choices, we are assuming that no options are available to us — that we are in some way a victim of our situation or luck. But there are always options. You may not like the consequences of these options, but the options are there regardless. It may be useful now to list those areas of your life where you feel you have the least choice. These may be to do with your work, your boss, your kids or your relationships, for example. As you go, begin to generate a list of different ways forward in each of your chosen areas without evaluating the consequences. Are you beginning to see that there are always choices available?

The Austrian psychiatrist Viktor Frankl, who was tortured in the Nazi concentration camps of the Second World War, wrote in his book *Man's Search for Meaning* about the constant availability of choice — what he calls the last of the human freedoms:

> *We who lived in the concentration camps can remember the men who walked throughout the huts comforting others, giving away their last piece of bread.*
>
> *They may have been few in number, but they offer sufficient proof that everything can be taken away from a man but one thing — the last of the human freedoms. To choose one's response in any given set of circumstances, to choose one's own way.*

As this humbling example clearly testifies, you can always choose your own way no matter what your situation.

Because it can be difficult to see real choices from where you are now, it is helpful to have a process to help you generate options and to give you confidence that you can successfully move to where you want to be. Here are five steps to making the fact of choice real for you:

1 *Vision*. Where are you now? Where do you want to be? Can you clearly see where you want to get to? Don't worry about the 'how' at this point.

2 *Plan.* What are the options for getting to where you want to be? Generate several options; be creative. Do some options seem better than others? What feels right?

3 *Effort.* Are you willing to put the work in? What is holding you back? Decide to put the plan into action.

4 *Persistence.* Keep going no matter what setbacks you encounter. See your 'failures' as 'learning'.

5 *Patience.* Be willing to wait.

As you become more confident about the existence of choices, your life will take on a marvellous energy that comes from deep within you. The power of choice is to know that you can always move to a different, and better, future.

Affirm your beliefs

To accomplish great things, we must not only act, but also dream, not only plan, but also believe.

— ANATOLE FRANCE

John Assaraf, who began life as a street kid and gang member, tells an amazing story in his book *The Answer*. The story relates events from a Tuesday morning in May 2000, when Assaraf and his son Keenan opened a cardboard box that had been sealed for five years. Assaraf, now a very successful businessman and owner of OneCoach (a leading provider of coaching and consulting services), tells how the box contained his old 'vision boards', where years earlier he created images of how he wished his life to be. The boards had images of his lifestyle, his relationships and what he wanted to do for a living, including pictures cut out from magazines of cars, watches and even a dream house.

As father and son opened the box, it became clear that Assaraf had indeed achieved all the things that were on those vision boards from all those years ago. What was even more amazing was that the picture of the dream house was the exact house they were living in that day! Without even knowing it, and against all the odds, Assaraf had ended up purchasing his dream home.

Now, I am not saying that this will happen to you, but I would nevertheless strongly encourage you to write down some affirmations based on your most important beliefs. As we saw in chapter 3 when we explored the power of affirmative statements, you can bring your beliefs to life by writing them down. There is just something that I can't fully explain about writing things down. The act of writing must in some way harness the attention of your subconscious mind, thereby making you more alert to possibilities and opportunities as they present themselves.

Do your beliefs match your ULP?

The greatest danger for most of us lies not in setting our aim too high and falling short, but in setting our aim too low, and achieving our mark.

— MICHELANGELO

As you become a student of your beliefs, you'll begin to notice the belief patterns of other people and, in particular, those of successful people you are seeking to emulate. Along the way, you may decide that some of your old beliefs are no longer 'fit for purpose' and that you would like to establish some new beliefs for yourself. If this happens to you, congratulations! You are well on your way to becoming a truly successful person.

The most important thing is making sure your beliefs are in alignment with, and supportive of, your Unique Life Purpose statement. You'll know your beliefs are right when they 'feel' right to you — invariably, this will be when they clearly correlate with your ULP.

As we come to the end of this chapter, I am reminded of a movie that I encourage you to watch — *The Shawshank Redemption* (1994), based on a short story by Stephen King. Tim Robbins plays Andy, an innocent man serving a life sentence for the murder of his wife and her boyfriend. While in prison, Andy becomes best friends with Red (Morgan Freeman) — also a convicted murderer. In one scene, both men are in the exercise yard sitting against the high wall talking about what they will do if and when they get out. Red is of the belief that he is there forever, while Andy sees a future for himself in a small Mexican town where he can look at the stars, touch the sand, wade in the clear blue water and feel free. Both men find themselves in exactly the same situation but with different outlooks. Andy concludes that their difference in perspective is down to their beliefs and a simple matter of choice: 'get busy living or get busy dying'. Indeed.

Ideas for Action

- Take some time out to review your journal and, in particular, your list of beliefs. Ask yourself, are my beliefs true? Are they helpful? Are they in alignment with who I really am and who I want to be?

- Once you are excited by the beliefs you hold to be true, write down some corresponding affirmations that you can refer to often.

- Watch *The Shawshank Redemption*, and be inspired!

By changing my beliefs, I can change who I am.

—JAMES ALLEN

Energy — synchronising your body and mind

We are what we repeatedly do. Excellence, then, is not an act but a habit.

— ARISTOTLE

When you manage your energy, you manage your life. Our energy sources aren't just food and sleep (although these are important); they are physical, mental, emotional and spiritual, and each of these areas deserves deliberate care and attention. Most of us incorrectly assume that our aim should be to demand more and more of our energy levels in each of these four areas; recent research, however, shows that the key to high performance in any endeavour is knowing how to balance periods of exertion with periods of rest. That is, instead of looking at life as some kind of marathon, it is better to view it as a series of short races. As we'll learn in this chapter, managing your energy in this way can positively influence all aspects of your life.

We need to take a much more active interest in energy management than our forebears had to. Several centuries ago, people's everyday lives were more in tune with their natural energy cycles. But the unique demands, expectations and opportunities of modern life constantly challenge us to make deliberate choices if we are to live our best lives. Let's consider some examples.

First, there is the problem of sedentary lifestyles. For many of us, the jobs we have are not very physically demanding. Since the industrial revolution the developed world has been able to deploy machines to do most of our hard work, and the jobs we now have reflect the incredible advances in science and technology that have become part of our everyday lives. Even at home we have gadgets to do most things, and professionals available to come in for the bigger jobs. In contrast, our forebears were far more likely to do everything for themselves, to work physically demanding jobs and, in consequence, to get the right level of daily exercise. For them, work and the management of their physical energy was often one and the same thing.

Second, consider our eating patterns. We now have a vast range of foods available to us in quantities that would astound those who lived just 50 years ago. Some of these are healthy and nutritious, while others are designed to make us feel good in the short term, but are not very good for us overall. And then, of course, there is the volume of food we consume—most times, far more than we actually need, especially when you consider our sedentary lifestyles. Again, we need to make active and deliberate choices when it comes to food.

A third pitfall of modern life is our frequent obligation to commute long distances. Working away from where we live is a fairly recent phenomenon. Long commutes affect every aspect of our lives because we are likely to experience increased stress, reduced time with our families, and the possibility of unhealthy city noise and smog.

Finally, there is the pace we live at. Few would argue that the pace of life hasn't increased enormously over the past decades. The mantra seems to be 'more, more, more—now, now, now'. While technology has certainly played its part, there is also strong evidence that we have become more self-absorbed and less community-minded.

These trends, and many others, have contributed to a way of living that, if left unchecked, will become unhealthy and less than fulfilling. The only way to avoid these problems is to deliberately manage and respect your physical, mental, emotional and spiritual energies. Unfortunately, when we were born, we did not come supplied with a comprehensive user manual to help us adjust the voltage of our various energies! It is my wish that this chapter, in combination with your many life experiences, will allow you to finally write that manual for yourself.

Your unique energy cycle

Knowing others is wisdom; knowing the self is enlightenment. Mastering others requires force; mastering the self needs strength.

—LAO TZU

The very first step in changing something is increasing your awareness of what it is you are seeking to change. When it comes to your energy, this means developing an acute awareness of the ups and downs of the various energies you have available to you. Taking your physical energy, for example, you will probably know when this peaks at certain times each day. For many people this will be in the morning, but others get a tremendous burst of energy and enthusiasm late in the evening. It's important to know your peak times, because you can then make sensible choices about when to go about your most important tasks and activities. You will know from your own experience that work done at your peak time is generally some of your best and there is a certain 'flow' to how you get the work done. (I talk more about your unique energy cycle in chapter 9.)

In his *Harvard Business Review* article 'Manage Your Energy, Not Your Time' (co-authored with Catherine McCarthy), Tony Schwartz claims that individuals, teams and whole organisations can, with some straightforward interventions, increase their capacity to get things done. In his more recent book *The Way We're Working Isn't Working*, Schwartz builds upon his original research with even more compelling evidence that it is the proper management of your energy that has the greatest impact on your performance.

The key to better energy management is to deliberately focus your attention on each of the four areas I highlighted at the start of this chapter:

1 *Physical energy.* The maintenance of our physical bodies is absolutely essential to the proper management of the remaining three energies. Without a strong, flexible and healthy body our alertness and vitality—essential for managing our creativity, our emotions and our mental endurance—is severely compromised. We simply do not have the fuel to power our lives if we do not take care of our physical energy.
2 *Mental energy.* The proper cultivation of your mental capacity has an enormous impact on your concentration and creativity. This energy, which can be significantly enhanced over time through further education and learning new skills, gives you the toolkit to work in ways that are highly productive and highly valued.
3 *Emotional energy.* Your capacity to manage your emotions plays a significant role in the results you get in your life. The key attributes of someone with emotional energy are self-confidence, self-control,

empathy and social skills. If you have a wellspring of emotional energy, and you can regulate it well, you have the capacity to solve bigger and bigger problems. The bigger the problems you can solve, the more valuable you become.

4 *Spiritual energy.* This is not strictly about your religious beliefs but rather is about your sense of purpose. To feel motivated, we need to know that what we're doing matters. The energy we get from knowing that we are on a meaningful journey can overcome all kinds of obstacles that might be in our way. Strong spiritual energy ignites our will to step outside what's comfortable and makes us passionate.

As you become aware of these four energies operating within you, you'll get better at noticing when they are up and down, and, consequently, at knowing how to work with rather than against them. Let's now look at some practical ways of doing just that.

Focus on your physical wellbeing

The secret of staying young is to live honestly, eat slowly, and lie about your age.
— LUCILLE BALL

When you become fully aware of the importance of your body and your physical wellbeing, you begin to make better choices about what you eat, how much you eat and the exercise you take. You also become sensitive to just how much your performance is influenced by the choices you make in these regards.

In simple terms, we can think about food as fuel, which gives us the energy to do the things that we want to do. An excess of fuel in the body leads to a heaviness that results in sluggish performance, and to potential weight gain that can dull our sharpness. Developing a good understanding of the nutritional value of different food types is an essential first step in planning your ideal diet. Many people are unaware of their eating patterns and don't know (or, rather, choose not to think about) the impact their food choices have on their lives.

Each of us has a relationship with food. While we all need a certain amount of sustenance to stay alive and healthy, the satisfaction of our nutritional needs isn't the only reason we eat. From childhood on, every person develops a set of expectations, habits, associations and states of mind related to food. Our family dynamics, our cultural backgrounds and our individual attitudes and tastes all influence how this situation develops. We could call the sum total of these expectations, habits, associations and states of mind our 'relationship' with food.

One good way to become aware of your relationship with food is to record, for one week, what you eat, when you eat and your feelings as you consume different types of food. If you're like most people, you'll discover some distinct patterns. Armed with this information, I recommend that you review your eating habits so that the foods you consume are in your best interests. Planning your food intake on paper one week ahead is a really worthwhile strategy.

Food writer Michael Pollan has developed 64 simple guidelines for good eating in his book *Food Rules*. Here is some of the practical advice he gives:

- Don't eat anything your great-grandmother wouldn't recognise as food.

- Avoid foods that have some form of sugar or sweetener listed among the top three ingredients.

- Don't eat anything with more than five ingredients.

- Eat food cooked by humans, not corporations.

- Don't get your 'fuel' from the same place your car does.

- Drink plenty of water and reduce your alcohol consumption.

- Do all your eating at a table — not at a desk, while working, watching television or driving.

As well as paying close attention to what you eat, it is also really worthwhile to examine *how* you eat. In his excellent book *I Can Make You Thin*, Paul McKenna reveals what he calls the 'secrets of naturally thin people'. One secret is to eat 'consciously'. When you eat consciously and enjoy every mouthful, your brain more quickly recognises when you are getting full and you stop yourself from overeating. The key to eating consciously is to eat slowly and to eliminate distractions so that your attention is on taste, texture and when it's time to stop. The proper regulation of your diet is a critical step in boosting your physical energy. The positive feelings that reward self-control will in turn motivate you to continue your efforts!

As well as planning your food intake, it is equally important to plan for the proper maintenance of your body in other ways. Given our lifestyles today — where most of us do not get enough exercise on a daily basis — we must make specific plans for increasing our cardiovascular activity and also for stretching our bodies.

Generally, the advice is to have five exercise sessions per week. Three of these should be one-hour long, every-other-day cardiovascular workouts where the focus is on increasing your heart rate and keeping yourself working at that level for extended lengths of time. Working out at a gym, participating in sport or vigorous walking are ideal ways of getting this type of exercise. The remaining two exercise sessions should be aimed at muscle stretching and/or strength building. For both forms of exercise, choose activities that make sense for you and will be sustainable in the long term.

For those who can afford it, a coach or personal trainer is an excellent investment. If you are new to exercise, your trainer can help you construct a program that will work for you, and design it so that the impact of any pre-existing injuries can be minimised. A personal trainer can also motivate you by giving you an element of external accountability — you have to show up because he or she is expecting you! Whichever way you do it, when planning your program of exercise it is important to choose activities that are varied so that boredom is reduced. Remember, your exercise program will ideally be part of your life for good. Make it fun.

Finally, before embarking on a new diet or exercise regime, it's best to start off slowly, build up momentum and then maintain the new habits with regularity. Also check with medical practitioners to ensure your plans make sense for your unique circumstances.

Know your sleep cycles and patterns

If you watch how nature deals with adversity, continually renewing itself, you cannot help but learn.

—BERNIE S. SIEGEL

Most of us need between seven and eight hours of sleep every night. While we can keep going with less for short periods, eventually our bodies start to wane, and we need to recharge them with good sleep. To be deliberate about your sleep is to bear in mind your unique sleeping patterns—to know what you need to perform at your best. We have an internal clock—the body's circadian rhythm—that tells us when it's time to sleep and wake up. This inner timekeeper is sensitive to light, the time of day and our core body temperature, and works in tandem with adenosine, a neurotransmitter that builds up during the day as our bodies burn energy. The more adenosine that builds up in the brain, the sleepier a person feels.

As we sleep, our body goes through a series of sleep cycles. The average adult experiences four to five full sleep cycles over an eight-hour period. Each cycle lasts about 90 to 110 minutes and comprises five different stages. Stages one to four are non-REM sleep. During stage one, you sleep lightly; during stage two, your sleep gets progressively deeper. Stages three and four are when you sleep most heavily. Stage five, known as REM (rapid eye movement) sleep, is marked by significant physiological changes—accelerated respiration, increased brain activity, rapid eye movement and muscle relaxation. People dream more actively during REM sleep.

Exercise, diet, medications, drugs or alcohol, stress, sleep disorders and sleep deprivation are all factors that can influence and disrupt sleep cycles. Gender and age can also play a role—women tend to sleep more soundly than men and, as we age, we sleep more restlessly. It's important to be alert to your sleeping patterns and try to avoid things that may disrupt a full sleep cycle, because the quality of your sleep will have a direct bearing on your energy levels. This explains why sometimes we wake up restless or still tired, even though we may have been asleep for, say, eight hours—perhaps most of that time was spent on stage one or even stage five (REM) sleep.

As you become aware of your sleep cycles and patterns, it is helpful to consider the following seven tips in planning how you can get the most from your sleep:

• Try to get to sleep and wake up at the same time every day—including weekends. This helps your internal clock to be always in synchronisation with your body. If you are feeling extra tired, go to bed early rather than sleep in late.

- Establish a pre-sleep routine that you find calming and relaxing. Perhaps trade the television watching or computer work for reading an enjoyable book or taking a bath.

- Invest in the best bed and pillow you can afford.

- Have your room as dark as possible.

- Don't eat or drink for two hours before going to sleep.

- If you are one of those people who keep themselves awake with busy thoughts (these might be habitual worries or sudden inspirations), try keeping a notebook and pen close to your bed. If you wake up during the night, writing your thoughts down can help you get back to sleep.

- Get up when you plan to get up.

For some people, including me, it is a good idea to have an afternoon nap. Studies have suggested that regular naps (an important part of life in many cultures) are worthwhile both in terms of refreshment and other medical benefits. Researchers at Harvard and the University of Athens Medical School conducted a six-year study of nearly 24 000 Greek adults, finding that those who took midday naps on a regular basis (around 20 minutes at least three times per week) decreased their risk of dying from heart disease by more than one-third.

As with everything else, be deliberate with your sleep—it will help you every hour you are awake.

Nurture your mind

Don't be too timid and squeamish about your actions. All life is an experiment. The more experiments you make the better.

—RALPH WALDO EMERSON

The second energy source that you need to actively manage is your mental capacity. With proper nurturing and the right challenges, your brain will become sharper and actually improve its performance as you get older. You are probably familiar with the claim that we use only a tiny proportion of our full mental capacity—according to some scientists, as little as 5 per cent. Why is this? Well, the main reason is that we have mistaken beliefs about the operation of the mind. For instance, some believe that our brain cells die off as we get older, or that our memory or capacity for creativity diminishes over time. However, when you look at the research from the past 30 years, many studies show that there is no limit to how much you can improve your mental faculties.

Deepak Chopra, a medical doctor who has carefully documented his experiences with patients in his book *Ageless Body, Timeless Mind*, clearly shows that the mind and body are inseparable. Indeed, Chopra maintains that the careful management of our mental processes can actually reverse the effects of ageing on our physical bodies. As he says, 'People don't grow old. When they stop growing, they become old'.

The very best way to mentally grow is to deliberately put yourself into new learning situations. Expand your interests into the unknown, and move away from what is comfortable and familiar. Stretch yourself. One way to do so is to see yourself as a lifelong student—always learning new things and challenging what you already think you know about. Such an approach will ensure you never get complacent enough to think you know it all.

In my seminars, I sometimes say that education is wasted on the young. As you get older and have some life experience to draw on, you can really value what education has to offer. Unlike many younger people, as adults we tend to take a big-picture approach to what we are learning—and, as parents and income-earners, we know the true value of the time we invest in educating ourselves. Accordingly, I suspect that many adults are capable of undertaking self-education with more motivation and application than the average undergraduate!

Seeing yourself as a lifelong student is an exciting way to think. It means that you will never be bored or boring.

The power of focus and attention

Any man who can drive safely while kissing a pretty girl is simply not giving the kiss the attention it deserves.

—ALBERT EINSTEIN

Of all the mental abilities to be nurtured, your power of attention is undoubtedly the most valuable. Your ability to focus your attention for extended periods of time underpins everything else you do in your life.

Without mastery of your attention, your life can easily turn into a series of incomplete, half-started activities that don't add up to much. You may be an ambitious multi-tasker but, without the capacity to really focus, your efforts will yield little. The good news is that, like a muscle, your powers of attention can be strengthened, and the way to do this is through the practice of mindfulness. Mindfulness is the energy of attention, and is the capacity in each of us to be 100 per cent 'present' in the moment.

In his book *The Miracle of Mindfulness*, the Vietnamese monk Thich Nhat Hanh teaches that in our everyday lives we often miss out on the present moment because we are thinking of something else and, therefore, living more out of our minds than in them. To illustrate this point, Nhat Hanh tells this lovely story of a time when his friend Jim Forest came to visit:

> *I usually wash the dishes after we've finished the evening meal, before sitting down and drinking tea with everyone else. One night, Jim asked if he might do the dishes. I said, 'Go ahead, but if you wash the dishes you must know the way to wash them.' Jim replied, 'Come on, you think I don't know how to wash the dishes?' I answered, 'There are two ways to wash the dishes. The first is to wash the dishes in order to have clean dishes and the second is to wash the dishes in order to wash the dishes.*

As the story illustrates, if, while washing dishes, we think only of the cup of tea that awaits us, thus hurrying to get the dishes out of the way as though they were a nuisance, then we are not 'washing the dishes to wash the dishes'. What's more, we are not fully alive in the moment, but rather thinking about the near future.

As you become more mindful, you'll realise how frequently your thoughts wander away from the task in front of you. An excellent strategy for anchoring yourself in the moment and letting go of distracting internal commentaries is to pay close attention to your breath. Sitting quietly for a while, simply follow each breath as it enters and leaves your body. While this can be harder than it sounds (your internal dialogue will keep trying to intrude), it gradually gets easier. When you are in tune with your breath, you are really present in the here and now, and your ability to focus on other tasks with equal concentration will improve markedly.

In the corporate world, the practice of mindfulness is gaining widespread recognition as a way of creating more harmonious workplaces and increasing productivity. Consultants Daniel Goleman and Jon Kabat-Zinn have pioneered the practice in many Fortune 500 companies with notable success.

Later in this chapter we will look more closely at the practice of meditation, which is really just a more concentrated form of mindfulness. The difference lies in the fact that while meditation is an activity we might engage in once or twice a day, we can aim to be mindful all of the time.

Manage your emotional energy

No-one can make you feel inferior without your consent.

— ELEANOR ROOSEVELT

The third type of energy we can deliberately manage is our emotional energy. Like all other energies, our emotional energy can be actively managed through the conscientious development of certain skills.

Emotional intelligence, or EI, is essentially the ability to recognise your feelings and the feelings of others, and, where your own feelings are concerned, to be able to constructively moderate them. Sometimes, feelings give you important information about your life and your relationships. Other times, however, they interfere with your ability to perform at your best and to reach your true potential. Most people don't try to adjust their emotions because this seems like too hard a task. To an extent, it is. But feelings can be adjusted indirectly. While you may not be able to change the way you *feel*, you can change the way you *think*. This will then influence your emotional life in the long run.

When we lack emotional control, we end up making poor choices that produce undesirable consequences in many areas of our lives. I'm sure you can recall some examples from your own experience. If you trace these examples back, you'll likely discover that decisions were made too quickly and you did very little thinking about the downstream implications of what you were about to do.

The problem is familiar enough, but what can you do about it? Essentially, you have to become self-aware to the extent that you recognise a feeling as it happens. Being able to observe your life and what you are doing with a certain detachment is a vital skill; it allows you to put your feelings in a proper perspective. I have observed that many successful people are skilled managers of their emotions. They characteristically achieve exactly the kind of constructive detachment I am talking about, whereby you create a space or 'gap' between the immediate situation and your emotional response to it. This 'gap' has many advantages, as follows:

- You tend to make better judgements because you have the opportunity to reflect before you act.

- New information often comes to light as you pause to reflect, resulting in a better informed response.

- When you reach for positive thoughts, you come up with more positive solutions.

Following a seminar I gave, one of the participants sent me a postcard from London. On that card were the words 'Mind the Gap'—the message that is constantly played through platform speakers on the underground train system as passengers enter and leave trains. I only wish that many more people knew what 'Mind the Gap' really means!

Banish energy sappers

The art of being wise is the art of knowing what to overlook.

—WILLIAM JAMES

We all know certain things or circumstances in our lives trigger negative emotions that just sap us of our energy. These may be:

- drinks we consume

- events we attend

- food we eat

- memories we recall

- music we listen to

- news or chat groups we belong to

- people we meet

- phone calls we make or receive

- radio stations we tune into

- smells we smell

- television programs we watch

- websites we visit.

As you cultivate your self-awareness, you'll become more sensitive to any negative feelings that come with these encounters. You'll also learn to put in place routines or rituals to minimise their impact on you. When you look at each area, you'll be able to identify specific actions you can take — ahead of time — to protect yourself from their negative consequences.

Of course, the best way to reduce the impact of energy sappers is to avoid them altogether. The key here is to be aware of the choices you are making and to challenge yourself to find alternative ways of doing things. For example, if you find certain people or events mentally draining, does it matter if you say a polite 'no' now and then? Is your attendance really crucial? Does the maintenance of this relationship or friendship really matter? You may be surprised by what you'll discover.

There are times, however, where some potentially negative encounters are simply unavoidable. This might be because of the nature of your work or because of family responsibilities that require your direct involvement. Think here, for example, of the 'unwelcome' relatives coming to stay with you for an extended time, or the boss who always leaves you feeling deflated. By developing certain pre-event rituals you will minimise their impact on you. In the case of the visiting relatives, you could plan — before their arrival — other activities that you find particularly refreshing or some time alone that will allow you to get your energy back during their stay. And before you meet with your boss, you can take some time out to prepare yourself mentally by perhaps reviewing your ULP or reading some specially written affirmations. These strategies will help you to remember what is truly important and put the potentially negative encounters in their proper context. During the event itself, I would encourage you to remember the words of Eleanor Roosevelt: 'No-one can make you feel inferior without your consent'. It's your choice.

Similarly, carefully choosing such things as the kind of food you eat, television you watch and internet sites you engage with can significantly help you to get better control over your emotions and how you feel. Remember that carefully managing how you feel is very important because how you feel governs your behaviour, and it's your behaviour that ultimately gives you the results you get in your life.

Increase your spiritual energy

It's only when we truly know and understand that we have a limited time on earth—and that we have no way of knowing when our time is up—that we will begin to love each day to the fullest, as if it was the only one we had.

—ELISABETH KÜBLER-ROSS

The fourth energy you need to nurture is your spiritual energy—that which gives meaning and significance to your life. From time to time, all of us can feel like a run-down battery that needs recharging. It is easy to be so busy doing things that we forget the 'why' behind what we are doing. Like the other energies we have discussed, spiritual energy, and the way it can be recharged, is different for each person; some of us, for example, might need a good sleep or a long walk alone to recharge our spiritual energy, while others, who draw energy from social encounters, might find a dinner party the perfect restorative.

Again, the key is to know where your spiritual energy is at, and then to come up with ways of recharging yourself. In your work life this is particularly important because long hours can cause you to lose your effectiveness. Leonardo da Vinci had the right idea:

Every now and then go away,
have a little relaxation,
for when you come back to your work
your judgement will be surer;
since to remain constantly at work
will cause you to lose power of judgement...

Go some distance away
because the work appears smaller
and more of it
can be taken in at a glance,
and a lack of harmony
or proportion is more readily seen.

Gaining perspective, then, is crucial if you are to manage your spiritual energy. But why do we lose our perspective to begin with? I believe that it is in our nature as humans to put ourselves at the centre of things. We incorrectly assume that it's all about us—what I think, what I'm doing and so on. We mistakenly put ourselves at the centre of our own little universes and behave as if the entire world revolves around us. In this way, we become overly attached to what we are doing, and forget that we are but part of a much larger world.

One way to get perspective is to connect with nature. Again, thanks to our modern lifestyles, we can easily live our lives surrounded by a barricade of technology that reinforces our self-importance. Nature takes us back to who we really are. This is very true for me. There is nothing I like better than going for long walks along the beach with waves crashing beside me, walking through a forest where I can feel the crunch of twigs beneath my feet, or closely examining the beauty of a flower. I also like to look at the vastness of the sky on a clear night.

I encourage you, therefore, to think about creative ways of finding that energy that you just know in your heart makes all the difference.

Meaning matters

Great minds have purposes, others have wishes.

—WASHINGTON IRVING

The ultimate way to connect with what is most important to you is to regularly look at and feel great about your ULP statement. Over the years, many people have told me that the crafting of their ULP is probably the single most significant thing they have ever done. And because your ULP is created within the context of deeply held values and aspirations, it should always be a joy to read. It gives what I call the '3 Ms' to life: meaning, motivation and mojo. So, if you are in need of a spiritual energy boost, take your ULP from your wallet or your purse and just see where it takes you.

The practice of meditation

Only in quiet waters do things mirror themselves undistorted. Only in a quiet mind is adequate perception of the world.

— HANS MARGOLIUS

The practice of meditation, or more accurately mind training, taps into, and revitalises, all four of the energy sources I have been discussing in this chapter: physical, mental, emotional and spiritual. Very simply, meditation cultivates and strengthens your inner resources so that you can more confidently deal with the ups and downs of life.

Interestingly, the majority of successful people I have studied practise daily meditation in some shape or form. While precise practices vary, the development of a lifelong interest in meditation is closely linked to achieving real success. In the Western world, however, meditation is widely misunderstood. It is often confused with religion (in particular Buddhism), and with various forms of mind control and manipulation. The truth is that meditation is none of these things. Simply put, meditation is a learnt technique to help the mind become free, lucid and balanced.

So, how does it work and, perhaps more importantly, why does it work so well? The goal of meditation is to calm the mind. Every day, sometimes every minute, we experience agitation and various forms of inner turmoil that keep us from experiencing our authentic selves. Meditation, through the attainment of inner stillness, is a process of getting to know your own mind — the real you. When you are in touch with yourself in this way, you are calmer, clearer in your thinking and more in control of your emotions.

In their comprehensive book, *Meditation — An In-Depth Guide*, Ian Gawler and Paul Bedson trace the early practice of meditation to around 5000 BC in China, 1500 BC in India and 750 BC in the West. While there are variations in how meditation can be practised, generally all methods involve the cultivation of an alert yet passive mode of being, and sensitive attention towards one's moment-to-moment experience. Some methods encourage focus on the body (in particular the breath), while others direct attention to a sound or a mantra repeated aloud or in the mind. Irrespective of the method, the objective is always the same: to get away from living 'out of the mind'—which is to say, in the past or future—and into the present moment. Most traditions also follow what is known as the 'seven-point meditation posture':

1 Sit quietly in a comfortable but balanced posture (on a chair or on a cushion on the floor is fine).
2 Rest your hands in your lap. This can be done by resting your palms either upwards or downwards on your knees, or cupping your hands together in a relaxed and natural way.
3 Keep your back straight, yet relaxed. Because your spine is the main conduit of your central nervous system, a straight back encourages the energy to flow freely, and you will be able to meditate for longer and longer periods. Try to imagine the spinal vertebrae as a pile of coins delicately balanced one on top of the other.
4 Gaze downwards with slightly open eyes. Many newcomers to meditation find it easier to concentrate with the eyes fully closed. While this is not wrong, closed eyes can encourage sleepiness or the creation of dreamlike images that interfere with meditation.
5 Your mouth, jaw and tongue should be relaxed—not slack or tight—with the teeth slightly apart, and the lips lightly together.
6 Place the tip of the tongue behind your front teeth, so you can help control the build-up of saliva and the need to swallow.
7 Tilt your head forwards just a little so your gaze is directed to the floor in front of you. Don't drop it too low: this encourages sleepiness.

This seven-point posture keeps the body and mind comfortable and free of tension—you are now ready to enter the meditation itself.

The simplest form of meditation for beginners focuses on the breath. The technique simply involves being aware of the breath as it enters and leaves the body. Once you are in your meditation posture, begin by breathing as naturally as you can, counting each inhalation or exhalation up to 10. Counting is an aid to concentration and helps to prevent the mind from wandering. Some people find it helps if they focus their attention on the tip of the nose or the inside of the nostrils as the breath enters and leaves the body. Others use the movement of the abdomen to focus their attention on. If you find your attention wandering — as it will — don't be put off: simply bring your attention back to the breath and start again on the next inhalation. It is important not to follow these stray thoughts, and to keep gently redirecting your attention.

For beginners, 10 minutes of meditation is an excellent start. Gradually, for maximum benefit, increasing each sitting to 20 minutes twice a day is ideal. With practice and further study you can advance to other forms of meditation such as those based on mantras (for example, transcendental meditation), external objects, music, bodily sensations, visualisations and even the rhythm of walking. Each form of meditation has its own advantages.

If you want to know more about these techniques, I recommend that you enrol yourself in a meditation course — these are easy to come by. An experienced teacher will guide you towards the right method and help you overcome any challenges you encounter as you are learning.

So, that's the very basic 'how to' of meditation. But what are the benefits and why do those benefits come about? With regular practice, you set yourself up for a lifetime of good health and wellbeing. It is now well documented, through hundreds of scientific studies, that the benefits of meditation are physical, psychological and indeed social. Many of these studies have involved EEGs (tests that record the electrical activity of the brain), MRI scans, blood and hormone sampling, and a host of other cutting-edge research methodologies. Detailed analysis has linked meditation to cardiovascular, cortical, hormonal and metabolic benefits, along with several positive behavioural effects (for example, improved emotional intelligence and more positive self-perception). According to one research team in a study entitled 'The Physical and Psychological Effects of Meditation' (1996), led by Michael Murphy and Steven Donovan from California's Esalen Institute, *everyone* seems to benefit from these improvements — regardless of gender, race or life circumstance.

Among the proven physical benefits (from Murphy and Donovan's 'The Physical and Psychological Effects of Meditation') are:

• increased energy levels and stamina

• shorter recovery periods after illness

- the significant reduction of blood pressure
- the alleviation of pain caused by arthritis, back injury and other ailments
- the significant reduction of stress and stress-related illnesses such as heart disease, hypertension and insomnia
- improved response time, motor skills, coordination and other physical responses
- the improvement (in terms of frequency and severity) of asthmatic attacks and other allergic reactions
- a slower ageing process.

In other studies specifically designed to measure the psychological and social impacts of meditation, researchers such as Richard Davidson at the University of Wisconsin, Jon Kabat-Zinn at the University of Massachusetts Medical School and Daniel Goleman at Harvard have identified the following benefits:

- lessened anxiety and depression
- greater emotional stability
- increased social confidence
- heightened creativity
- increased concentration
- a greater sense of independence
- improved judgement
- improved memory and IQ
- improved emotional intelligence and sensitivity to others.

In his classic book *How to Meditate*, Lawrence LeShan says the benefits of meditation come about because we deliberately put ourselves in a unique physiological state in which we are not asleep, hypnotised or overly stimulated. When we meditate we are fully awake but also fully relaxed. By focusing the mind on just one object—say, the breath—the number of signals sent to the brain is greatly reduced, allowing the mind to settle down into a deeply relaxed yet highly alert state. This deep rest, combined with quality 'alone time', cultivates a sense of stillness within us that empowers every aspect of our lives. As well as meditation, other practices such as yoga and Pilates are also well worth your investigation.

The 'Recommended reading' section on p. 267 lists a number of books that teach simple meditation techniques. Such techniques can be easily integrated into even the busiest of lives—and, in fact, the busier your life is, the more worthwhile you'll find them. Why not give one or two a try?

Ideas for Action

- Starting next Monday, plan your meals for the week ahead, including the following weekend. Make sure you have a good variety of food groups and a nutritionally balanced menu for each meal—including snacks.

- Also starting next Monday, try to eat your meals consciously. Eat slowly, putting your knife and fork down often, and chewing your food more completely. Eliminate any distractions (such as television) as you eat in this way. After the week is over, write in your journal what you have learned.

- Begin the practice of meditation for just 10 minutes per day—the morning is often the best time to start. Using the seven-point meditation posture, try simple breath-awareness meditation with an open mind and an open heart.

Silence is one of the great victims of modern culture... One of the reasons so many people are suffering from stress is not that they are doing stressful things but that they allow so little time for silence.

—JOHN O'DONOHUE

Responsibility—accepting and taking ownership

Destiny is not a matter of chance—it's a matter of choice.

—W. J. BRYAN

A client of mine—let's call him Gary—arrived at his coaching session with me driving a late-model BMW. From the outside, it looked like Gary was truly successful—as well as the car, he had a good job, his kids in private school and a house in a stylish suburb. But on the inside, as he told it, he was a 'total mess'. It transpired that Gary was almost financially bankrupt and deeply unhappy with many aspects of his life.

As our coaching session unfolded, I asked Gary why he chose to have such an expensive car and to live in an exclusive area of town. His answers were as much a surprise to him as they were to me. According to him, he did not *choose* these things as such, but fell into making decisions without thinking through the consequences. Indeed he 'fell into' his whole life. His career as an accountant began many years previously because he had been good with numbers at school, but he had never really wanted to be an accountant—his real passion was to teach. Over the years, as Gary's escalating lifestyle required more funding, he accepted more senior roles and soon enough he was hooked. To feed his habit of 'more' he needed greater seniority and a bigger pay cheque. Now a partner in an accounting firm, Gary needed bigger and bigger clients to fund his lifestyle. What really troubled Gary was that there was no end in sight.

The key to helping Gary was to help him realise that he, and he alone, was responsible for the situation in which he found himself. Regardless of whether he fell into these decisions or not, he *chose* to continue in a career he did not enjoy: he *chose* the cars, the house, the private schooling and all the other burdens that were now causing him so much unhappiness.

There is a little bit of Gary in all of us. The purpose of this chapter is to find this part and to put the responsibility for who we are and what we do squarely back on our two shoulders. When you take the step of accepting 100 per cent responsibility for your situation—the good and the bad—you essentially take full control of your life. With this control comes the power to make changes and to become the person you really want to be.

Research into the psychology of success has shown that the acceptance of personal responsibility for one's current circumstances is absolutely vital. One such study, with findings that are presented by Jack Canfield in his book *The Success Principles*, identified 64 different 'success factors'. Among these, taking responsibility for one's life was listed as the most important factor of all. Canfield writes:

> *If you want to be successful, you have to take 100% responsibility for everything you experience in your life. This includes the level of your achievements, the results you produce, the quality of your relationships, the state of your health and physical fitness, your income, your debts, your feelings—everything!*

The good news is that accepting responsibility and taking ownership of your life is entirely possible. It is a matter of disciplining yourself and developing skills of self-mastery and self-control that, I assure you, are learnable. To acquire these skills is to graduate from a state of semi-childhood to full adulthood. You'll have finally grown up.

Accept 100 per cent responsibility

> *It is easy to dodge our responsibilities, but we cannot dodge the consequences of dodging our responsibilities.*
>
> —E. C. MCKENZIE

The word *responsible* comes from two words: *response* and *able*. Being responsible means that while you can't always choose your circumstances in life, you are always able to choose how you respond to them — however challenging they appear to be. It is no accident that those who are unhappiest and least successful in life are also most resistant to the idea that they are response-*able*. If you ask them how they got to where they are, you will likely hear a long tale of misfortunes, obstructed opportunities and 'bad luck'. Such people refuse to acknowledge not only their role in creating their situation but also their ability to respond differently to it. In doing so, they choose a path of blame and victimhood, rather than a path where they can actively make choices and influence the outcomes they are getting in their lives.

Taking 100 per cent responsibility means just that. This is a crucial point. With anything less than total responsibility, you leave the door open for blame and feelings of victimhood to enter. The moment you do this, you relinquish control over your own life. Sure, you may not control all the circumstances in your life, but you do have full power over how you *react* to these circumstances. Of course, this can mean hard work. If it were easy to take ownership of all the not-so-great aspects of one's life, everyone would be doing it. Facing your problems head-on isn't easy, and sometimes it takes a lot of guts. Winston Churchill once said that 'the price of greatness is responsibility'. You will always know when someone is aiming at greatness because of two things: first, they don't blame others and, second, they have given up the excuses.

Blaming others and coming up with excuses is such an engrained way of thinking in our society that we hardly notice it anymore. But if you stop and honestly assess the situation, you'll notice the part you alone played in the results you are getting. Think about the following (adapted from Jack Canfield):

- You are the one who ate the junk food.

- You are the one who didn't exercise.

- You are the one who took the job.

- You are the one who stayed in the job.

- You are the one who chose that relationship.

- You are the one who bought it.

- You are the one who didn't take care of it.

- You are the one who didn't trust your intuition.

- You are the one who said 'yes'.

- You are the one who said 'no'.

- You are the one who gave up on your dream.

I know that looking at your life in this way is hard medicine to accept. But the upside of truly accepting responsibility and of taking ownership is enormous. For a start, your life will take on renewed vigour as you realise that you don't have to depend on others or outside circumstances to get what you want. The knowledge that you alone are responsible for creating your reality can lead to exciting futures and possibilities. The ball is in *your* court, and *you* get to decide what your next shot will be.

A large body of psychological research has demonstrated a strong link between accepting responsibility and personal happiness. The Locus of Control Theory (developed in the 1950s by Julian B. Rotter) states that people with an internal locus of control feel that they are in complete control of their lives and this, in turn, results in them feeling strong, confident and powerful. With these strong feelings comes an optimistic attitude that gives power and energy to their actions. By comparison, people with an external locus of control feel controlled by external factors — their boss, their childhood problems, their partner, their financial situation and so on. They effectively hand over their power to someone or something outside of themselves.

The more you say 'I am responsible!', the more you strengthen your internal locus of control. The result is confidence and power — as well as a sense of release from long-held feelings of resentment and blame. Accepting and taking ownership in this way is a deliberate, liberating act.

Your unique situation and how you created it

There is a choice you have to make in everything you do. And you must keep in mind the choice you make, makes you.

—ANON.

When you really think about it, everything in your life today is the result of decisions and choices you made yesterday. One good way to fully understand the impact of yesterday on today is to see everything you do as a decision. Even doing nothing is a decision! Whether you like it or not, you contributed to the current state of your life in three ways:

- *As a causative agent.* The choices you made led directly to your current situation. For example, you worked hard to get a degree, which allowed you to enter a career you enjoy; your excessive spending put you in financial trouble and now you have credit card debt; you choose to work on the weekend, and you feel tired when it's only Tuesday.

- *By your response.* The event or circumstances may have been completely out of your control, but the way you responded did not improve the situation. For example, your boss was trying to give you constructive feedback, you were not open to learning and now there is an unhealthy tension between you; your partner was late home for dinner, you were annoyed and said some hurtful things, and now your relationship is damaged.

- *By your lack of response.* You may not have contributed to your circumstances, but instead of responding to your situation you chose to do nothing. By choosing not to respond, you have made a choice. For example, your workload was increasing but you did nothing, and now you feel stressed and unable to function; you could sense that you needed to spend more quality time with your kids, but instead you continued a selfish lifestyle, and now your teenage child will not discuss his or her troubles with you.

It is important when looking at your past decisions that you simply note the choices you made without dwelling too much on what might have been. To endlessly replay the past does not do anybody any good and can lead to frustration on your part. It can be comforting to acknowledge that you made the best decisions possible based on the tools and information available to you at the time — as most people do. The trouble with hindsight is that it surveys the past through the lens of now. The best approach is to look on the past as a way of learning for the future. Successful people tend not to waste energy by dwelling on the past for too long; they know that the quality of their life is determined by the decisions they make today.

If there is anything that you are unhappy about, it is up to you to take the necessary steps to change and improve it so that it is more to your liking. As the saying goes, 'If it's to be, it's up to me!'

The future can be different

Life shrinks or expands in proportion to one's courage.

— ANAÏS NIN

As a young boy, I remember the circus coming to our town. One of the most amazing sights was the elephants as they carried the massive wooden poles that formed the structure on which the big top circus tent would be built. With their powerful bodies, the elephants, working with their keeper, lifted, carried and hauled until the tent was ready for the show. I was always impressed by their effortless strength. Then I noticed something very unusual. If the keepers wanted to prevent the elephant from wandering around the field, they simply fastened a small rope around the elephant's leg and secured it by hammering a small peg into the ground. The massive animal would not dare to move beyond the reach of the little rope. Why would the elephant stay? Clearly, it could easily have pulled the peg from the ground and gone wherever it wished.

Well, to understand why, we need to consider the life of baby circus elephants. As infants, their keepers would have tethered them with a mere rope because of their small size, and they would have quickly learned that their world was confined by its length. And, of course, being elephants, they never forgot! In the same way, we too can restrict our futures by not realising the extent of our freedom to choose. As a deliberately responsible person, you should become acutely aware that it is the decisions and choices you make *today* that determine your future. You are not tied by your past.

Consider the following simple formula:

$$E + R = O$$
$$(\text{Event} + \text{Response} = \text{Outcome})$$

In discussing this formula, Jack Canfield says that if you are not happy with any aspect of your life, you basically have two choices. First you can blame the event (E) for your lack of results (O). With this approach you locate the 'cause' of your problems outside yourself and seek refuge in your inability to control events. It's a hopeless state where you have an excuse for everything. The second approach is to simply change your response (R) to the events (E) until you get the outcomes (O) you want. This means that as a response-*able* person you can deliberately change your thinking, change your mode of communication, change the pictures you hold in your head—and change your behaviour.

Choice is always available

The best years of your life are the ones in which you decide your problems are your own. You don't blame them on your mother, the ecology, or the president. You realise that you control your own destiny.

—ALBERT ELLIS

In seminars and in coaching sessions, people frequently argue with me that they are different from others in that they don't have many choices. For whatever reason, the circumstances of their lives restrict what's possible for them. When this happens I do two things. First, I strongly disagree with their point of view and, second, I give them a book to read before I will argue any further with them. In every case, the person has come back to me with a change of heart.

The book I recommend is Viktor Frankl's *Man's Search for Meaning*, published in 1959 but still readily available. Dr Frankl—whose story I mentioned briefly in chapter 5—was one of millions of Jews placed in Nazi concentration camps during the Second World War. The Hitler regime took virtually everything away from him: his wife, parents, home, medical practice and all his worldly possessions. He was thrown into a prison camp where he experienced every form of human degradation possible. Frankl watched several of his friends be killed in that concentration camp. He also saw many men commit suicide, while others simply lost the will to live, gave up and died.

As he sat in the squalor of his freezing hut, Frankl was determined to find something he still had that the Nazis couldn't take; something important enough to sustain his will to live. He decided that there was one thing that no-one could take away: his ability to choose his own attitude.

Viktor Frankl not only survived the atrocities of the war, but also went on to become one of the world's most respected psychiatrists. Through his unique approach of logotherapy (the Greek word *logos* may be interpreted broadly as 'meaning' or 'reason'), he has helped thousands of people who were ready to give up on life gain a renewed will to live by showing them that, no matter what their circumstances, they still have choices. As Frankl recognised, it is essentially choice that gives our lives meaning. He calls our ability to choose our own attitude in any given set of circumstances 'the last of the human freedoms'. The key, he says, is to know that what we become is the result of an *inner* decision.

Realisation that you are free to choose is, then, the foundation stone of a meaningful and responsible life. The recognition of choice places you in the driving seat. What happens if you simply don't see any choices? What can do you? Here are some strategies to consider:

- *Take your time and take a step back.* When we don't see possibilities, it's often because we are trying to rush decisions or because we don't want to put the hard work into generating further options. However, if you slow things down, you'll notice a space (what I referred to as a mental 'gap' in the previous chapter) opening up between whatever has happened and your response to it. Invariably, from this period of quiet reflection possibilities begin to emerge. One of the most practical ways of generating such a space is to sleep on a decision overnight, and come back to it the next day. You have no doubt experienced for yourself just how constructive and illuminating a single night's sleep can be when it comes to problem-solving.

- *Think with an open mind.* With an open mind you begin to see all sides of a situation, to be more understanding and to be aware of your own limitations. One of the best ways to open your mind is to practise creative thinking techniques such as the 'Six Thinking Hats' technique taught by Edward de Bono in his book of the same name (see chapter 4). These techniques allow you to generate new ideas and, therefore, new choices in a very short space of time.

- *Do things outside of your normal routine.* Shaking things up a bit from time to time can heighten your awareness of available choices. For example, decide to drive home using a different route, walk under ladders just to show it can be done, order different meals at restaurants or walk through puddles just because!

- *Think for yourself.* One of Ralph Waldo Emerson's most famous writings is his essay 'Self-Reliance' (1841). It is a powerful statement about our need to think for ourselves. Emerson felt that too many people were taking the easy way out by choosing 'to live after the world's opinion'. Instead, we need to be brave enough not to be swayed by popular opinion. Otherwise, if we let others do the thinking for us, we never experience what Emerson calls 'the integrity of our own minds'.

- *Seek external advice.* It's amazing what a fresh pair of eyes can see. Because other people can look at an issue without preconceived biases, they can help you see options that were always there, but were obscured by your way of thinking.

Of course, in those situations where time is of the essence, you need to balance the process of generating options with the need to take reasonably swift action. Sometimes, the luxury of time simply isn't there: decisions have to be made more or less on the spot, according to the information available to you. The danger here is the 'paralysis of analysis', or having so much information available that you struggle to make a decision, which can lead to missed opportunities and other negative outcomes.

While you need to recognise this danger, it remains true that in the majority of cases pause for thought is constructive. Sometimes the rush we are in to make decisions is subjective and unreliable: how urgent is the situation really? What would happen if you delayed action for two or 24 hours? Wherever possible, in other words, I encourage you to deliberately seek out options and to recognise that you *always* have choices. Your ability to choose, and especially to choose your own attitude, is the single most important resource you have for succeeding in life.

Things won't always work out as planned

Freedom is not worth having if it does not include the freedom to make mistakes.
—MAHATMA GANDHI

Responsible people know that living their best lives involves taking risks and living with the possibility that sometimes things will not work out as planned. In life there will always be unexpected problems and roadblocks that frustrate your best efforts and intentions. This being so, truly successful people make decisions, take action, work hard, *and* are willing to accept whatever comes into their lives. Less successful people, on the other hand, tend to be so cautious and risk averse that they take action only when guaranteed success. They live 'safe' but unfulfilled lives.

The biggest obstacle that holds people back from achieving their true potential is the fear of failure. They look upon failure as something to be avoided at all costs. Successful people, on the other hand, feel the fear along with the rest of us but they don't let it keep them from doing anything they want to do. They understand that fear is something to be acknowledged, experienced and learned from. They have learned, to borrow Susan Jeffers's famous phrase, to 'feel the fear and do it anyway'. If you want to seize an opportunity, you must be able to take risks. If you want to grow, you must be willing to face your fears and make mistakes.

Two of the most famous failures I can think of are Albert Einstein and Thomas Edison. Our greatest mathematician and our greatest inventor, long before they were honoured for their achievements, suffered through years of trial and error, mistakes, disappointments and defeats. When Edison was looking for ways to keep a light bulb burning, he tried more than ten thousand combinations of materials. When someone asked him how he could continue after failing so many times, he said he didn't see it as failure. He said that he had successfully identified more than ten thousand ways that didn't work and that each attempt brought him closer to the one that would. Likewise, Einstein said, 'I think for months and years. Ninety-nine times the conclusion is false. The hundredth time I am right'.

The key to overcoming your fear of failure is to better understand what is known as your 'explanatory style'. Your explanatory style is how you interpret what happens to you. Working with his colleagues at the University of Pennsylvania, Martin Seligman, author of *Learned Optimism*, shows how we can develop greater resilience by seeing our failures as temporary and not personal to us. The good news is that your explanatory style is a learnt behaviour and, therefore, can be changed by the choices you make.

Learn from failure and move on

Would you like me to give you a formula for success? It's quite simple, really. Double your rate of failure.

—THOMAS J. WATSON

When you take full responsibility for every aspect of your life, including the consequences of all your actions, both positive and negative, you come to realise that things happen as they are supposed to happen. You begin to look for the good in every situation, even when you fail, and to recognise that something good always comes out of adversity. Consider this story, for example:

> *Nasrudin and his master were hunting in the forest. The master cut his thumb while shooting his bow and arrow because he held them incorrectly. Nasrudin stopped the bleeding and bandaged the deep wound as his master moaned in pain. In an attempt to console his master, Nasrudin said, 'Sir, there are no mistakes, only lessons, and we can learn from them if we're willing.'*
>
> *The master became enraged. 'How dare you lecture me!' he barked. And with that he threw Nasrudin into a deserted well and continued on without his devoted servant.*
>
> *A little farther on, a group of forest people captured the master and took him to their chief for human sacrifice. The fire was roasting hot, and the master was about to be thrown into it when the chief noticed his bandaged thumb and set him free. It was a rule that all sacrificial victims had to be perfect specimens. Realising how right Nasrudin had been, the master rushed back to the well and rescued his faithful servant. Acknowledging his unjust actions, the master pulled Nasrudin out and asked his forgiveness for the terrible mistake he'd made.*
>
> *Nasrudin assured him that he had not made a mistake at all. On the contrary, he insisted that another lesson was concealed here. Nasrudin told the master that he had done him a great service by throwing him into the well. He thanked the master for saving his life, explaining that if he had continued with him into the forest, the forest people would have taken him for sacrifice and surely he would have died.*
>
> *'You see,' Nasrudin said, 'there are no mistakes, only lessons to learn. What we call our mistakes can be a blessing in disguise, if we're willing to learn from them.'*
>
> *This time the master smiled and nodded in agreement.*

Thinking of mistakes and failures as lessons can help you develop an optimistic frame of mind. Mistakes viewed as lessons build confidence and success while mistakes viewed as failures undermine these things. Simply by reinterpreting your failures, you instantly feel more upbeat and are more likely to take positive action. I learned one of the greatest lessons of my life when I was a junior management consultant with PricewaterhouseCoopers (PwC) in Europe. One day a more senior consultant told me, 'David, we never make mistakes here, we only *add* to our experience'. In fact, when you think about it, this is exactly why clients pay high fees to PwC and others—they want to tap into their experience, so they don't make the same mistakes themselves. I have never forgotten that lesson.

In a fascinating study of business leaders and how they view failure, Warren Bennis interviewed 70 top performing people in numerous fields of endeavour. None of them used the word failure to describe their mistakes. Instead, they referred to learning experiences, detours or opportunities for growth.

While it's important to be upbeat about our failures, it's still critical to understand that as humans we go through a predictable cycle when it comes to handling failure and the associated grief in our lives. Elisabeth Kübler-Ross famously wrote about the stages that a person goes through in dealing with the death of someone close. These stages—denial, anger, blame, depression and acceptance—are similar to what you go through when you're dealing with setbacks in your professional or personal life. Ideally, they will be followed by three further stages: resurgence, taking responsibility and taking control. Research shows that people who are more successful are able to get through the first five stages quicker than others, so that most of their energy can be spent on constructive recovery.

Your first reaction to a major setback will often be *denial*. You will be shocked and feel that the problem cannot be happening to you. You may react by shutting it out—ignoring what is happening and hoping that it will just go away.

The second stage is *anger*. You may have a frustrated sense that 'things like this are always happening to me'. You may even deepen the problem by behaving in an irritable or aggressive manner towards others.

The third stage is *blame*. Here the natural tendency is to make people, organisations and events outside your control responsible for the situation in which you find yourself. In the business world, this is the typical 'witch-hunt' for someone to shoulder the responsibility for what happened.

In the fourth stage, *depression*, the reality of the setback begins to sink in. Along with the sense of a new reality, you may feel sorry for yourself and wonder 'why me?'

Acceptance is the fifth stage, where you come to terms with the failure or setback and start looking towards the future. This is the crucial stage, because without it you cannot move on to *resurgence*—the point at which you take complete responsibility for charting the way forward.

When you really understand failure, you begin to see it as one of life's greatest teachers. When seen in this light, everything is good, even the bad stuff. A positive approach to failure has several important advantages:

- You won't be so judgemental about events. Life is life. What happens, happens. And everything that happens is instructive one way or another.

- You won't get stuck in bad situations for long because you aren't resisting them. What you resist persists. Instead, you will simply take action. You will move through the stages of grief knowing that *you will* eventually come out the other end.

- Instead of complaining, you make the most of your current situation.

- Failure teaches us humility. It shows us our limitations and teaches us that we are not invincible.

- Failure teaches us about the strength of our character. It challenges us to dig deeper into our resources. Failure teaches us about perseverance. It asks us whether we're going to quit or become more determined and keep on trying. It makes us stronger.

As we have seen, the question isn't whether we're going to fail, because all of us are. The question is *how* we're going to fail. Essentially, like everything else, we have two choices. We can choose to regard failure as something negative and, therefore, something to be avoided. Or we can make friends with failure and use it to propel us forward to become fully alive, responsible adults. The choice is yours.

Know when to apologise

I've learned that people will forget what you said, people will forget what you did, but people will never forget how you made them feel.

— MAYA ANGELOU

People with a strong sense of responsibility have learned how to apologise when they get things wrong. They know how to say 'I'm sorry' and really mean it. Refusing to apologise is one of the biggest obstacles to becoming successful because it keeps us tied to the past and unable to move forward with our lives. If you just think of how bitter you felt when a friend failed to apologise for hurting you or letting you down, you'll recognise that these negative feelings can stay with you long after the event itself has passed. The irony, of course, is that all the fears that lead us to resist apologising — the fear of losing face, admitting we made a mistake, being vulnerable — are actually eased by the apology. When you say 'I'm sorry', you turn people into your allies and sometimes even your best supporters.

Apologising forces everyone to let go of the past. In effect, an apology is saying to the other person, 'I can't change the past. All I can say is I'm sorry for what I did. I'm sorry for hurting you. I care about you. There is no excuse for what I did and I will try to do better in the future. I would like you to give me some ideas about how I can improve. Can you forgive me?' Apologising, then, is a sign of strength, not weakness. The handling of the Tylenol crisis by Johnson & Johnson in 1982 provides a great example of how to apologise. Tylenol is Johnson & Johnson's own brand of painkiller and it held 35 per cent of the market share until seven people died after taking the product. It turned out that a psychopath had contaminated the product with cyanide after the product reached the shelves — clearly no fault of Johnson & Johnson. The company immediately apologised, accepted full responsibility, and recalled 31 million bottles of Tylenol. For customers who already had Tylenol, they could get their money back or swap for the new product in redesigned tamper-proof packaging.

This rapid and open response, spearheaded by CEO Jim Burke, firmly established Johnson & Johnson as a company that genuinely cares about its customers. Although the exercise cost more than $100 million, and although Tylenol's market share dropped to 7 per cent, the product survived and quickly regained consumer confidence. Indeed, since the 1982 incident, Johnson & Johnson has positioned itself as a trustworthy company that puts people before profits.

While there are many reasons for shying away from apologising, I strongly encourage you to deliberately practise saying that you are sorry. You'll be amazed at how liberating it is and how helpful it is in moving you from where you are to where you want to be. It also does wonders for the quality and depth of your relationships.

The main thing to remember with apologising is that you are not excusing your behaviour. In effect, you are saying 'please forgive me' and waiting for the other person to respond. How the person responds is up to him or her—you have done your best, and now the fate of your relationship is with the other person. Most times, the other person will sense your sincerity and agree to move on. If he or she doesn't, I suggest you move on anyway, because there is nothing else you can do.

With apologies, it's best not to delay. Apologise simply. Don't try to justify what you did. Be sincere.

Say 'no' to responsibilities
that are not yours

When we learn to say a deep, passionate yes to the things that really matter, then peace begins to settle onto our lives like golden sunlight sifting to a forest floor.

—THOMAS KINKADE

One of the main reasons we need to apologise is because we said 'yes' to something when we really should have said 'no'. Saying 'yes' creates expectations of follow-through. With a 'yes', we assume the responsibility to do something whether we like it or not. And if we don't deliver on our promises, we need to say sorry and ask forgiveness. Today, more than ever, we need the courage to say 'no', because we have so many things we are asked to do. For many people, refusing can feel harsh, unhelpful and selfish; often our first inclination is to say 'yes', to help out, irrespective of how we might feel inside. Agreeing to do too much, too often, is the root cause of anxiety and stress in many lives.

The perils of saying 'yes' too often are entertainingly illustrated by the movie *Yes Man*, starring Jim Carrey and Rhys Darby. Carl Allen (Carrey) is challenged in a self-help seminar to say 'yes' to everything for an entire year. As you can imagine, such indiscriminate choice-making leads Allen into all sorts of trouble and adventures. While, of course, grossly exaggerated for comic effect, the movie does an excellent job of showing how the results we get in our lives are the direct consequence of saying 'yes' or 'no' to every choice we face.

This idea was brought home to me some time ago when I was coaching a woman who was feeling stressed by the many responsibilities in her life. She complained that she felt she never had any time left to do the things she really wanted to do. During the session I asked her how she spent her time in a typical week. As we talked, it emerged that much of her out-of-work time was spent on various community projects, which often involved attending meetings and working with volunteers. One of these organisations was her local kindergarten where she held the role of secretary and finance officer. On average, this work took 10 hours of her time every week — and sometimes more at the beginning of each school term. The interesting point was that this woman's own children had long since left kindergarten (they were now in their twenties), yet she still continued with the role, even though she did not even really enjoy it anymore. Once we talked about the idea of saying 'no' to responsibilities that are no longer in alignment with what's important, she soon realised that many of the responsibilities in her life were out of date; she needed to rethink many of her commitments. Do you have any 'historical' responsibilities that need to be reviewed?

For many people, the idea of saying 'no' to things induces feelings of guilt and regret. This is especially difficult for people who are people-pleasers and who fear the negative reactions of others. But there is good news — there is a better way to think about it. Instead of seeing 'no' in a negative light, think of it instead as saying a 'yes' to something more important. No actually means yes! In his book *Good to Great*, Jim Collins makes the same essential point when he says, 'The good is the enemy of the great'. In other words, when you say 'no' to something good, you create space to say a resounding 'yes' to something great — something that truly matters in your life. Thinking this way takes away any feelings of guilt you may have about saying 'no'.

Sometimes instead of refusing to do something, it may be best to *negotiate* what is being requested of you so that you can honour your promises to people you care about. There are three basic grounds for negotiation:

- *The 'what'.* For example, 'I won't be able to write the full report, but I would be happy to write the introduction, and sections 4 and 6'; 'I can't attend all the sports games, but I am able to attend every second event'.

- *The 'when'.* For example, 'I can't visit the client on Wednesday, but I can do it today'; 'I won't be able to do the shopping tomorrow, but I can do it on Friday'.

- *A combination of the 'what' and 'when'.* For example, 'I can't get the entire accounts done by Friday, but I can get the receivables done by this Wednesday'; 'I can't get the whole room painted by the end of the week, but I can have the ceiling finished for the following Sunday'.

In situations involving different levels of authority — your boss, for example — you may not be in a position to negotiate everything. However, that being so, you can still negotiate within limits, or at least highlight the consequences of the responsibility you're taking on; for example, 'Yes, I can get the report done by Friday, but this will mean pushing the office filing into next week, and coming in at 6 am for the next five days'. The important point here is to be aware of the promises you make and clear about what is involved in honouring them. It is far better to only make promises you can keep than to over-promise and underdeliver.

As a deliberate person, you may find it helpful to make a list of those things you don't want to do as an aid to your everyday decision making. By identifying some of your important 'nos' you can create clarity where you might otherwise have experienced a dilemma. Some of my 'don't do' items are:

- I don't provide coaching to people who have not attended my workshop. I find it better to give people tools at workshops, and then coach on the application of those tools.

- Although I am qualified and can do it, I don't lecture on subjects outside my immediate interest of personal development and personal mastery.

- I don't give free talks to charities or other non-paying organisations. I am not a charity and if I want to donate to good causes, I'll do so directly in cash.

- I don't lend my books to other people. They rarely come back, and they are the tools that enable me to do what I do. I will, however, buy extra copies of books that I can give away.

- I don't do any significant maintenance on my home. I am not good at it, I don't enjoy it and I can afford to get professionals to do it for me.

Ralph Waldo Emerson wrote in his journal that he likes the 'sayers of no' better than the 'sayers of yes'. And Leonardo da Vinci said, 'It is easier to resist at the beginning than at the end'. If you aren't able to say 'no' right up front, you end up being reluctantly involved in things that are not aligned with what's important to you. Sometimes you simply must say 'no' to the good to make room for the great.

Take responsibility for stress in your life

To make the right choices in life, you have to get in touch with your soul. To do this, you need to experience solitude … because in the silence you hear the truth and know the solutions.

—DEEPAK CHOPRA

As we have seen, the choices you make by saying 'yes' and 'no' within your daily life determine the results you get. Despite our best efforts, however, we can sometimes experience unhealthy stress as a consequence of the choices we make. This stress can be brought on by the emergence of unforeseen events, new demands that we did not anticipate, or not making as much progress on existing projects as we had planned. The important point in dealing with such unhelpful stress is to acknowledge it, own it, and then find ways of moving forward.

Stress in itself is not harmful. It's an integral part of life, and some stress is good for us, in that it creates the motivation that enables performance. This good stress is called 'eustress' and is the type of positive energy that helps us achieve our goals. There comes a point, however, when a line is crossed, and that positive stress turns to an uncomfortable feeling of overload or anxiety, which compromises performance.

So how do you know if you have crossed that line? To answer that question, we need a definition of unhealthy stress. Unhealthy stress is a set of reactions (thoughts, feelings, physical sensations and/or behaviours) we experience when we perceive that the demands of a situation are greater than our perceived resources to cope with them. You will notice that this definition of unhealthy stress makes reference to what we *perceive* to be true about a situation and our ability to deal with it. People experience stress when the demands they face exceed their real or imaginary capacity to deal with them. Whether these perceptions are real or not does not matter to the person experiencing stress. Stress is stress.

If you are a deliberate person and you honestly accept full responsibility for what happens to you, you'll be acutely aware of the signs of stress operating in your life. You'll know that when you begin to cross that line, you can put yourself in the driver seat and make different choices to help yourself take a step back.

Stress has a purpose. It's a signal that you need to take action or change your thinking patterns (or both). When you are in control of your life, you actually welcome stress because you know it's a hidden opportunity for growth that will enable you to become a better, more resilient person. In fact, good management of your stress levels is a key to managing your entire life.

Be a role model

If you're lucky enough to do well, it's your responsibility to send the elevator back down.
——KEVIN SPACEY

Over the years I have observed that the best way to learn something is to teach it. When it comes to learning about personal responsibility, it's a good idea to find ways of putting this message across to those around you. For example, if you hear someone complaining or blaming, you could simply remind them that they have the power to think in a different way about the situation in which they find themselves. You may be pleasantly surprised by the positive impact this can have and by the way people respond to you.

Of course, while talking about accepting responsibility is good, actions always speak louder than words:

> *You are writing a gospel,*
> *A chapter each day,*
> *By the deeds that you do,*
> *And the words that you say.*
>
> *People read what you write,*
> *If it's false or it's true,*
> *Now what is the gospel*
> *According to you?*

If you become a role model to those around you, you'll experience tremendous satisfaction knowing that you can spark new thinking that can positively influence the lives of many people.

In this chapter we have looked extensively at what is involved in taking full responsibility and ownership of what's happening in your professional and personal life. Your entire life up to now has been determined by the choices and decisions you have made or failed to make. If there is anything you are unhappy about, it's up to you to make changes so the results you get are more to your liking.

Peter Drucker, in his article 'Managing Oneself', published in the *Harvard Business Review,* found that people who ranked in the top of their field tended to share a trait that distinguished them from their colleagues. These top people had a habit of viewing themselves as self-employed throughout their careers, no matter who their employer was. Effectively, they saw themselves as the CEOs of their own lives. And as CEO, they were fully responsible for every part of their life and career. I encourage you to adopt this attitude too.

Always remember that the choices you make, make you.

Ideas for Action

- Review how good you are at accepting responsibility for your life. What decisions do you now regret making? What things do you wish were different? Do you blame others? If so, who? Why? Does it make sense?

- Knowing what you now know, what would you not do again? What lesson can you take from these experiences?

- Is there anyone you need to say 'sorry' to? Perhaps at work, within your family, maybe a friend? If you need to make an apology, plan to do it sooner rather than later.

This above all: to thine own self be true
And it must follow, as the night the day
Thou canst not then be false to any man.

—WILLIAM SHAKESPEARE (*HAMLET*)

Action — getting work done

Action may not always bring happiness, but there is no happiness without action.
— BENJAMIN DISRAELI

Action is magical because, without it, no real success can happen in your life; with it, there is no limit to what can be achieved. Many people spend their lives wondering why it's so difficult to get things done — important tasks just seem to keep slipping down the list of things to do. Deliberate people, however, have strategies for getting things done efficiently. They know that taking action is the key to achieving real success.

As an introduction to this important idea, consider the following story:

> *There was once a man who had to travel 10 miles to attend to some work. It was late at night and very dark. His lantern could at most light only a couple of steps ahead. Because the journey seemed so long, and the night so dark, he felt unsure of reaching his destination.*
>
> *While he stood at his door feeling frustrated and helpless, a wise man appeared and asked him why he was standing there with a lantern. The man replied that he really did not know what to do; though he was all set for the journey, he was worried that his light would be inadequate on such a night.*
>
> *The wise man explained to him that it was not necessary to have a light big enough to illuminate the whole way. 'As you proceed,' he said, 'the light moves with you, so the next one or two steps will always be clear. All you need to do is to hold on to this light and start walking'. So the man did and he reached his destination.*

Like the man with the lantern, many of us are on the doorstep of our lives when it comes to taking action. We may hesitate by procrastinating too much or, if we do set off on our journey, we torment ourselves with unhelpful thoughts and anxieties that make each step more difficult than it needs to be.

The purpose of this chapter, then, is to provide you with some practical tools that will help you to take action in your life. Our aim will be to cultivate 'present-moment awareness'—a good phrase because it reminds us that action is always tied to the present moment, not to the past or future. While this may sound like a simple idea, putting it into practice is another matter. The wisdom traditions of the world have traditionally spent a great deal of energy encouraging present-moment awareness, because it is both at the very core of effective action and inherently challenging. Why should this be so? Surely, if the benefits are so great, we should be motivated to stay in the now? To answer these questions we need to understand the nature of the mind and how it operates moment to moment.

At any one time, the mind is focused on one of three places: the past, the future or the present. There are no other possibilities. When the mind is focused on the past, it works from memories that are often imperfect or filtered through a subjective lens. When it is focused on the future, it builds pictures in the imagination. While these can be based, in part, on memories of the past, the future is always an illusion of possibilities. It is only *now* that we can experience full reality. Yet when we look honestly at our lives, we begin to realise how little time we actually spend in the now. How often have you been driving from A to B and, upon reaching your destination, find you have little memory of the road travelled? Or made yourself a cup of tea or coffee only to finish it without tasting anything? If the quality of our lives was measured by how much time we spend in the now, undoubtedly we would be shocked.

The mind finds it challenging to be in the now because it is naturally drawn to the past or the future. There are at least five reasons for this. The first is that we are addicted to keeping our minds occupied. Especially when we have little to do, or are just resting, the mind will conjure up something to think about. It will find an 'old movie' to watch, or create some future fantasy.

The niggling attraction of unresolved issues is the second obstacle between us and the present moment. Feelings of anger or grief, and anxieties of all kinds habitually come into our mind without invitation. And because they represent unfinished business they can nag at us for a long time, using up valuable mental energy. The mind loves to replay issues even when there is nothing to be gained by doing so.

The third reason we spend so much of our time in the past or future is to do with our tendency to devalue the present moment. For whatever reason, we often find the now less interesting than the past or the future. Thoughts of the immediate future—even the next few minutes or seconds—are especially distracting. We are like a politician shaking hands: even as we have one person's hand in our grip, we are already looking for the next hand to shake. In such moments we're there, but not *really* there.

Fourth, unfulfilled desires are a major and pervasive distraction from the present. Thoughts of the medium- and long-term future endlessly take us out of the present moment with the promise that tomorrow will be more satisfying than today. Our happiness becomes conditional on some future achievement or event. The result is that we are always seeking, always looking forward, and never fully enjoying the now.

Finally, the fifth distraction is the incessant commentary that goes on in the mind. We are forever passing judgement upon ourselves and others—generally in a negative and unhelpful way. Even a walk down the street is an occasion to pass comment: she's fat; who does he think he is; that's a nice shirt; I wish I had one of those; and so on. Such judgemental commentaries take us out of the present moment and—while they may make us feel better in the short term—ultimately wear us down.

The consequences of a life lived away from the now are far reaching. For a start, our minds can be so full of activity and clutter that we don't appreciate what is right in front of us, a reality that can only be fully experienced as it unfolds. Sometimes not being alert to the demands of the present moment can cause us unnecessary problems—forgotten commitments or misheard instructions, for example, can result in some nasty surprises. And because of our many preoccupations, we are often prevented from looking at situations with fresh eyes, and unable to come up with solutions that are innovative.

The good news, however, is that all these distractions from the richness of the present moment can be reduced when you step in and take more control of your mind. This chapter shows you how to do exactly that.

Act upon your ULP

I'm absolutely convinced that if someone has a long-term goal and writes it down, and starts thinking about it, then everything will gravitate towards that thought.

—MICHAEL HILL

The key to a fulfilling life is to do things in the now that are in alignment with your highest values. When you are living in accordance with what you really value, you are most fully alive and most fully yourself. If your experience is anything like mine, you'll notice that when you do things that are genuinely in alignment with what's important to you, you *want* to do them and the work involved is almost effortless. Rather than having to muster motivation, you are drawn like a magnet. Action executed under such conditions is always worthwhile and, therefore, always enjoyable.

In their eagerness to get started, many people make the mistake of diving into action without first establishing a strong connection between the task in front of them and their reason for doing it. They lack clarity of purpose. Within no time, as the inevitable obstacles to completing the task appear, they waiver in their determination and too easily give up. Clarity, then, must precede action. The clearer you are about what you want, why you want it and what you have to do to achieve it, the easier it will be for you to overcome procrastination and to be in the now as you execute the task in front of you.

This clarity can be quickly achieved by bringing to mind your ULP statement and the associated campaigns you identified in chapter 1. Your ULP supplies the 'why' for any given task. It is the motivating force in your life and reflects your deepest values. For this reason, at the beginning of this book I recommended that you commit your ULP to memory and also carry a copy in your wallet or purse, so you can refer to it often.

Clarity of purpose produces results in your professional and personal life. When you and those around you know the 'why' of things, energy is released and tasks are undertaken with a positive frame of mind. You feel good about what you're doing because of the clear connection between where you are and where you want to be. As you work, you'll find it easy to be fully present in the moment because you have consciously chosen to be right here, right now, doing things that truly matter to you.

Beat procrastination

So ... be your name Buxbaum or Bixby or Bray or Mordecai Ali Van Allen O'Shea
you're off to Great Places! Today is your day! Your mountain is waiting. So ... get on
your way!

——DR SEUSS

One of the biggest barriers to doing what needs to be done is the self-inflicted problem of procrastination or, more precisely, *negative procrastination*. In itself, procrastination is not necessarily a bad thing. Sometimes a decision to delay action for another time can be constructive if the likely benefits of the delay outweigh the advantages of doing it right away. This is what we call positive or creative procrastination. For example, you could begin writing the report today, but instead you decide to begin it tomorrow when you'll have more complete information or when you'll be fresher and in a more productive state of mind. You could also procrastinate over things that are of limited significance to you—in other words, prioritise things that are more significant. The key here is to make a conscious decision and to then feel good and guilt-free about the decision you have made.

Most people engage in unconscious procrastination. They procrastinate without thinking about it. As a result, they waste precious time when faced with big, valuable tasks that might have significant long-term consequences for them. You must avoid this common tendency at all costs. Your job is to deliberately put off tasks that are of low value so that you have more time for the ones that can make a big difference to your life and work.

Negative procrastination is not just delay, but irrational delay; that is, the procrastinator voluntarily puts off tasks despite believing he or she will be worse off for doing so. When we negatively procrastinate, we know we are acting against our own best interests.

Interestingly, procrastination seems to be on the rise. In *The Procrastination Equation*, a major study of procrastinators and their behaviour, Piers Steel showed that impulsivity and distractibility are the traits most strongly associated with negative procrastination. Steel found that in 1978 only about 5 per cent of Americans thought of themselves as chronic procrastinators; today, that figure is 26 per cent. Further,

Steel found that dislike of a task and doubt over its achievability — that is, fear and self-doubt — are its principle causes.

Because understanding *why* we irrationally put off important tasks is a vital step towards replacing procrastination with action, let's consider the root causes — and their antidotes — in more detail:

- *The task seems unpleasant.* This is the most common reason for procrastination. For some people, just getting started on a seemingly unpleasant task is the hard part; when they do begin, they wonder what all the fuss was about. The problem is caused by our *perception* of the task rather than the task itself. In times like this, the best strategy is simply to make a start. Suspend your judgements and internal commentaries, and just put one foot in front of the other until you build momentum. It's a bit like starting to climb a hill: if you are standing at the bottom looking at your destination, the task can seem daunting. If, on the other hand, you focus on the next step, you'll be at your destination before you know it. Here are some strategies to help you get started:

  - *Do it first thing in the day.* If you can do an unpleasant task before you've had much time to think about it, it will seem easier. In his book *Eat That Frog*, Brian Tracy says that if you have a 'frog' to eat, you should do so quickly so that it is not looking at you all day. If you have two frogs to eat, you should do so in quick succession.

  - *The night before, place the task, or a reminder of it, where you can't miss it.* When you walk into your workspace the next day, the task will be hard to avoid and you will be less likely to be distracted by other work. I sometimes write sticky notes to myself that I place on my keyboard to remind me of a task to be done first thing in the morning.

  - *Make a list of advantages and disadvantages.* Just thinking about the benefits of completing a task and seeing them written down can help you to overcome any anxieties you may have about beginning.

  - *Delegate.* Perhaps what you find unpleasant, someone else might enjoy.

More often than not, the seemingly unpleasant task will turn out
to be enjoyable on some level. Completing such tasks is also a
great boost to your self-confidence and your resolve to tackle more
difficult challenges in the future.

- *The task seems overwhelming.* In this case, the task is not necessarily
  unpleasant — in fact, you may even look forward to doing it.
  However, you perceive it to be so huge and overwhelming that
  you just don't know where to begin. Generally, the problem here
  stems from a lack of planning around how the task is going to
  be accomplished. Here are some ideas to make a task seem more
  achievable:

  - *Break it down.* Henry Ford once said that 'nothing is particularly
    hard if you divide it into small jobs'. No matter how complex
    your task, it can be thought of as a series of small jobs that
    connect with each other. The trick is to delay making a start on
    the task itself and instead put your energy into thinking about the
    project so it can be broken down into more manageable chunks.
    Then, when you do make a start, you'll feel great knowing that
    what you are working on contributes in some important way to
    the larger project.

  - *Think on paper.* Instead of trying to keep everything in your head,
    write on paper or, for bigger projects, perhaps use a computer
    tool (project-planning software or mind maps, for example).
    The goal is to externalise the project so that you can gain some
    objective distance from it. Sometimes, a solid hour of planning
    can be more constructive than a full day of work.

  - *Find a solitary place.* Once you have the information you need, find
    a workspace out of the road of distraction and temptation.

- *The task generates fear.* Procrastinators have three main fears:

  - *Fear of failure.* If you don't do it, you won't get judged.

  - *Fear of success.* If you do it, you'll be expected to produce more.

  - *Fear of being controlled.* By not doing it, you're saying, 'You can't
    make me'.

The key to overcoming these fears is to take some time out, reconnect with your ULP, your campaigns, your beliefs about success and failure, and any positive affirmation you may have crafted for yourself. If you can successfully connect with the bigger picture of your life, you'll see the 'why' behind what you are doing. Once you see this clearly, fear will lose its power to inhibit you.

- *The task overcommits you.* Many people are so eager that they take on far more than they should — at work, at home or in their communities. A range of factors may drive this tendency: the inability to say 'no', an unrealistic desire to please, unbridled ambition or such an active interest in everything that prioritisation flies out the window. Procrastination in these circumstances is caused by a basic incapacity to get everything done. My best tips for overcoming this form of procrastination are:

  - *Review your commitments.* What do you really want to do? Where can you uniquely add value? Where is your true passion?

  - *Make decisions.* Can you prioritise your commitments differently? Is delegation an option? Is the deadline negotiable? Can you just say 'no'?

- *Delay generates adrenaline.* Some people procrastinate because they believe that doing things at the last minute brings out the best in them. This is false logic and simply untrue. If this is one of your habits, I strongly encourage you to break it. There are several problems with the 'last-minute' strategy:

  - *Mistakes are more frequent.* There is no question that work done at the last minute is more error prone and more likely to require rework.

  - *Quality is compromised.* Because there is no time at the end, the all-important finishing touches don't get done.

  - *The unexpected may happen.* From experience we all know that no amount of planning can prevent a crisis from happening at the least desirable moment. In a last-minute situation, both the task and the unexpected demand will suffer, and you will experience high levels of unnecessary stress.

These five underlying causes give us some insight into the psychology of negative procrastination. Procrastination is not only the thief of time, it is also the thief of present-moment awareness because it takes us away from acting now. The best advice I have heard on this matter is to procrastinate later!

Get in the zone

The first law of success is concentration—to bend all the energies to one point, and to go directly to that point, looking neither to the right nor to the left.

—WILLIAM MATHEWS

When you talk to high-performing people about present-moment awareness and being in the now, they invariably make reference to what it feels like to be 'in the zone'. Sportspeople, artists and other creative people frequently refer to how this state of mind enables them to perform at their highest level. You too may have had this experience while engaged in a task you enjoy or feel passionate about: time stands still and there is absolutely nothing else on your mind. The psychologist Mihaly Csikszentmihalyi (pronounced chick-SENT-me-high) calls this state 'flow' and has popularised the term in his seminal book *Flow: The Psychology of Optimal Experience*. He defines flow as 'being completely involved in an activity for its own sake. The ego falls away. Time flies. Every action, movement, and thought follows inevitably from the previous one...your whole being is involved, and you're using your skills to the utmost'.

Researchers such as Timothy Gallwey, Joel Spolsky and Charles Snyder have all found that being caught up in an activity that completely engages us without distraction, and where there is no fear of failure or time awareness, is extremely good for our psychological health. When we are in a state of flow there is a perfect balance between a stimulating challenge and our skill level. Work that lacks challenge is boring and encourages the mind to wander, while a task that is beyond our skill level will be frustrating. When we enter the realm of flow, we merge with our environment and whatever we are doing; activity seems effortless and refreshes rather than drains our energy. In short, it's a state of being perfectly in the now—in full awareness of the present moment. The great news is that getting into this special zone is a learnable skill. With practice, you can teach yourself how to achieve a state of flow every day.

Understanding that you always have choices, and then making good decisions, is fundamental to spending more time in your zone. You want to organise your life so that when you work on a task, you work on that task alone and do not allow yourself to become distracted. It's really a matter of improving your self-discipline and self-control.

In an optimum state of flow, your powers of attention focus like a laser on the work you are doing. This superior focus is what brings out the best and finest energy you have, resulting in work to the highest quality. As Csikszentmihalyi writes, 'It is the full involvement of flow, rather than happiness, that makes for excellence in life'. Indeed.

The power of non-attachment

When asked, 'How do you write?' I invariably answer, 'One word at a time'.
— STEPHEN KING

'The Muddy Road' is an Eastern story told about two monks, Tanzan and Ekido, who were once travelling together down a muddy road. Coming around a bend, they met a lovely girl in a silk kimono and sash unable to cross the intersection because of the stream from the heavy rain. 'Come on, girl,' said Tanzan and, lifting her in his arms, he carried her over the mud to the other side of the stream. Ekido did not speak again until that night when they reached a lodging temple. Then he no longer could restrain himself. 'We monks don't go near females,' he told Tanzan, 'especially not young and lovely ones. It is dangerous. Why did you do that?'

'I left the girl there,' said Tanzan. 'Are you still carrying her?'

Like Ekido, many of us harbour unhealthy attachments to things, events and feelings that cause us all kinds of difficulties when it comes to doing our work. Instead of putting our attention on what needs to be done, we distract ourselves with thoughts that are frustrating, distracting and often unhelpful. Instead of simply working on the task in front of us, we start to imagine what life will be like when it is done, and in that instant we lose that all-important present-moment awareness. As a result, errors can creep into what we are doing and the quality of our work can suffer. We are there, but not really there. When you develop the skill of non-attachment, you work with no thought of reward.

The best way to practise non-attachment is to approach your work with what is called a 'meta-mind'. With a meta-mind, you develop the capacity to observe your own mind in action. You notice what you are thinking, your emotions, and how these thoughts and emotions are influencing the results you are getting. In essence, you become an observer of your own life. You ask yourself, 'What am I thinking here?', 'Is this kind of thinking helpful?' and 'Can I let these thoughts go?' Simply letting go is the key to reducing the impact of unhelpful attachments.

Yet another story, as told by the Indian philosopher Shantanand Saraswati illustrates the value of letting go. A special trick is used to catch monkeys in the wild. A round earthen pot with a small mouth is buried in the ground. Pieces of tasty food are put inside. When the monkey smells the food, it comes close and puts its hand inside to clutch the food. With its hand full, it cannot pull away from the jar. To free itself, all it has to do is release the food but, like us, the monkey strives to be free while remaining attached.

Sensory awareness

The secret of health for both mind and body is not to mourn for the past, worry about the future, or anticipate troubles; but to live in the present moment wisely and earnestly.

— BUDDHA

Another good way of maintaining strong present-moment awareness and letting go of unhelpful thoughts is to deliberately connect with your senses — sight, touch, smell, taste and hearing — as you go about important tasks. As your mind wanders, you can bring your attention and focus back to the work in front of you by using the following simple exercise.

Exercise

Sitting quietly, connect with your breathing until the mind settles. Then experience each of your senses in turn. Feel the weight of your body in the chair. Feel the warmth and movement of the various energies in your body—the breath and the heartbeat, for example. When this is reasonably well established, connect with sight, then with taste and smell, and finally with what you can hear. Listen for different levels of sounds, including those near and far; for example, the sound of a clock ticking, the humming of air conditioning, voices in the distance or a car far away. Try to hear each sound individually and then hear all the sounds together. If thoughts or dreams take you away, gently return to your body in the chair. Try to hold this awareness for a few minutes.

The purpose of this exercise is to help us to get away from living our lives inside our heads—where our overactive imaginations habitually relive the past or project into the future—and to recall us to the rich potential of the present moment.

The practice of learning to live in the now is admittedly a lifelong endeavour. While as a concept it sounds very simple, living with a high level of present-moment awareness takes practice and dedication. If you are interested in pursuing this further, I highly recommend the books of Eckhart Tolle: *The Power of Now* and *A New Earth*. Tolle further explores the idea that all of our struggles and frustrations come from either thinking too much in the past or trying to anticipate the future. Tolle, in common with so many other influential thinkers, teaches that we can only be truly happy and content in the present moment. By actively living in the now, we distance ourselves from what he calls our 'false selves' and all those ego-driven behaviours that prevent us from experiencing life as it really is. As Tolle puts it in *A New Earth*:

> *The present moment is the field on which the game of life happens. It cannot happen anywhere else. Once you have made peace with the present moment, see what happens, what you can do or choose to do, or rather what life does through you. There are three words that convey the secret of the art of living, the secret of all success and happiness: One With Life. Being one with life is being one with Now. You then realise that you don't live your life, but life lives you. Life is the dancer and you are the dance.*

When you apply this way of thinking to the work you do, you'll become very aware of how easily wayward thoughts divert your attention. These diversions determine how long it takes you to perform a task and, indeed, the quality of your work. In his classic book *Zen and the Art of Motorcycle Maintenance*, Robert Pirsig captures the essence of the problem:

> *So the thing to do when working on a motorcycle, as in any other task, is to cultivate the peace of mind which does not separate one's self from one's surroundings. When that is done successfully, then everything else follows naturally. Peace of mind produces right values, right values produce right thoughts. Right thoughts produce right actions and right actions produce work which will be a material reflection for others to see of the serenity at the centre of it all.*

Developing the practice of being in the now has many benefits in both your professional and personal life. It brings life and energy to everything you do. Because your mind becomes much calmer, the quality of your thinking and the results you get markedly improve.

For me, living with present-moment awareness is akin to walking instead of driving. Imagine, for example, that you are travelling to the next town by car. As you journey, the view through the front windscreen remains much the same; if you look out the back windscreen the same thing happens, except this time the view is receding. Now imagine that you are making the same journey on foot. You are now taking in your surroundings in much more detail. You see the wild flowers on the roadside, the little bird flying past and the blades of grass glistening in the sun. And so it is when we live with present-moment awareness. We become aware of all the many finer aspects of life that we often miss as we hurtle towards the future, so eager to get to our destination, or so busy looking in the rear-view mirror, that we miss the journey along the way. The real action is happening out the side windows.

As Henry Miller once observed, 'The moment one gives close attention to anything, even a blade of grass, it becomes a mysterious, awesome, indescribably magnificent world in itself'.

Cultivate effortlessness

At the still point of the turning world ... at the still point, there the dance is.
— T. S. ELIOT

A few years ago I spent a full day on a golf course watching Tiger Woods. For 18 holes, I followed him as he teed off, took tricky shots from the rough and provided a masterful display of putting excellence. As Tiger played, it struck me that he was able to achieve a special mental state just before he stepped up to hit the ball. Then, when he did swing the club, the stroke seemed almost effortless. I also noticed that despite the cheering from the crowd, Tiger was incredibly composed. His stillness and calmness was almost palpable.

Working with highly successful people, I have seen that they too demonstrate these essential characteristics: efficiency of movement and a deep-rooted stillness or calmness. For the person watching, it seems that high-performing people operate in a special zone that makes what they're doing seem *effortless*. For the people performing, that external appearance corresponds to a feeling of total absorption. They aren't thinking about other people or how they are seen, and they don't feel like they're in a race against time. They are 100 per cent involved in the task right in front of them.

In her wonderful book *The Art of Effortless Living*, Ingrid Bacci makes an important distinction between living from a philosophy of doing and from a perspective of being. *Doing* is associated with activity and busyness, while *being* is associated with relaxing, being present and trusting yourself. In a chapter titled 'Action', you might have expected me to extol the virtues of *doing* over all else—but not so. Research clearly shows that the most productive, creative and healthy individuals are those who, by doing less—and living with a present-moment awareness mindset—paradoxically achieve more.

The Eastern mystic, Swami Vivekananda, put it this way:

> *The calmer we are, the better it is for us and the greater is the amount of work we can do. When we let loose our feelings we waste so much energy, shatter our nerves, disturb our minds, and accomplish very little work. The energy which ought to have gone into work is spent on mere feeling, which counts for nothing. It is only when the mind is very calm and collected that the whole of its energy is spent in doing good work... The man who gives way to anger or hatred or any other passion cannot work; he only breaks himself to pieces and does nothing practical. It is the calm, forgiving, equable, well balanced mind that does the greatest amount of work.*

Without question, then, my best advice is to learn how to live with less effort. You'll end up achieving more!

Follow through on prioritised tasks

You are never given a wish without also being given the power to make it true. You may have to work for it, however.

— RICHARD BACH

In *The Attention Economy*, business consultants Thomas Davenport and John Beck conclude that 'understanding and managing attention is now the single most important determinant of business success'. It seems that in our information intensive world, our ability to keep focused on our real priorities is an essential skill that needs to be nurtured. It's important because, unlike during the industrial age, when life was arguably simpler and work much more structured, the information age offers us far greater flexibility and, correspondingly, far greater distractions.

While looking at the topic of ADHD (attention deficit hyperactivity disorder), I came across the following anecdote, which can be found from multiple sources online, that illustrates the modern-day challenges many of us face.

As I turn on the hose in the driveway, I look over at my car and decide it needs washing. As I head towards the garage, I notice post on the porch table that I picked up from the postbox earlier. I decide to go through it before I wash the car. I put my car keys on the table, put the junk mail in the recycling box under the table, and notice that the recycling box is full.

So, I decide to put the bills back on the table and take out the recycling first. But then I think, since I'm going to be near the postbox when I take out the recycling paper anyway, I may as well pay the bills first. I take my cheque book off the table and notice that there is only one cheque left. My extra cheques are in the desk in my study, so I go into the house to my desk where I find the cup of coffee I'd been drinking. I'm going to look for my cheques but first I need to push the coffee aside so that I don't accidentally knock it over. The coffee is getting cold, and I decide to make another cup.

As I head toward the kitchen with the cold coffee, a vase of flowers on the worktop catches my eye—the flowers need water. I put the coffee on the worktop and discover my reading glasses that I've been searching for all morning. I decide I better put them back on my desk, but first I'm going to water the flowers. I put the glasses back down on the worktop, fill a container with water and suddenly spot the TV remote control. Someone left it on the kitchen table. I realise that tonight when we go to watch TV, I'll be looking for the remote, but I won't remember that it's on the kitchen table, so I decide to put it back where it belongs, but first I'll water the flowers.

I pour some water in the flowers, but quite a bit of it spills on the floor. So, I put the remote back on the table, get some towels and wipe up the spill. Then, I head down the hall trying to remember what I was planning to do.

At the end of the day, the car isn't washed. The bills aren't paid, there is a cold cup of coffee sitting on the bench, the flowers don't have enough water, there is still only one cheque in my cheque book, I can't find the remote, I can't find my glasses, and I don't remember what I did with the car keys.

Then, when I try to figure out why nothing got done today, I'm really baffled because I know I was busy all day and I'm really tired. I realise this is a serious problem and I'll try to get some help for it, but first I'll check my email.

Although a little extreme, the story may strike a chord with you. But why are we so easily distracted? And, can we do anything to reduce the unwanted consequences of such destructive behaviour?

As always, an important step in solving the problem is to understand your role in its creation. In this case, the starting point is to fess up and take personal responsibility for allowing yourself to become distracted. When you think about it, you and *only* you chose to direct your attention away from what you were doing to some other activity. Your choices got you to where you are.

In my experience, there are three reasons we allow ourselves to be distracted: boredom, thinking we need a break and nearing completion. The first of these, boredom, is by far the most frequent reason cited for stopping what we are doing and (hopefully) coming back to it later. We convince ourselves that the energy we have is running low, the task we are working on is not exciting enough and if we temporarily switch to some other task we'll be invigorated when we come back to it. Once we reach this point in our thinking, we actively start looking for reasons to switch our attention onto something new. As usual, we find something within no time.

The trouble with the boredom justification is that we rarely get 'invigorated' about the task later. In practice, it is much more difficult to pick up a task that we earlier put down and labelled as 'not exciting'. When we drop a boring task, we invoke what is known in economics as 'switching costs'—a price that we will have to pay at some future time to get to the level of thinking that will allow us to continue with the task.

For example, think of some writing you might have been doing in the recent past. If you stopped before it was completed, your mind will take perhaps 10 or 15 minutes just to get back to where it was, before you can write another word. If you put something on hold for several months, you may need several days to be able to pick up where you left off, and so on.

If you are tempted to switch tasks for reasons of boredom, I would encourage you to keep working on the original job if at all possible. More often than not, you'll find that you can break through the barrier and go on to finish the job—persistence is where the true invigoration lies. The entrepreneur Estee Lauder once remarked, 'When I thought I couldn't go on, I forced myself to keep going. My success is based on persistence, not luck'.

The second justification, thinking you need a break, is a trickier one to handle. You would indeed benefit from a break if you have reached a point in your work where persistence is not helpful. Perhaps the quality of what you are doing *would* be enhanced if you came back to it later. If this is truly the case, taking a break is an excellent idea. Other times, however, we come up with the excuse of 'needing a break' as a way of giving ourselves permission to go on to something else that has more immediate appeal. And if we keep doing this, we end up with a plethora of half-finished tasks that are all awaiting completion. These unfinished tasks drain you of energy. As David Allen observes in his book *Getting Things Done*, these 'incomplete loops' remain active in your brain and produce a sense of annoyance far greater than the actual effort required to finish the task.

So my advice is to push ahead and finish incomplete tasks as often as possible; if you do decide to take a break, be sure to stop at a place where it will be easy to pick up again. At least that way you'll feel better about resuming work on the task and the 'incomplete loop' will not play on your mind so much.

The third reason we allow ourselves to become distracted and lose focus is that we see the finish line of our current task. Because there is 'only a little left to do', we stop too early without finishing the job. Often we never get around to finishing the task completely and the quality of our work suffers. It's a very common problem, and one that is responsible for many anxieties and unnecessary stresses.

The Russian novelist and historian Alexander Solzhenitsyn incisively describes the challenge of 'the last inch' in his novel *The First Circle*:

> *Now listen to the rule of the last inch. The realm of the last inch. The job is almost finished, the goal almost attained, everything possible seems to have been achieved, every difficulty overcome—and yet the quality is just not there. The work needs more finish, perhaps further research. In that moment of weariness and self-satisfaction, the temptation is the greatest to give up, not to strive for the peak of quality. That's the realm of the last inch—here the work is very, very complex but it's also particularly valuable because it's done with the most perfect means. The rule of the last inch is simply this—not to leave it undone. And not to put it off—because otherwise your mind loses touch with this realm. And not to mind how much time you spend on it, because the aim is not to finish the job quickly, but to reach perfection.*

By not allowing yourself to be distracted and endeavouring to do complete work, you give yourself the mental space and the clarity to tackle the next task with high energy and enthusiasm. Remember, really successful people get things done because they do the things that matter most, irrespective of how they might feel about them. And they take things to completion.

Take short pauses between tasks

Learn to pause ... or nothing worthwhile will catch up to you.

—DOUG KING

One of the very best ways of removing unwanted distractions from your mind is to ground yourself in present-moment awareness just prior to beginning work on a new task. I call this *micro-pausing* and it works as follows:

- After finishing one activity and before starting something else, sit quietly and go through the sensory awareness exercise outlined in the section 'Sensory awareness' earlier in this chapter.

- When you feel calm and relaxed, bring your ULP to mind. Repeat it in your mind or quietly to yourself. Allow yourself to feel good about your ULP.

- Before you begin the new task, mentally form a link between the task in front of you and your ULP.

- Begin working on the new task.

With practice, the above exercise should take about one minute to complete. The power of micro-pausing is that it deliberately breaks your thought patterns and any built-up feelings as you move from one activity to the next. When you start work on a new task in this way, you come into it 'clean' because you have left behind the residual thoughts, emotions and energies from the previous task. When you take a deliberate micro-pause, you give yourself the best possible chance of remaining in a state of present-moment awareness as you complete your work.

If, while working on a task, you find yourself drifting and losing contact with the present moment, take another pause and then get back to work. I personally find micro-pausing to be one of the most effective mental tools I have ever used. It's extremely simple and can be applied in all areas of your life.

Avoid multi-tasking

We first make our habits, then our habits make us.

—JOHN DRYDEN

In my workshops, we often have heated debates about the value of trying to do several things at once. Some people argue that their ability to multi-task is what allows them to accomplish so much, while others believe that rushing around trying to do several things at once is fundamentally inefficient. So, where do you stand on the issue? Are you a fan of multi-tasking? Are you good at it?

It is important to be clear about what multi-tasking is and is not. In reality, at any given moment we can only do one thing at a time. Yes, we can switch our attention very quickly between different activities—for example, watching television and talking on the phone—but at any one instant our attention must be on one thing or the other. In reality, when we talk about multi-tasking we are really referring to *rapid task-shifting* between different activities. Let's consider an example.

You are working on a report and the phone rings. You answer the phone while still looking at the report. You are talking on the phone and looking at the report when someone comes up to interrupt you. You are now doing three things at once. Or are you? When you break it down and look at what just happened in slow motion, you'll agree that at any one instant your attention can only be directed at one of the three demands — the report, the phone call or the drop-in visitor. You find yourself re-reading lines from the report, or asking the person on the phone or the drop-in visitor to repeat a question he or she just asked as your attention shifts between the three. While it *seems* that you are doing three things at once, you are really only doing one thing while neglecting the other two. Sure, you can quickly shift between them, but the full focus of your attention is scattered and diluted. In effect, we have a situation of rapid task-shifting, not multi-tasking.

The distinction here is important, because while our human ability to engage in rapid task-shifting can be a wonderful asset, it can also get us into a lot of trouble. If we unconsciously allow ourselves to switch between tasks willy-nilly, we can easily get ourselves into a situation where nothing gets completely finished, or everything takes far longer than it needs to. A better approach is to practise rapid task-shifting deliberately and with clarity of purpose.

In some cases, it might make sense to task-shift; for example, stirring a boiling pot while listening to the radio or putting things into a box while casually chatting to a friend. In these cases, the level of concentration required for each task is relatively low. The 'switching costs' (covered in the section 'Prioritise, then follow through', earlier in this chapter) we incur by rapid task-shifting are minor and, therefore, we are willing to pay the price in order to advance several activities at the same time. Such deliberate multi-tasking makes rational sense.

Where we get ourselves into trouble is when we combine activities that each require high levels of concentration if we are to do them well. In our professional lives, I suggest that the majority of our tasks fall into this category. For a certain period of time, they demand single-minded attention.

Research into multi-tasking is fairly conclusive. One laboratory study conducted by David Meyer and Jeffrey Evans, both at the University of Michigan, found that substantial time was lost when people switched repeatedly between two tasks of varying complexity. The more complex the task, the greater the time lost. Time costs also were greater when subjects switched to tasks that were relatively unfamiliar to them. And productivity expert Brian Tracy suggests that when you concentrate single-mindedly on your most important task, you can reduce the time required to complete it by 50 per cent or more.

On the back of this evidence, then, I recommend the practice of deliberate multi-tasking. If you are going to multi-task, do so knowingly and only for activities that are relatively routine. When it comes to your most important tasks — those that give you the most value — do things one at a time and wherever possible take them to the point of completion. This requires you to develop the essential skill of self-discipline: the ability to make yourself do what you should do, when you should do it, whether you feel like it or not.

Stop when it's time to stop

Action is character. What a person does is what he is, not what he says.

—SYD FIELD

While it's important to overcome procrastination and to work without distraction, it's equally important to know when to stop. For some people, knowing when to stop is a real challenge. They may simply not know when the task they are working on is complete or, more likely, they may be unsure about whether or not what they have done is of sufficient quality. Still others are perfectionists and keep working on a task unnecessarily, sometimes stealing much needed time away from the next task and placing themselves under inordinate pressure. No matter what the underlying reasons, to keep working on something when you should have really stopped is a habit to be carefully avoided.

One good question to ask yourself is the following: 'Will more effort on this substantially improve the outcome?' If you can truthfully answer 'no', it's time for you to finish with the current task and move on to the next thing.

In his provocative book *The 80/20 Principle*, Richard Koch gives an insightful modern-day reinterpretation of the well-known Pareto principle, which states that 80 per cent of your results will be driven by 20 per cent of your activities. When we apply this principle to our own activities, we become very discerning about where we direct our efforts. Of course, the trick is to clearly identify *which* 20 per cent of your activities will give you the greatest return. Thinking strategically in this way helps to combat perfectionism and ensures that you give your utmost attention to the things that matter most.

In this chapter we have explored the benefits of present-moment awareness and focused effort. To me, these strategies are the very bedrock of effective action and, therefore, a key to success. By fostering stillness and calmness in the place of frenetic and disordered industry, moreover, these strategies allow you to feel good about yourself and what you are achieving every day.

Although the journey ahead of us might be long and uncertain, I encourage you, like the man with the lantern, to trust the lamp of present-moment awareness to shine sufficient light on every action you take.

Ideas for Action

- Recall a time when you were 'in the zone', completely absorbed in what you were doing. What did it feel like? In what ways were the results you got influenced by the quality of your work? Perhaps ask a friend to share his or her experiences too.

- If negative procrastination is an issue for you, ask yourself why this is so. What specific strategies can you put in place to help in the future?

- Unproductive multi-tasking is a problem for most people. In your journal, write about a time when you caught yourself multi-tasking on complex or important tasks. How did your choices impact on the results you got? What will you do differently in the future?

Success is simple. Do what's right, the right way, at the right time.

—ARNOLD H. GLASGOW

Time — achieving your priorities

The Gift of Time
You can buy a gift,
Of anything you like,
To help someone today,
In their time of strife,
But the most desired gift,
Is the precious gift of time.
Time is there for comfort,
To listen and to speak,
Time is a gift for everyone,
That doesn't cost a cent.

—SINÉAD KEANE, AGE 12

Every significant choice, every important decision we make, is determined by our perception of time. Do we see time as elusively slipping by? Do we see it as flexible? Do we mostly spend time, or do we make it? Most of us aren't accustomed to answering such questions. We rarely get the opportunity to step back from the hustle and bustle of our daily lives to reflect on this deeply. In this chapter, however, we'll do exactly that—take a step back and really come to grips with what time means for you. How can you make the most of it? Almost 40 years ago, the time-management expert Alan Lakein had this to say:

> *Time is Life. It is irreversible and irreplaceable. To waste your time is to waste your life, but to master your time is to master your life and make the most of it.*

My own interest in time management was ignited several years ago when I observed two facts, both of which are entirely self-evident. The first is that everybody has exactly the same amount of time available to them. Each week, we all have precisely 168 hours to spend. There are no exceptions. This means that, like you, Leonardo da Vinci, Thomas Edison and Steve Jobs were given the same 168 hours each week. The second fact is that, most likely, we have just around 30,000 days and nights in our lifetimes. When you look at it like this, and factor in your current age, the number of days and nights you have left may seem surprisingly few. Given their ever-dwindling number, it makes sense to examine how we are spending our days before it's too late!

Time, and its value, has been a subject of interest for centuries. Consider these classic quotations:

- 'Pythagoras, when he was asked what time was, answered that it was the soul of this world.' Plutarch (c.46–c.120)

- 'Nothing is so dear and precious as time.' François Rabelais (1490–1553)

- 'All that really belongs to us is time; even he who has nothing else has that.' Baltasar Gracian (1601–1658)

- 'Dost thou love life? Then do not squander time, for that is the stuff life is made of.' Benjamin Franklin (1706–1790)

- 'You can ask me for anything you like, except time.' Napoleon Bonaparte (1769–1812)

- 'Time is at once the most valuable and the most perishable of all our possessions.' John Randolph (1773–1833)

- 'Time is the coin of your life. It is the only coin you have, and only you can determine how it will be spent. Be careful lest you let other people spend it for you.' Carl Sandburg (1878–1967)

I have found that many successful people share a particular characteristic: they know that time is their most valuable resource because, unlike money, gold or silver, it is both perishable and irreplaceable. It is perishable in that it cannot be stored up or saved in any way. It is irreplaceable to the extent that once a minute goes by, that minute will never be lived again — it is gone forever. Time can only be spent, not saved. Thinking like this can positively alter your relationship with your most valuable resource.

How you 'see' time is strongly influenced by your culture and by the shared values of the people you interact with most. Western culture, for example, tends to view time as a scarce resource to be managed with maximum economy. We put our efforts into techniques such as time management, daily planning, the creation of 'to-do' lists and the like. But for other cultures — for example, in the Pacific Islands of Fiji and Tonga — time is seen as elastic and flexible. For these peoples, the clock is secondary, with the primary focus being on the 'nowness' of the moment. It's a case of 'we'll get to what needs to be done in the future once we are finished with what we're doing now'.

How you regard time — what I call your time orientation — determines your whole outlook on life. I prefer the notion of 'time orientation' to 'time management' because, if you stop and think about it, there is no such thing as 'managing' time. It marches on irrespective of our feelings and wishes. All we can really do is change our approach, or our orientation, towards time.

Weekly planning

Like as the waves make towards the pebbled shore,
So do our minutes hasten towards their end.

—WILLIAM SHAKESPEARE (*SONNET 60*)

Of all the possible orientations towards time you might adopt, I strongly advocate what I call a seven-day perspective. In my experience, most people view their lives in 12-hour blocks. They plan their day ahead, check off items from their daily to-do list, respond to their emails and deal with unexpected things as they crop up each day. The trouble with a daily time orientation is that it engulfs our attention with things that are short-term, pressing and local. By contrast, a weekly time orientation facilitates 'bigger picture' thinking. As we'll see later in this chapter, thinking in terms of weeks rather than days is especially suited to the pursuit of your ULP and associated campaigns. For this reason, I always encourage participants of my workshops to get into the habit of weekly planning.

Here is what I find works best:

- The afternoon or early evening before you begin your working week is the best time for planning—for most of us this means Sunday. Because we are generally more relaxed on this day, we are more likely to think about our lives as a whole and to put our working lives into a larger perspective. For those who don't want to mix their professional and personal lives, I suggest planning your next working week on Friday afternoons before you leave work. Then on the weekend you can plan for your personal life only.

- When you plan, consider the full seven days ahead, including the following weekend and activities outside of your work life. Amazingly, most people do a reasonable job of planning their work lives, but are poor at using all the other hours.

- If you have a family situation, consider doing your weekly planning in the kitchen or another shared family space, because this allows others to get involved and better coordination between family members.

- Planning on paper rather than using an electronic medium seems to work best, partly because paper can be posted in your kitchen for everyone to see. You can always transfer the plan to your electronic diary afterwards. If you would find it useful, a template seven-day planner can be downloaded from this book's website at www.artofdeliberatesuccess.com.

- As well as planning your work and personal activities for the week ahead, also plan your meals—especially your dinners. There is space on the planner template available on the website for doing this. Experience shows that when we plan our meals a week ahead, we are more likely to eat healthier food and reduce wastage.

Developing a weekly time orientation has a lot to recommend it. It mentally sets you up for the 168 hours ahead, allowing you to sleep better on Sunday night. And even if, during the week, some unexpected crisis takes you away from your plan, you only have to wait until the next Sunday before you are back on track again.

Later in this chapter, we'll learn how to plan using our ULPs and campaigns as reference points.

The urgent/important distinction

The most important choice you make is what you choose to make important.

— MICHAEL NEILL

One of the most useful conceptual frameworks for thinking about time is the Eisenhower Time Matrix. Although it's been around for a long time, authors such as Charles E. Hummel and Stephen Covey have recently reinvigorated the matrix and now it's widely adopted by time-management coaches. My experience, however, is that while many people have heard of the matrix, few really understand how it works — and fewer still know how to integrate it into their daily lives.

The basic idea that Dwight D. Eisenhower came up with was that everything we do should be evaluated by its importance and urgency. The importance of a task is gauged by how *significant* it is, while urgency is measured according to some kind of a *time dependency*. The critical point is that importance and urgency are entirely distinct concepts. In other words, a task that is important is only made important to the extent that it is significant, and not because it is urgent or otherwise. Similarly, urgent tasks are only urgent because of their time dependency, and not at all influenced by their perceived level of importance. Simply put, important tasks are significant, while urgent tasks are only urgent because of a perceived 'ticking clock'.

Working with these two concepts, it is possible to come up with a time matrix, which comprises four quadrants that we can apply in our everyday lives. Table 9.1 (overleaf) is an example of a matrix containing different tasks classified according to their perceived levels of importance and urgency.

Table 9.1: the time matrix

	Urgent	Not urgent
Important	**1 Crisis quadrant** Crises Pressing problems Imminent deadlines Windows of opportunity Serious physical accidents Major communication breakdowns Mechanical breakdowns Unpaid bills Legal demands	**2 Value quadrant** Formal learning Long-range planning Work not due yet Anticipating client needs Prevention and maintenance Constructive delegation Nurturing relationships Building networks Regular family time Recreation Improving health and wellbeing
Not important	**3 Distraction quadrant** Some phone calls, emails, mail, meetings Other people's priorities Organisational politics Unimportant reports Unsolicited information and offers	**4 Wasted quadrant** Gossip Internet surfing Mindless television Low-value reading Addictive computer games Excessive shopping Stuff More stuff

You will notice that each of the four boxes is individually named and numbered, starting at the top-left and finishing at the bottom-right. Let's explore each of the quadrants in turn.

The crisis quadrant

The crisis quadrant (Quadrant 1) includes tasks that must be tackled when dealing with a crisis or when a deadline is fast approaching. Tasks in this quadrant have high priority, and not doing them will lead to significant consequences. Any delay will be undesirable or make the task more difficult to do as time goes on.

One of the features of tasks in this quadrant is that they can pop up unexpectedly, and no amount of planning or forethought can anticipate their arrival. Needing to take your sick child to hospital and your car breaking down (hopefully not at the same time!) would fit into this category. Other tasks, however, find their way into Quadrant 1 simply because they were not taken care of before they became urgent—unpaid bills, for example. Of course, even the car breakdown could be caused by the neglect of necessary maintenance. Many people spend much of their lives in Quadrant 1. Such people seem to be rushing around between activities, yet they never seem to achieve much. They are busy—frantic even—but when it comes down to it, too much time in Quadrant 1 can be exhausting and not very satisfying. Some people are even 'addicted' to the adrenaline rush that comes with racing around doing things at the last minute.

In his book *Freedom from Tyranny of the Urgent*, Charles E. Hummel captures exactly why excessive Quadrant 1 activity is such a problem:

> *The urgent task calls for instant action...The momentary appeal of these tasks seems irresistible and important, and they devour our energy. But in the light of time's perspective, their deceptive prominence fades; with a sense of loss we recall the vital task we pushed aside. We realize we've become slaves to the tyranny of the urgent.*

Indeed, it is the momentary appeal of Quadrant 1 tasks that can trick us into erroneously thinking that we are spending our time well. Without question, there will always be Quadrant 1 tasks—genuinely unexpected, time-bound, important tasks—that should get our full attention. However, under honest examination, how many such tasks really result from a lack of care and forethought?

The value quadrant

Ideally, tasks and activities in this quadrant (Quadrant 2) should constitute your main workload. It is called the value quadrant because time spent here, doing important but non-urgent things, is a real investment. And, like all good investments, your efforts here will be rewarded many times over. As the examples in table 9.1 show, everything in this quadrant is associated with fulfilling long-term goals and aspirations. It includes all forms of planning, self-maintenance, relationship building and care.

The main reason most people do not spend enough time in Quadrant 2 is very simple: unlike Quadrant 1, which grabs your attention (primarily because of the urgency), work in Quadrant 2 never seems pressing and, therefore, we tend not to do it. As Charles Hummel says, these tasks are 'costly casualties of the tyranny of the urgent'. A further reason for neglect of Quadrant 2 is lack of clarity surrounding what is truly important to you. Obviously, in order to classify tasks as important or not, you'll need a strong sense of which is which. And only *you* can determine what is important to you. This is where the work we did in chapter 1 — on your ULP and your campaigns — comes in. With this foundation work done, you now know what's important and what's not.

Attention to tasks and activities in Quadrant 2 is what divides really successful people from others. Most of the truly important things in our lives are not urgent. They can be done now or later. In many cases, they can be postponed forever, and in many cases they are. They are the things we never get around to and, because we don't, we end up not achieving our full potential. Don't let that happen to you. Decide now to become a Quadrant 2 person.

The distraction quadrant

In the distraction quadrant (Quadrant 3) belong all those things that clamour for our attention but, upon close examination, are revealed to be a low priority for us. Yet, because of the anxiety brought about by their perceived urgency, we find ourselves investing time that we later regret. The key to better understanding Quadrant 3 is to ask yourself the question 'Important to whom?' Most times, you'll find that it is not you but someone else who has endowed the task with its sense of urgency.

Quadrant 3 tasks are responsible for many of the stresses in our lives. They induce stress (and guilt) because we find ourselves working on things that we know deep down are not important to us. The problem is further exacerbated when we put effort into Quadrant 3 tasks when we know we should really be attending to Quadrant 2 or even Quadrant 1 tasks.

Why do we prioritise Quadrant 3 when we know we shouldn't? The answer is that many of us have not developed the skill of managing such tasks effectively. You will notice that tasks in this category will not go away of their own accord, but rather keep clamouring for your attention. They can take a considerable amount of time as well — you may think you can quickly get them out of the way before settling in to Quadrant 2 tasks, but doing so then takes up most of your day.

Resolving this problem involves having a conversation with the person who gave you the Quadrant 3 task to begin with. This may mean your boss, a co-worker, a client, your family or a friend. The purpose of this conversation is to help you to clarify the true importance of the task — is it or is it not Quadrant 3? Following this conversation, the item may move to any of the other remaining quadrants. For instance, you may now understand that the task is indeed important as well as urgent (Quadrant 1), or you and the other person may agree that the item is in fact important, but the timeline has changed (moving it into Quadrant 2) or, finally, everybody agrees that no further action is actually needed (Quadrant 4). Sometimes the result of the conversation will be to delegate the Quadrant 3 work to someone else, and this is a good outcome. If the conversation is honest, you will conclude that it's better all-round that another person takes responsibility for this item. Perhaps the completion of the work draws on his or her strengths (making it a Quadrant 2 task for that person), or frees you up to tackle important things for which you are uniquely qualified.

In any event, your goal should be to deal constructively with such distractions as soon as possible. The longer you leave it, the more difficult it will become.

The wasted quadrant

Tasks in the wasted quadrant (Quadrant 4 — neither important nor urgent), are the easiest to resolve: simply don't do them. Nobody cares — not even you. You will notice from the examples given that everything in Quadrant 4 is done to excess. As a rule, value is diminished in exact proportion to the degree of excess. It's therefore critical to know at what point an activity turns from being useful, and so important, to being a mere waste of time. Watching television is a good example of this. I am sure you'll agree that television can be a good thing — many of us use it to relax, to unwind and to refresh — but there comes a point when we just find ourselves mindlessly watching shows that simply do not interest us. This kind of excessiveness is not at all relaxing; it induces laziness and feelings of guilt, and keeps us away from the truly rejuvenating and healthy activities of Quadrant 2.

The best way to handle Quadrant 4 activities is to nip them in the bud the moment you detect you are in excessive mode. To help raise your awareness of Quadrant 4 (as well as the other quadrants), you may be interested in keeping a time journal for a week. In this journal, record where and how you spend your time and what's going on in your life. Many people report that this is an excellent way to assess where their time is actually going. You'll notice that what we *think* we do with our time and the reality of the situation can be quite different matters. I predict that you'll see all kinds of patterns that you were unaware of. A time journal template can be downloaded from this book's website at www.artofdeliberatesuccess.com.

The time matrix is an excellent tool if you want to develop a deliberate time orientation. Quite simply, by spending more of your time in Quadrant 2 you will achieve more. The key is to give the lion's share of your attention to tasks and activities that are important but not urgent — especially those that are in danger of becoming urgent if you leave them. By the way, this is exactly the opposite of what the vast majority of people do. But then, they don't know the secret of real success!

Plan with your energy cycle in mind

Extreme busyness, whether at school or college, kirk or market,
is a symptom of deficient vitality.

— ROBERT LOUIS STEVENSON

Are you a morning lark or a night owl? Or do you come alive in the late afternoon? As we saw in chapter 6, everybody experiences natural peaks and troughs in their energy levels each day. Helpfully, these usually conform to some sort of recognisable pattern. The science behind this phenomenon — chronobiology — shows that changes in our brain chemistry, enzyme production, blood-sugar and hunger levels, and even sleeping patterns all account for how much energy we have at different times of the day. As you develop your own personal time orientation, it's important that you become familiar with your energy cycle so that you can work with rather than against it. Your most important tasks should be tackled when you are at your peak.

Therefore, I encourage you to study yourself. Clues to your energy cycles and preferences lie in the way your days operate. For example, if you keep promising to wake up at 6 am to exercise, but haven't made it to the gym even once, it's probably a safe bet that getting up with the early birds doesn't jibe with your body. We often feel that we ought to get up early, but perhaps late afternoon or early evening would work better for you.

Most of us already have a good idea of our peaks and troughs. Knowing what you know about yourself, write down the ways you'd complete the sentences shown in table 9.2.

Table 9.2: working out my peaks and troughs

Mornings are the best time for me to _____, and the worst time for me to _____.
Afternoons are the best time for me to _____, and the worst time for me to _____.
Evenings are the best time for me to _____, and the worst time for me to _____.
Late at night is the best time for me to _____, and the worst time for me to _____.

Understanding your natural preferences gives you a point of negotiation; you might not always be able to do things at your optimal time, but if you're aware of when this time is, and willing to make the effort, you can schedule many of your tasks for when you are at your best. For most people, this peak period constitutes one or two hours in every day. This is called the 'golden hour(s)' and, for about 75 per cent of us, is the two hours after you have been awake for an hour (for example, between 7 am and 9 am if you get up at 6 am).

Too often we spend the first of these golden hours checking email and seeing what everyone else needs from us. The problem here is that if you postpone your most important work until after you've taken care of everyone else's needs and your own lesser tasks, you've wasted your peak-performance hours and the burden of what needs to be done hangs over your head all day, weighing you down with dread and guilt. If you knock it off first thing in the morning when you're at your peak, not only are you likely to get through what needs to be done more quickly, but also the relief buoys you up all day long, energising and boosting your productivity as you tackle the rest of the items on your schedule and as your energy starts to lag.

One helpful approach is to decide the night before exactly what you are going to tackle during these hours. Ask yourself, 'If tomorrow flies out of control, what one task (not two or three) would I be excited/relieved to get done? What's most important?' Sometimes I write my answer on a sticky note that I place on my keyboard so I see it first thing in the morning. The energy you'll feel from accomplishing that one task will fuel you all day long.

People who are more successful tend to be very deliberate in recognising and working with their unique energy cycle and using their golden hour(s) well. When thinking about their time, what they want to accomplish, and the ups and downs of their energy, they are masters of synchronising themselves with their daily agenda. The following points provide some guidelines.

When you're *fully alert*, schedule:

- large, involved and important projects (Quadrant 2)

- critical, pressing and important matters (Quadrant 1)

- important reading and material that's potentially boring

- any meetings with your boss

- meetings and phone calls of importance where you mostly listen

- anything that requires you to be calm and reflective

- anything that should not be interrupted.

When you're *alert*, schedule:

- meetings with colleagues or those you supervise

- moderately interesting reading

- mathematical activities (for example, preparing a budget) where, by definition, your mind will be active

- responding to emails

- most computer work

- physical work that requires concentration (for example, driving).

When you're *sluggish*, schedule:

- short-duration projects and brief tasks
- activity that requires physical movement where concentration is not critical (walking, moving boxes, filing)
- calls or meetings with people you like
- interactive computer work (for example, online learning that's engaging)
- things you find extremely interesting.

Pay attention to when you feel most alert and try to schedule your most important tasks during that time. With practice, you'll find yourself achieving more than you ever thought possible.

Plan according to your campaigns

You can't always control the wind, but you can control your sails.

— ANTHONY ROBBINS

Developing a personal time orientation, then, requires you to take action on a number of counts. I have recommended that you:

- make a firm habit of weekly planning
- devote most of your energy to matters that are important but not urgent
- carefully observe your unique personal energy cycle, keeping a temporary journal if necessary.

All this sounds straightforward enough in theory, but you may be asking yourself, 'How do I know what's important and how can I get all this down to a manageable weekly plan? And how much is realistically achievable day to day?' Well, thankfully, there is a way to clarify these areas of uncertainty—the 5-Step Weekly Process (performed every Sunday). Over the years, I have taught it to thousands of people, and many of them have come back to say how this one idea changed their lives.

Figure 9.1 shows the process and the following sections then discuss each step in some detail.

Figure 9.1: the 5-step weekly process

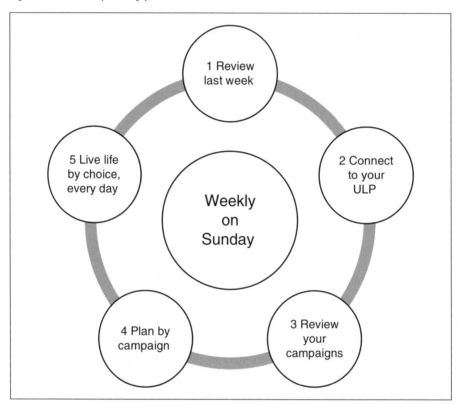

Step 1: review last week

Since last Sunday, how did your week unfold? Did the things you planned to do come to fruition? What went well? Were there unexpected opportunities? What could have gone better? What, if anything, can you learn that might help you plan the week ahead?

The purpose of this review is to help you to positively learn from the past, so, if possible, undertake this review in an upbeat kind of way, looking for the positives and not being too hard on yourself. When you have had a bad week, work hard at identifying things to be grateful for and review the week from this perspective.

Step 2: connect to your ULP

As we saw in chapter 1, your ULP is that short, inspiring statement that provides you with an infallible compass for living. It is firmly based on your deepest values and reflects what you want to have, be and do in life. Reading your ULP at this time every week reminds you of what is truly important. And because it is written in an inspiring way, it should uplift your spirits and put you in a good mental space for planning the week ahead.

If you have a copy of your ULP handy (in your wallet or purse, for example), I encourage you to read it aloud to yourself. Affirming your ULP in this way puts your current concerns and responsibilities into immediate perspective, reminding you why you are investing energy in some activities and deliberately avoiding others.

Step 3: review your campaigns

Your campaigns, which we also worked on in chapter 1, should likewise be inspiring, uplifting and motivating. They stem directly from your ULP and together represent all the aspects of your life that deserve time and attention each week. Each campaign represents an important part of your life that you want to move forward so that, over time, you are advancing in a direction that makes sense for you. The important point about campaigns is that they can each be acted upon in some way *most* weeks.

Step 4: plan by campaign

Using your seven-day planner, answer this magic question for *each* of your campaigns: 'What will I do, this week, on this campaign?' As you come up with ideas, book them into your planner. Be as specific as possible, noting when you plan to start and finish each task or activity. For example, if one of your campaigns is to take care of your body, you might initially plan to go for an energetic walk after work on Monday, Wednesday and Friday, between 5.30 and 6.30 pm. If, however, you know you're going to be travelling on the Wednesday, you might then schedule the walk *before* work on that day — say, at 7 am. Vague plans are easily overridden, so the point is to think about what you're going to do in plenty of detail.

For best results, you need to be realistic and come up with ideas that you can 'see' yourself doing. As we saw in chapter 3, visualisation is a powerful tool for getting things done. Moreover, if you keep your tasks practical and wherever possible *enjoyable*, you're more likely to actually do them, and you'll feel great knowing that you achieved what you set out to do at the beginning of the week. Over time, you'll feel better and better as you keep promises to yourself.

Step 5: live life by choice, every day

The final step in the process is to let your week unfold according to what you had planned on the Sunday. The secret to making this happen is to see every moment, and every decision you make, as a *deliberate* choice. You are either *deliberately* choosing to stick to the plan, or you are *deliberately* choosing not to stick to it. The choice—and consequences—are 100 per cent yours.

Typically, when you start weekly campaign-based planning, a number of questions arise. Some examples, and answers I suggest, include the following:

- *Should all campaigns get attention every week?* In any given week, your focus might be on a restricted number of campaigns, but on a monthly basis *all* your campaigns should be moving forward at least a little. For example, some weeks may have a prominent work or study focus, while other weeks could have a strong element of leisure or recreation.

  If you find that one or two of your campaigns are never getting touched, you should review your list. Perhaps these campaigns are not that significant to you after all? If they are, you need to put greater effort into building them into your weekly plans. If you are struggling for some reason, start off with small commitments and build up from there.

- *How much should I plan and to what level of detail?* I have already mentioned the importance of planning in detail and being realistic—you need to begin each week with a reasonable degree of certainty that what you do plan will actually happen.

I would only add that it's best to focus on your big tasks and activities, leaving plenty of space for others to arise as the week unfolds. Remember, the goal is not to get the most done in the least time, but to get things that matter most done first, when you have most energy.

- *What if I miss a week?* The good news is that because there is a new Sunday every seven days, you only have a short time to wait before you can get back on the horse.

Weekly campaign-based planning is the critical link between what you do every week and what's important to you, and its power cannot be overstated. This one tool, if used consistently, will guarantee that you spend *much* more of your time doing things that are actually important to you. The impact on your professional and personal life will be enormous. I would even go so far as to say that sitting down on a Sunday to plan should be among your highest priorities. You can miss a meal, but whatever happens don't miss your weekly planning session!

Time chunking

Good habits are formed; bad habits we fall into.

— ROBIN SIEGER

With your weekly plan in place, you'll begin every day with a strong sense of purpose because you'll know where your effort and energy is going to go. Instead of aimlessly being driven by events as they unfold, you'll have a plan in your mind that will give shape and direction to your day. While your weekly plan is your chief guide for the week, it's also very useful to create a plan for each day. This plan is in the context of the weekly plan, but is more detailed and also takes into consideration events that may have happened since Sunday.

The end of the day is a good time to prepare your plan for the next day. Beginning with your weekly plan as a base, list the tasks you want to achieve tomorrow, bearing in mind your preference for non-urgent but important Quadrant 2 activities and also your personal energy cycle. As you make the daily plan, you should consider 'chunking' your tasks. For example, if you have phone calls to make, make them all at the same time. If you have emails to respond to, do them together rather than dabbling throughout the day. This approach allows you to build momentum and reduce those 'switching costs' I spoke of in chapter 8.

One helpful idea is to write down your daily plan on paper and, as your day unfolds, 'check off' what you have completed. This approach gives you a real sense of accomplishment and ensures that you keep focused on tasks that really matter. You'll be more likely to stick with important tasks longer and less likely to drift into activities that are distracting or of low value.

Chunking and writing down your tasks in this way allows you to concentrate your focus and thereby make the very best use of every day.

Value your time

Gather ye rosebuds while ye may,
Old Time is still a-flying:
And this same flower that smiles to-day,
To-morrow will be dying.

— ROBERT HERRICK

A key part of developing your time orientation is to know — in dollar terms — what your time is worth. One simple way to cost your time is to divide your annual salary by 2000 (40 hours × 50 weeks). Let's take an example. If your annual salary is $50 000, your hourly rate is $25 per hour. And if it's $100 000, you are looking at $50 per hour. These numbers are on the conservative side as they do not include any overheads and they also assume that each hour of your eight-hour day is equally productive. If you're like most people, your real number of productive hours will be more like five.

Professionals such as accountants, lawyers, consultants and trades-people of all kinds already know their hourly rate because they use it every week in order to charge for their services. If you don't know yours, I suggest you calculate it now. When you know your number, you'll look on everything you do with new eyes. In particular, you'll become aware of the monetary value of the minutes passing by, and you'll begin to find yourself making different choices about what you will and will not do. For example, if you find yourself doing tasks that are low-value and for which you are overqualified, it will make sense to delegate these to others.

In your personal life, too, there may be an opportunity to 'outsource' some low-value tasks and activities. Often in coaching, for example, I'll recommend to busy mums and dads that if they are struggling to spend more quality time with their kids, they should carefully look at their household chores (such as laundry, cleaning, gardening and filing tax returns) and consider getting them done by professionals. Unless you enjoy these activities, it makes sense to outsource them if you can possibly afford to do so.

Learn to say 'no' to things that aren't important

Besides the noble art of getting things done, there is the noble art of leaving things undone. The wisdom of life consists in the elimination of the nonessentials.

—LIN YUTANG

Chapter 7 has a section on the importance of saying 'no' to things that aren't your responsibility, but it is also worth covering here the importance of saying 'no' to things that aren't important to you. Your ability to say 'no' to things that are not important has an enormous impact on what you can achieve and, therefore, the results you get in all aspects of your life. You will find that people who are truly successful have mastered the art of refusal so that when they say 'yes' they really mean it and are always able to deliver on their promises. Real success is not a matter of being 'nice' or even 'cooperative' but rather is about being assertive when you need to be. Far from getting a reputation for avoidance, you'll become known as a reliable and trustworthy person.

Why is it that most of us find it so challenging and uncomfortable to say 'no'? The fundamental problem is that mentally we associate a 'no' with a negative experience. We assume that to decline something will hurt people's feelings or spoil our chances for the future. But that's only our perception and it's unlikely to be true. In chapter 7 I recommended that you overcome such anxieties by interpreting refusal positively: saying no to one thing is actually saying yes to something else that you have determined to be more important and more significant.

This is not to say, of course, that people's feelings are never hurt when we decline an invitation or request. There is a certain art to saying 'no' tactfully. Marc Mancini, in his book *Time Management*, offers these helpful guidelines:

- *Give a reason*. When people understand your reasoning, they may come to accept the reason you said 'no'—they may, in fact, agree with you and think you are being reasonable. However, be prepared that sometimes—no matter how reasonable you are—the other person will not accept your perspective. In these cases, remind yourself that, 'sometimes you cannot please all people, all of the time'. You have done your best, and now it's time to move on.

- *Be diplomatic*. How to say 'no' is a skill to be learned and developed. The way you say it can make a great difference between coming across as rude and uncaring, or considered and honest. The key here is to be direct but not aggressive. Examples might be, 'I'd love to be involved, but I've already got plans' or 'It's nice to be asked, but I can't help you at the moment'.

- *Suggest a trade-off*. Most times, there is more than one solution to every difficulty. If you can find another way that's better for everyone, you and the person you are dealing with can *both* be satisfied.

- *Get your boss involved*. If your boss is asking you to take on another task and you really can't juggle it, it's important to put the responsibility back on your boss to help you. You could say, 'Well, this is what I'm working on at the moment—which task should I prioritise?'

As well as the obvious and clear-cut ways of saying 'no' to direct requests, you should also be aware of more subtle ways of becoming entrapped in potentially low-value tasks and activities that use up your time and energy. One very common workplace scenario is discussed by William Oncken Jr and Donald L. Wass in their *Harvard Business Review* article 'Management Time: Who's Got the Monkey?'. The article begins:

Let us imagine that a manager is walking down the hall and that he notices one of his subordinates, Jones, coming up the hallway. When they are abreast of one another, Jones greets the manager with, 'Good morning. By the way, we've got a problem. You see ... ' As Jones continues, the manager recognises in this problem the same two characteristics common to all the problems his subordinates gratuitously bring to his attention. Namely, the manager knows, (a) enough to get involved, but (b) not enough to make the on-the-spot decision expected of him. Eventually, the manager says, 'So glad you brought this up. I'm in a rush right now. Meanwhile, let me think about it and I'll let you know.' Then he and Jones part company.

Let us analyse what has just happened. Before the two of them met, on whose back was the 'monkey?' The subordinate's. After they parted, on whose back was it? The manager's. Subordinate-imposed time (stealing) begins the moment a monkey successfully executes a leap from the back of a subordinate to the back of his superior and does not end until the monkey is returned to its proper owner for care and feeding.

If you are a manager, the only way to end this unnecessary upward delegation is to politely refuse to accept other people's monkeys. Again, it's a matter of saying 'no' so that you can give a resounding 'yes' to tasks and activities that are truly important and significant.

Developing good delegation skills, managing monkeys and saying 'no' when appropriate will free you up to focus on more of your Quadrant 2 activities. Where the art of delegation is concerned, here are some more guidelines to consider:

- Look for ongoing or recurring projects that will give you a long-term return for the time and effort you invest in training someone else to do them. Choose tasks that take up a lot of your time but others can do.

- Match the person to the job. Choose people with the right skills or people who are capable of learning those skills.

- Agree on what is to be done. At the outset, walk the person through the task, clarifying expectations and establishing standards of quality.

- Make yourself available for support and advice, but don't do the work yourself. Let the person find a method of working that suits his or her style and personality.

According to the motivational speaker Brian Tracy, in his book *Eat That Frog,* our aim within our professional lives should be to answer the following four questions:

- What are my highest value activities? What are the things that I do that contribute the greatest amount of value to my work?

- What are my key result areas? What specific results have I been hired to accomplish?

- Why am I on the payroll? Why do they pay me money at my job? What specifically have I been asked to do?

- What can I, and only I, do that, if done well, will make a real difference? If I don't do it, it won't get done. But if I do it, and I do it well, it will make a significant contribution to my work and my life. What is it?

Clearly identifying what your job *is* will highlight exactly what it *isn't*. Everyone, eventually, has to accept that they cannot do everything. It was well put by Charles Spurgeon: 'Learn to say "no"; it will be more use to you than to be able to read Latin'.

Avoid time wasters

Shortage of time is the greatest shortage of our time.

—FRED POLAK

When you become more aware of your personal time orientation, you'll become very conscious of how productive you really are. For many people, keeping a time journal highlights some surprising patterns of time wastage in their daily lives. It is important that you develop this awareness so that you can minimise the impact of these time thieves. As you carefully examine where your time goes, you may discover that many of your time wasters are 'habits' that have evolved within you and now seem to be an established part of your identity. They are generally Quadrant 4 activities — the kind that have little or no value and distract you from much more important priorities. While it might be disturbing to acknowledge how little of your day is actually productive, there is nothing more constructive than looking your time wasters in the eye.

The following sections cover the 'Top 10' time wasters, along with some helpful recommendations.

Uninvited interruptions

According to a study published by Cubesmart Inc. ('Social Interruption and the Loss of Productivity'), we experience, on average, one interruption every eight minutes, or approximately six or seven interruptions per hour. While some of these will be welcome — even necessary — everyone needs to work undisturbed at certain times.

Interruptions, of course, are an essential part of what we get paid to do. Talking with customers, dealing with colleagues, responding to a call from your boss — this is what many jobs are all about. Having said that, extensive research shows that your ability to manage interruption is absolutely essential if you are to succeed. The key lies in not treating every disruption equally. Here are some useful strategies:

- Begin the conversation with 'What can I do for you?' not 'How are you?'

- Rehearse a few comfortable 'exit' lines such as, 'I'm in the middle of finishing a project; can we talk this afternoon?' or 'This sounds important and I want to give it my full and undivided attention. But I'm busy right now, so let's schedule a time to meet'.

- If you work in an open-plan office area, develop a signal indicating whether you are available for interruption. Perhaps putting your headphones on or creating a small sign will be enough to communicate your wishes to your colleagues.

Your boss

Our natural tendency is to do what our boss wants or expects. If you are a 'pleaser', you will tend to build your timetable around his or her requests. Truly successful people, however, do not work in this way. While they want to deliver, they also want to proactively manage their boss so they can give their attention to tasks and activities that make the greatest contribution to their organisations. Instead of being on standby and responding to various ad hoc requests, it's far better to think of working in partnership with your employer. Here are some ways of fostering better partnerships:

- Think about your boss's style of working. What are his or her strengths and weaknesses? How can you best work together?

- Ask for clarification. Time spent clarifying expectations before you begin on a task is worthwhile. What's required? When does your boss want it? Why? To what quality level?

- Discuss priorities with your boss, requesting brief regular meetings if necessary. This is particularly important if he or she keeps piling work on you.

In their classic *Harvard Business Review* article 'Managing Your Boss', John J. Gabarro and John P. Kotter encourage us to invest time and energy into better understanding our bosses with the single aim of having 'unambiguous mutual expectations'. If you do this, both of you will be far more productive and effective.

Too much television

Surveys suggest that, on average, we spend between four and five hours every day watching television. While some television watching is relaxing, educational or even productive, I am certain that much of it is none of these things. Beyond a certain point, too much television robs us of valuable time that would be much better spent elsewhere. Here are ways to avoid this particular time thief:

- When you write your weekly plan, take a look at the TV guide. Are there certain programs you find relaxing and enjoyable? If so, schedule to watch them.

- If possible, record the programs you want to watch for the week ahead. This means you can watch them according to *your* timetable.

- When you have not consciously decided to watch television, turn it off. If your experience is anything like mine, you'll free up an amazing amount of time that you didn't know you had.

Too much internet surfing, gaming and texting

Like excessive television watching, excessive online activity can eat into the time we have available. It's now very clear from the research that too much online activity is addictive in much the same way as food, caffeine, gambling, alcohol, or any overused substance or activity is addictive. One research study conducted by a team from Stanford University's School of Medicine found that online addictions can alter our personalities, make us less socially adept and have a negative impact on our mental health. Again, like television, it's *excessive* use that brings about problems. Here are some ideas to think about:

- Put daily or weekly limits on the amount of time you spend online.

- Instead of endless social networking activities with your friends, why not meet them in person?

- When you are working on your computer and you don't want to be distracted by the temptation of online activities, consider disconnecting the internet.

- Have internet-free days, weekends and even holidays.

Too much shopping

These days, shopping is an important social and recreational activity, and is even thought of as 'therapeutic'—a way of relieving unwanted stress and anxiety from our lives. But as we learned in chapter 2, material acquisition is never going to satisfy our deepest wants and needs. It's worthwhile, therefore, to review the role of shopping in your life. Are your spending habits more recreational than necessary? Do you experience a temporary lifting of spirits when you make a purchase that perhaps you're addicted to? Again, shopping in and of itself is a fine activity—it's the excess that robs us of time and money and gets us into trouble. If you think it is a problem for you, you could:

- Limit how much time and money you spend shopping every week. By planning weekly, you take care of this automatically.

- Shop according to your needs rather than your wants.

- If you're an impulse buyer, try letting a couple of days pass before you make any given purchase. Often the impulse will go away and you'll discover that your 'need' was emotionally driven, and not that important after all.

Looking for things

I read that according to one poll we waste up to three hours per week trying to find lost things. Of course, things really don't get lost; they get misplaced. The old adage, 'a place for everything, and everything in its place' is the best prescription if you suffer from the 'Where did I put that?' syndrome. Here are some practical strategies:

- Invest time and effort on deciding where to store different items. Is your filing system robust and serving you well? How about your computer files?

- If clutter is a problem for you, take action to resolve it (see chapter 2).

- Put important things where you can easily locate them later. For example, always put your keys in the same place. Do the same for things like your wallet or purse, phone and diary.

Gossip

Gossip, unlike 'organisational intelligence', is of no value. While there is unquestionable value to be gained from being in touch with what is going on around you, gossip for its own sake is neither helpful to you, the other person, or your organisation. Here's how to steer clear of it:

- Resist the temptation to spread gossip about anyone. People will respect you for it.

- Ask yourself the question, 'Would I say this if the person was right in front of me?' If not, hold your tongue.

- Have some exit lines ready for when you want to remove yourself from gossip-driven conversations. For example, 'I'm on a deadline', or 'I'm back to work'.

A slow computer

Because most of us spend so much time working on computers, it makes sense to have yours working in an efficient way. You'd be surprised how much time we waste just waiting for our computers to boot up, do something or even power down. Here are some suggestions for speeding things up:

- Up-to-date virus protection is critical.

- When working on a task, only have the software applications you actually need open on your desktop. This will free up computer memory *and* stop you from being distracted while you work.

- Occasionally — say, weekly — defragment your hard disk and remove unwanted files.

- From time to time, restore your computer to its original condition by reformatting your hard disk and reinstalling software programs. Make sure you have a complete backup of all your important files before doing this!

Low-value reading

As in the case of television, some leisure reading is enjoyable and, therefore, valuable. What concerns me, however, is the sheer quantity of low-grade reading material that's out there. Even what we now classify as 'news' is questionable. Much of it is sensationalism designed simply to sell newsprint and magazines. When reviewing your diet of reading material, consider the following:

- Is there much variety in my reading matter? Is my 'diet' balanced?

- What sources do I depend on? What are their credentials? Have they done their research?

- Do I learn much from the things I read, or is it pure escapism?

Waiting

If you do keep a time journal, you may be surprised to find how much of your day is spent waiting for things to happen. This might be a result of dead time between meetings, other people's lateness or things not quite going according to plan. My best advice here is to expect the unexpected and be prepared to use these times well. Instead of staring blankly or absently surfing your smartphone, always plan to have things to do with you. Perhaps you'll read a chapter of your book, complete your expenses report or update your journal.

The secret to using these times well is to:

- See them as welcome opportunities, not cause for frustration.

- Always have your daily plan handy in your bag.

- Sometimes, instead of doing things, deliberately decide to do nothing, and simply enjoy the silence. Be thankful for the opportunity.

As we have seen, you are surrounded by people and circumstances that have the potential to undermine your effectiveness all day long. The great news is, by developing a deliberate time orientation, you will learn the self-discipline required to free yourself from these time thieves and finally take control.

Live by choice, not by chance

Dwell not on the past. Use it to illustrate a point, then leave it behind.
Nothing really matters except what you do now in this instant of time.
From this moment onwards you can be an entirely different person,
filled with love and understanding, ready with an outstretched hand,
uplifted and positive in every thought and deed.

—EILEEN CADDY

In the 5-Step Weekly Process we discussed earlier (see p. 221), one of the critical steps was to 'live life by choice, every day'. When it comes to your time orientation, I encourage you to think about each of your 168 hours in every week as subject to deliberate choice-making on your part. *You* are the one who decides how to spend every moment of your time, *you* are the one who ranks your priorities, and *you* are the one who says 'yes' and 'no' to various opportunities as they arise. Looking at your time in this way puts the responsibility for the choices you make back where it belongs.

When you live your life with this philosophy in mind, you'll notice the following happening:

- The decisions you make about the use of your time will seem to slow down. Because you are now an active participant in your life, you'll put critical distance between yourself and the choices you make, becoming less emotionally overtaken and consequently spending your time more constructively.

- Your ability to weigh up the consequences of various choices will be greatly enhanced. Instead of 'going with the first option' you'll explore further, come up with alternatives and make more measured decisions.

- Once you have decided on a course of action, you'll feel much better about the choices you make because they'll always be informed and deliberate. All the regret and 'what-ifs' will evaporate.

- With practice, you'll begin to discern a 'gap' between what happens to you, your reaction to what happens to you, and the decisions you make next. You will become an active observer of your own life. Living your life by active choice-making rather than by chance, and with critical distance as opposed to emotional impulsivity, will be nothing less than liberating.

One way of looking at your life is to think of it as a series of choices. For me, in fact, reflecting on this at the beginning of each new day is one of my healthiest and most inspiring habits.

Be flexible

Begin at once to live and count each day as a separate life.

—SENECA

Throughout this chapter, I have been emphasising the importance of *formally planning* the use of your time. Specifically, we have considered the four quadrants of the time matrix, the usefulness of seven-day planning (using the 5-Step Weekly Process) and a range of practical strategies for banishing time wasters from our lives. Sometimes I am asked if all this planning and structure takes the 'fizz' out of life. Some have even suggested that it's all just too boring and predictable. And you know what, I agree!

If you were to live *every* single day of your life in the ways we've discussed, it would potentially cut you off from the enjoyment of spontaneity in your life. And yet, the opposite is also true: if you organise your time so that the most important things get done, it actually frees you up to do the unexpected and to make the most of unforeseen opportunities. It is those who leave urgent tasks to the last possible minute who will find their hands tied when a spontaneous invitation arises!

If you consistently use your time well, you'll discover that to deviate from a plan every now and then is no problem whatsoever. By always having an eye on what's important, you put yourself in an excellent position to seize opportunities as they arise. When you know that most of your campaigns are in good shape, you can enjoy the deviation because it is deliberate and, therefore, guilt free.

Someone once sent me the following poem by David L. Weatherford, which I think captures the sheer joy of appreciating every experience—planned or not. It's called 'Slow Dance' and I hope you enjoy it:

> *Have you ever watched kids on a merry-go-round,*
> *or listened to rain slapping the ground?*
>
> *Ever followed a butterfly's erratic flight,*
> *or gazed at the sun fading into the night?*
>
> *You better slow down, don't dance so fast,*
> *time is short, the music won't last.*

Do you run through each day on the fly,
when you ask "How are you?", do you hear the reply?

When the day is done, do you lie in your bed,
with the next hundred chores running through your head?

You better slow down, don't dance so fast,
time is short, the music won't last.

Ever told your child, we'll do it tomorrow,
and in your haste, not see his sorrow?

Ever lost touch, let a friendship die,
'cause you never had time to call and say hi?

You better slow down, don't dance so fast,
time is short, the music won't last.

When you run so fast to get somewhere,
you miss half the fun of getting there.

When you worry and hurry through your day,
it's like an unopened gift thrown away.

Life isn't a race, so take it slower,
hear the music before your song is over.

Although this has been a long chapter, I hope you have learned a little more about the value of developing a personal time orientation. Self-management with respect to time is going to be central to your future success. Quite simply, your ability to channel energy into your highest value activities will determine your rewards in life—a great thought!

Ideas for Action

- Download the seven-day planner template from the book's website at www.artofdeliberatesuccess.com and begin using it this coming Sunday. In preparation, have your ULP and campaigns ready, and identify any commitments you have in place for next week. What time on Sunday will you start your planning? Are you going to do it alone, or with others?

- Identify one area in your life in which you think time-wasting is a problem for you. Write down specific things you can do this week to reduce the problem.

- Keep a time journal (again available from the book website) for one week. Record what you *actually* spend your time doing. What patterns do you observe? Are there any you want to change? What practical things can you start doing today?

I am convinced, both by faith and experience, that to maintain one's self on the earth is not hardship but a pastime—if we live simply and wisely.

—HENRY DAVID THOREAU

Evaluate — managing your overall performance

We can only connect the dots by looking back on life.

— STEVE JOBS

The inspiration for this chapter came to me several years ago when reading the autobiography of Benjamin Franklin. Born in 1706, Franklin is considered the 'Founding Father' of the United States and lived a most remarkable life until his death in 1790 at the age of 84. In his autobiography, Franklin makes extensive reference to his 'Plan to Achieve Moral Perfection', which involved carefully tracking and systematically managing what he called his 13 moral virtues — qualities that Franklin wanted to actively and deliberately foster in his life. They were: Self-Control, Silence, Order, Determination, Economy, Productivity, Truthfulness, Justice, Moderation, Cleanliness, Peace, Chastity and Humility.

What fascinated me about Franklin's approach was his discovery that no matter how hard he tried to make a habit of each of the virtues, he found it much better to focus on one at a time. Each week, he concentrated on just one virtue — starting with self-control — leaving the other virtues to chance. At the end of the week, he reviewed his progress and prepared himself for the next virtue the following week. Each cycle, therefore, took 13 weeks to complete — making four cycles every year. Franklin began this practice of self-mastery in his early twenties and continued it throughout his life. According to Franklin, the method 'gave great results'.

In my work with clients, I too have learned that it is much better to deliberately measure and manage a few critical issues than to be too ambitious. We humans like clear, simple goals with clear targets.

The purpose of this chapter is to help you with the measurement and management of your overall performance. How are you doing with your campaigns? For each of the aspects of being DELIBERATE, how well are you progressing? Are there specific strategies you can put in place to give you better results in the future? The key lesson of this chapter is that consciously measuring your performance in these areas is a good thing. It should energise you and help you to lead a life of significant contribution and satisfaction. Many years ago, management writer Peter Drucker got it right when he said, 'If you can't measure it, you can't manage it'.

Learn from the past with the future in mind

What you get by achieving your goals is not as important as what you become by achieving your goals.

—JOHANN WOLFGANG VON GOETHE

One of the most remarkable things about really successful people is their approach to learning from their experiences. They look on *all* their experiences—good and bad—as opportunities for learning and growth. In contrast, less successful people dwell on the past with either a sense of regret or self-satisfaction, and do not carry lessons learned into their future. Successful people also have far more significant failures, losses and bitter disappointments. They take one step back and two steps forward with almost every challenge—and sometimes two steps back and one step forward. They harvest useful lessons and knowledge from what doesn't work, and they display a remarkable ability to bounce back from adversity. Developing such a mindset—whereby you actively look for ways of applying lessons from your past—is going to be nothing less than critical to your future success.

Writer Jim Rohn reminds us 'not to focus so much on what we have accomplished, but on what we are becoming'. In other words, we should continuously evaluate our performance, but from a forward-thinking perspective. The person you are becoming is determined by the choices you make and, therefore, entirely within your control.

In his wonderful book *Talent Is Overrated*, Geoff Colvin proposes that an ability to learn from experience is even more important than raw talent. People who are truly expert in their field — say, a Tiger Woods in golf, a Roger Federer in tennis, or a Garry Kasparov in chess — may well have practised more than anyone else, but they also will have squeezed more learning from each of their experiences. Indeed, Colvin makes the point that, on average, it takes 10 000 hours of experience — and learning — to become expert in any given domain.

In another fascinating book, *Bounce: The Myth of Talent and the Power of Practice*, table tennis champion Matthew Syed analyses his own success and concludes that almost anyone could have achieved his mastery in table tennis if they had had the same opportunities and had practised as much (amazingly, for 10 years or 10 000 hours). Syed goes on to debunk many of the myths of success, including the idea that some people are born with special talent that marks them out for greatness.

All this suggests that consistent practice and the skill of learning from experience are the two key ingredients when it comes to achieving excellence in most endeavours. Deliberate people know this secret and so look upon all their experiences as valuable learning opportunities.

Measure your success

However beautiful the strategy, you should occasionally look at the results.
— WINSTON CHURCHILL

Years ago I worked on a project to create an 'electronic dashboard' for a business executive who wanted to continuously track how his business was doing against predefined targets. The idea of the dashboard was that the critical numbers to be monitored were colour-coded — in the style of traffic lights — so the executive's attention could be directed to what mattered most. As this was in the early days of computing and our tools were fairly primitive, an important phase of the project was to isolate 'what was really important' because we only had one screen on which to display the results. I can clearly remember sitting with the executive and discussing which numbers to track and which to display on the screen. An interesting outcome from the project was not so much the dashboard we eventually delivered, but the clarity we ended up gaining about what was critical and what was not.

We too need to create a 'dashboard' to monitor what is important to us in our personal and professional lives. This dashboard should be designed to supply us with the critical information we need to make future choices. The challenge, however, is to select just *a few key measures* so we are not overwhelmed by too much information coming our way. How do we select which measures to put on our dashboard? The first place to look is your ULP and your campaigns. Because you have already articulated these as the most important elements in your life, it makes sense to measure your progress on these fronts. Are your campaigns inching forward in a direction that you are happy with? Are you on track with your ULP? Are most of your days lived in alignment with your purpose?

Fortunately, there are many books and articles that can help us to measure our performance. For instance, in their excellent article 'The Balanced Scorecard—Measures that Drive Performance' published in the *Harvard Business Review*, researchers Robert S. Kaplan and David P. Norton warn of the dangers of choosing measures that are too narrowly focused or too financially driven. Although they are primarily referring to measuring the performance of a corporate organisation, the essential lessons apply equally well to our own personal success. They advise that we take care to not only include the easy-to-measure financials, but also select *softer* measures that reflect progress towards more difficult-to-measure targets. For example, your income in any given year is easy to measure, while your progress towards improving your future career options or the expansion of your professional network is much more subjective—but no less important.

In another *Harvard Business Review* article, 'The Performance Measurement Manifesto', Robert G. Eccles offers practical suggestions for choosing measures that are more strategic and longer term in their orientation. In the corporate world, it makes sense to pay attention to quality, customer satisfaction, innovation and market share rather than focusing too much on purely historical financial data. At a personal and professional level, perhaps measuring your performance on critical metrics such as your ability to adjust to change, your creativity and your skill in bouncing back from defeat give more powerful insights. Again, the idea is to choose what you measure carefully. What you measure is what you make important, and what you make important will capture your attention.

With these caveats in place, we'll now explore the typical performance measures that deliberate people utilise in their lives:

- *Campaign/goal tracking.* With reference to your campaigns and goals, what measures can you put in place to measure your performance? For example, if you have a campaign for improved fitness and healthy living, how about counting the number of times in a month you exercised or meditated? If you have a campaign to become a more valuable team member, how would you measure that? Could you ask your colleagues or your boss for specific feedback?

- *Deliberate Quotient.* What is your most recent DQ Quiz score? What are your strong areas? Where could you potentially improve?

- *Physical health measures.* How well are you? Are your weight, body fat, cholesterol, blood pressure and so on at acceptable levels?

- *Financial health measures.* If financial management is important to you, can you carefully monitor your income and expenses against your budget for a set period of time?

- *Long-term net worth and investments.* Tracking your ongoing financial net worth shows you how decisions you make today influence your ability to become financially free in the future.

- *Inventories.* Listing and valuing what you own is an excellent way of heightening your awareness of where your resources go, what's involved in maintaining things and your attitude towards material acquisition more generally.

- *Relationship health.* Looking at your most important relationships in your professional and personal life, how well are you doing? On a scale of 1 to 10, where are you with each relationship?

- *Work-life balance.* Are you working to live or living to work? Is the balance between work and your personal life healthy? Is it sustainable?

- *Personal mastery.* How are you doing with your ongoing personal development? Are you a better person today than you were yesterday? Have you become better at making decisions? How is your program of reading and study going?

- *Spontaneity.* Are you too planned, rigid or structured? Do you really live life knowing that you always have choice, and do you exercise that choice? Do you take advantage of unexpected opportunities? Do you feel *alive*?

- *Happiness.* Looking at your life overall, how content are you? Again, on a scale of 1 to 10, where are you sitting right now?

With carefully selected performance measures you'll be well positioned to build your very own personal 'dashboard', which will give you valuable information, enhance your learning, and guide you in your future decisions. The French poet Paul Valéry once said that the 'best way to make your dreams come true is to wake up'. I can think of no better way of waking up to your life than honestly measuring your performance in the areas that matter most to you.

Collect performance information

Four steps to achievement: plan purposefully, prepare prayerfully, proceed positively, pursue persistently.

—WILLIAM WARD

The trick to getting maximum benefit from evaluating your performance is to identify what you intend to measure *in advance*—that is, by first identifying a small set of key measures that you actively want to track. Write down in your journal what you want to measure, including the reason you think this information will be valuable to you. Table 10.1 shows a way to list your responses.

Table 10.1: key performance measures

Measure	Why it's important

Well done. With these measures clearly identified, it will be much easier for you to capture the required information as your day-to-day life is unfolding. If, for instance, your goal is to improve your focus and execution of Quadrant 2 tasks (those that are important, but not urgent — see chapter 9), you might consider keeping a daily time journal and making notes as each day passes. In this way, the information you gather is accurate and you are spared the trouble of trying to remember how you spent your time in any given week. Similarly, if one of your campaigns is to increase your fitness level, you could make a note each time you complete an exercise session. The idea is to record details of your performance as close as possible to the actual event.

When designing your data-keeping system, make sure it's both maintainable and accurate. You want to capture information in a way that's easy and low fuss. This way, your records will always be complete and you'll be able to look back and to see clear patterns in your performance over time. One recording tool you may find helpful is the Campaign/ Goal Tracker Excel Spreadsheet that can be downloaded from the website supporting this book www.artofdeliberatesuccess.com. The spreadsheet is a simple table of 12 columns (for each month) and 31 rows (for each day of the month), with a space at the end to tabulate your performance. You can use the spreadsheet to track your daily performance on any campaign or goal you choose. As you complete tasks, make a tick in the appropriate box, and then, at the end of each month, simply add up the ticks to attain a 'score' for that month. As each month goes by you can calculate your cumulative success.

I have heard it said that 'forethought often prevents a headache' and this is definitely true when it comes to collecting information about your performance regularly rather than retrospectively. If you develop this habit, the information you collect will be more accurate, and it will only take a matter of seconds to note down.

Review your performance

The biggest adventure you can ever take is to live the life of your dreams.

— OPRAH WINFREY

So, with all this wonderful information in hand, how often should you sit down and review your performance? I recommend four forms of review, each directed at different levels of analysis:

- *Weekly.* As we saw in the previous chapter, the 5-Step Weekly Process is an indispensable tool for living deliberately. Step 1 of the process is to review how the preceding week went. How well did you follow your plan? Did you keep your promises and did you get to do your most important Quadrant 2 tasks? Where appropriate, did you remain flexible and take up unexpected opportunities? What did you learn this week?

- *Quarterly.* At the end of March, June, September and December, it is time to step back and ask yourself more penetrating questions. From experience, these questions seem to work well:

  - Are *all* of your campaigns moving forward in the direction you want?

  - Looking on your campaigns as a set, are they working well together? Do they support each other? If not, what can you do in the following quarter to reactivate progress?

  - Are there any performance measures to be reviewed? Are you on target? If not, what can be done?

  - How are things going with being a DELIBERATE person overall? Now would be a good time to re-take the DQ Quiz and see if there are any changes in your results. If you have been focusing on particular aspects of being DELIBERATE in the last quarter, how did you do in these? Which aspects do you want to target in the next quarter?

- *Annually.* Once a year or so, step back even further and review the campaigns themselves, and also formally review your ULP. The key questions to consider are:

  - Are your campaigns and your ULP serving you well? Do they still reflect your current priorities, and are they worded exactly as you wish?

  - When you look at your life, are you becoming the kind of person you've always wanted to be? Are you inspired? In other words, are your efforts paying off?

  - Are you truly accepting 100 per cent responsibility for the results you are getting in your life?

  If you are unhappy with your answers to any of these questions, it's time to question the campaigns you've chosen or the level of effort you're putting in, or to consider the obstacles — some of them perhaps out of your control — that you encountered during the year. What constructive things came out of these obstacles? What improvements might this year hold?

- *Five-yearly.* This perspective allows you to examine your life from the widest lens. It's a good time to review your situation, taking into consideration movement between the different stages of life. Perhaps your priorities are altering, your children are growing, the role of work in your life is now different, or you are financially free. As you review your life, you should consider writing some new campaigns or tweaking your ULP to see you through the next five years.

While each of these reviews has a different objective, they are supportive of each other. You will notice that being diligent with your weekly reviews will ensure that you are well prepared when it comes to the others.

Focus on *your* dreams and *your* goals

If a man does not keep pace with his companions, perhaps it is because he hears a different drummer. Let him step to the music which he hears, however measured or far away.

— HENRY DAVID THOREAU

Robert Frost, one of my favourite poets, is the author of a famous poem about choosing an independent course in life titled *The Road Not Taken*. His words apply to all areas of our lives and are particularly relevant to the task of performance evaluation. The last stanza of the poem speaks of 'two roads diverged in a wood, and I — I took the one less travelled by, and that has made all the difference'. The importance of choosing your own path — of not following the pack — is of critical importance. While virtually all really successful people intuitively choose this road, others are swayed by everyone else's opinions and expectations. Instead of being faithful to their ULP and their campaigns, they acquiesce to the popular vote. Don't let that happen to you! Follow your own dreams.

When you start evaluating your progress according to what is important to *you*, you'll find many stresses in your life simply disappear. For instance, you'll find yourself less concerned with comparing the results you are getting in your life with what others are getting in theirs. Similarly, many of the petty jealousies that form between people lose their significance.

Following the road less travelled can make an enormous difference in your life. In his inspiring book *The Element: How Finding Your Passion Changes Everything*, educationalist Sir Ken Robinson writes about what happens when people follow their dreams, irrespective of the opinions of others. Based on extensive interviews with people like Paul McCartney, Matt Groening (creator of *The Simpsons*) and Richard Branson, Robinson concluded that at the heart of success was discovering your 'Element'. This term is similar to Csikszentmihalyi's concept of 'flow', which I discuss in chapter 8; it describes the place where the things we love to do and the things we are good at come together. When you're in your element, time passes differently: you're vibrant, you're more alive and you feel more like your authentic self. People who know their element evaluate their performance according to their *own* definition of success, not according to the opinion of others.

Celebrate and reward your achievements

Success is to be measured not so much by the position one has reached in life, as by the obstacles which one has overcome while trying to succeed.

— BOOKER T. WASHINGTON

An important part of performance evaluation is celebrating what you have accomplished. If you're like most people, you'll be astonished by how much you actually achieve when you go to the trouble of writing things down and then working in a deliberate way every day. Soon enough, ambitions that were once only a vague thought come within your sights, and you learn that dreams can indeed become reality.

Most people don't take any time to celebrate, and this is a great shame. Perhaps it goes back to the old puritan work ethic that discouraged us from taking time out or patting ourselves on the back. Or it might be because many people feel that acknowledging their accomplishments is egotistical or even self-centred. But the truth is that rewarding yourself is one of the healthiest things you can do. By celebrating the key milestones in your life, you formally put them behind you and make room for what you want to do in the future. You close one chapter and build momentum for the next.

Little milestones can be celebrated too. For me, one of the main benefits of celebrating even small successes is that it helps me to focus on what I'm doing until it is 100 per cent complete. If you know that you are going to celebrate in a special way, you'll be more likely to avoid distractions and persevere with what you're doing, irrespective of how tiresome, boring or difficult it may feel.

'Celebrations' can be fairly minor — in my case, I'm often the only one who knows about them! For instance, when I finish writing this chapter, I plan to take a day off and go to a movie on my own. This small reward motivates me every day and helps me to be self-disciplined even though many other more attractive things could easily capture my attention. And because the writing of this book is my highest work priority, I know that getting this chapter done is a key milestone along the way.

In the same way, I encourage you to promise yourself rewards for the accomplishment of your goals, large and small. This simple technique will help you to stay focused on what matters most, and add pleasure to your life.

Build on your strengths

Use what talents you possess: the woods would be very silent if no birds sang there except those that sang best.

—HENRY VAN DYKE

Many of us think we have to do it all and be good at everything. It's part of our competitive spirit as humans. But what if you worked out what you're good at and then just focused on that? What if you became a master in that one thing, and delegated the rest? If you did this, you would be well on your way to becoming extraordinarily successful. Doing a lot of things fairly well is not nearly as valuable as doing one thing *extremely* well. Mastery is an art that takes time, practice and dedication, but the rewards of being really good at something repay this effort many times over.

Therefore, when you evaluate your performance in the different areas of your life, you should make it your priority to identify your strengths and build on them. If, for example, you enjoy communicating with a wide range of people with different needs — and you're good at it — it makes sense to seek out opportunities in which you can utilise this strength. On the other hand, if detailed analysis and number crunching is not your cup of tea, it's best to get assistance with these tasks or avoid them altogether.

Does that mean that you should give up on your weaknesses? Certainly not! You should work hard to compensate for them, but only to the extent that they are no longer problems for you. Tiger Woods is a classic example of someone who has 'done just enough' to prevent a potential weakness from undermining his entire golf game. Woods's long game — his ability to drive accurately off the tee — is unsurpassed, as is his tenacity around the putting green. What's less well known about Woods, however, is his inconsistent ability to chip out of bunkers — for a time, he ranked only 61st on the PGA tour. With the guidance of his coach, Butch Harmon, Woods improved his bunker play, but only to the extent that it was not going to compromise his overall game. Once that 'threshold' level of performance was reached, Harmon instructed Woods not to practise any more bunker shots, but to put even more effort into developing his strengths — his long game and putting — which is where he has the real edge on his competition. In the same way, when you evaluate your performance, identify and build on your weaknesses so they don't unduly influence what you are trying to achieve. But always give precedence to strengthening what you're already good at.

In the world of business, this focus on strength-building has gathered momentum with the publication of several books based on solid empirical research and analysis. Marcus Buckingham and Donald Clifton, authors of *Now, Discover Your Strengths*, give a comprehensive account of how leading organisations are beginning to encourage their employees to be 'different', to celebrate diversity and to identify their unique talents. Drawing on data from the Gallup research organisation, the authors present their case for 'strengths-based thinking' based on a detailed study of 198 000 employees across 36 companies. Similarly, Tom Rath, from the Gallup organisation and author of *StrengthsFinder 2.0*, has written about the popular online Strength Assessment tool that allows you to identify your top five strengths from a list of 34 possibilities. If you are interested to know more about your specific strengths, I encourage you to read these books and to take the online assessment for yourself.

Once you have recognised some areas for focus or improvement — be they strengths or weaknesses — here are some steps to take:

1 *Clearly identify your area of focus.* Are you attempting to improve on a known strength, or are you improving upon a weakness? It is helpful to articulate the scope of your focus, including what you are *not* focusing on.
2 *Plan with action in mind.* For each area of improvement, it's important to come up with *specific actions* you can take to move yourself forward. If you can't be specific, you'll end up with vague generalities that will only frustrate you.
3 *Document your plan.* By committing your plan to paper (or electronically) you'll clarify your thinking, solidify your commitment, and improve your chances of success.

4 *Act.* Every day, guided by your campaigns and your weekly plan, endeavour to become a better you. There are opportunities in every hour.

The purpose of identifying areas for improvement is to move yourself closer to the kind of life you really want. I recommend that you give up trying to be good at everything, and instead put your effort into developing your real strengths while at the same time minimising the impact of your biggest weaknesses.

Get help when you need it

To know the road ahead, ask those coming back.

—CHINESE PROVERB

The more you want to accomplish, the more help you'll need. Successful people don't get there all by themselves. Indeed, the more demanding your ULP and your campaigns, the more help, support, advice and encouragement you'll need, especially if you are going to do something big.

When you look at all the great achievers in history, you'll see that they have all been highly skilled at organising the people around them, and in getting them on board with their vision. Take, for example, the inventor Thomas Edison. While most of us have an image of Edison working away alone in his workshop, the reality is that Edison's greatness as an inventor resulted from his genius for organising teams of individuals—each with far more specialist knowledge than himself—around a common goal. In the same way, the best sportspeople, businesspeople and leaders of all kinds are masters when it comes to getting the best from their advisers, coaches and mentors.

As you evaluate your progress, actively look for ways of seeking help and involving other people in the pursuit of your ULP and your campaigns. There are three good reasons for doing so:

- *Accelerate learning.* An experienced coach or mentor will help you build the skills you require more quickly and more reliably than you are able to do on your own.

- *Avoid pitfalls.* Because your helper has seen it before, they will use their knowledge and expertise to guide you away from making unnecessary mistakes.

- *Increase accountability.* Having someone else or a team working on your side, investing his or her time and effort, heightens your own sense of responsibility and commitment.

Getting this support does not require you to spend a lot of money. If you can afford it, I recommend that you hire coaches or mentors with the expertise to hasten your progress. You'll find that sometimes the intervention of the right person at the right time can make all the difference because they can put you on the right track or they can teach you a critical skill. Often the investment you make — even for a short time — will pay itself back many times over.

An alternative low-cost way of getting help is to form a 'mastermind' group of like-minded people who commit to actively helping and supporting each other — and I discuss this strategy in chapter 2. According the Napoleon Hill, author of the classic success book *Think and Grow Rich*, 'When a group of individual brains are coordinated and function in harmony, the increased energy created throughout the alliance becomes available to every individual brain in the group'. Many successful people, including Andrew Carnegie and Henry Ford, attribute their entire success to the insights and power they acquired through their mastermind groups. Interestingly, Benjamin Franklin, who I discuss at the beginning of this chapter, organised his friends into a group that he called 'The Junto' with the express purpose of 'mutual self-improvement'. The Junto gathered every Friday evening and operated according to a strict set of rules so that their time 'would not digress into mere gossip or pointless disruption'.

A mastermind group can be an informal arrangement in which you call people individually, or you can set up regular weekly or monthly meetings in which all members of the group support each other. The most effective groups include people with diverse backgrounds — and, therefore, different perspectives — and stick to a formal structure so that meetings are productive for everyone attending.

A key part of evaluating your performance is for you to identify the people, groups and organisations that can help you to achieve what's important to you. Who are they?

Maintain a positive attitude

There is always an inner game being played in your mind no matter what outer game you are playing. How aware you are of this game can make the difference between success and failure in the outer game.

— TIM GALLWEY

You may have heard it said that 'your attitude determines your altitude'. When it comes to evaluating your performance a truer sentence could not have been uttered. Your attitude has a huge impact on how you take feedback on board and on how constructive you can be with the information you receive.

In his talk at TED (www.ted.com), Benjamin Zander — the conductor of the Boston Philharmonic Orchestra — tells the tale of the shoe factory that sent two marketing scouts to a region of Africa to study the prospects for expanding business. One sends back a message saying, 'Situation hopeless — no-one wears shoes'. The other writes back triumphantly, 'Glorious business opportunity — they have no shoes'. Attitude, then, is the critical factor that separates average from high-performing people. Author John Maxwell refers to it as 'the difference maker' and, indeed, has written an entire book on the subject.

As you know, I believe that your attitude is entirely under your control. Attitude is an inward feeling that colours your perspective; your perspective, in turn, is expressed by your outward behaviour. This means that you can choose your attitude irrespective of the circumstances in which you find yourself. I have observed that people who are more deliberate nurture their attitude so that they have the best possible chance of making it work for, rather than against, them. While many elements contribute to the make-up of your entire attitude, I would emphasise two in particular: persistence and self-discipline.

An attitude of persistence is fundamentally positive. You need it in abundance when you receive criticism and when you experience those inevitable feelings of self-doubt. The highest performers quite simply have more stick-at-it ability than others. Many years ago, the founder of *Forbes* magazine, B. C. Forbes, had this to say about persistence: 'History has demonstrated that the most notable winners usually encountered heart-breaking obstacles before they triumphed. They won because they refused to become discouraged by their defeat'. A good attitude will ensure that you don't quit too early.

The second key to a great attitude is self-discipline. Self-discipline is the ability to do what you should do whether you feel like it or not. Again, all deliberate people know the importance of doing the 'right thing' irrespective of their moods and inclinations. The great news about self-discipline is that the more you practise it, the easier it gets: as you reap the inevitable rewards, positive feelings replace any initial sensations of self-doubt or boredom. For this reason self-discipline is just like a muscle — with determined training, it gets stronger and stronger.

I encourage you to pay particular attention to your attitude. It colours every aspect of your life and will be tested every time you come up against setbacks. So make sure you choose the attitude you want — the one that will serve you and others best.

Remember REAL success

Once you accept your own death, all of a sudden you're free to live. You no longer care about your reputation. You no longer care except so far as your life can be used tactically — to promote a cause you believe in.

— SAUL ALINSKY

At the beginning of this book, I took care to define exactly what I meant by 'real' success. The reason I did this was to provide a context for the remainder of the book and to ensure that we were all on the same page before I introduced the concept of being DELIBERATE. Now that we are almost at the end, it's again important to remember that how you define real success for yourself is critical to evaluating your own performance. You want to make sure that the yardstick you are measuring yourself against is *your* definition of success.

You will recall that I defined real success as:

Being on the pathway to the achievement of worthwhile dreams—whatever these dreams may be.

Throughout the preceding chapters, I have repeatedly emphasised two important concepts that are embedded in the above definition. First is the idea of being on a pathway. Success is experienced *today*—not some ill-defined moment in the future. Looking upon success in this way keeps you grounded in the present moment and ensures that you appreciate the potential of *now*. Again, when evaluating your performance, you want to focus on what's happening in your life right now, not on what may or may not happen in the future. Remember, the length of your life is uncertain!

Second is the aim to achieve 'worthwhile dreams'. These dreams are defined by you and you alone, and your progress can only be measured according to what you consider important. While you no doubt take the wishes and needs of other people into consideration, success is all about living your life and not someone else's.

Having a clear definition of real success helps us evaluate our performance and put everything into context. Speaking of putting things in context, there is an old Taoist story called 'We'll See' that you might enjoy.

Once upon a time, there was a farmer in the central region of China. He didn't have a lot of money and, instead of a tractor, he used an old horse to plough his field.

One afternoon, while working in the field, the horse dropped dead. Everyone in the village said, 'Oh, what a horrible thing to happen.' The farmer said simply, 'We'll see.' He was so at peace and so calm, that everyone in the village got together and, admiring his attitude, gave him a new horse as a gift. Everyone's reaction now was, 'What a lucky man.' And the farmer said, 'We'll see.'

A couple of days later, the new horse jumped a fence and ran away. Everyone in the village shook their heads and said, 'What a poor fellow!' The farmer smiled and said, 'We'll see.' Eventually, the horse found his way home, and everyone again said, 'What a fortunate man.' The farmer said, 'We'll see.'

Later in the year, the farmer's young boy went out riding on the horse and fell and broke his leg. Everyone in the village said, 'What a shame for the poor boy.' The farmer said, 'We'll see.' Two days later, the army came into the village to draft new recruits. When they saw that the farmer's son had a broken leg, they decided not to recruit him. Everyone said, 'What a fortunate young man.' The farmer smiled again—and said, 'We'll see.'

The moral of the story? There's no use in overreacting to the events and circumstances of our everyday lives. Many times what looks like a setback may actually be a gift in disguise. And while gifts can turn out to be setbacks, these are always temporary. When we remember what real success is, all events and circumstances are gifts. They are gifts from which we can learn to do better in the future.

In this chapter we have discussed the importance of regular self-evaluation and identified some strategies for putting this into practice. As we found, self-evaluation works best as a long-term habit. It is a *process* that involves carefully identifying what you want to measure and then gathering performance information that enables you to evaluate how you're doing. Gauging your progress—and regularly rewarding yourself—is both informative and hugely motivating. It is one of the keys to your future success.

Ideas for Action

- Identify the goals you wish to achieve in your professional and personal life. What 'measures' can you put in place to track how well you are progressing towards them? Develop a system of self-evaluation that will allow you to look back on your progress over time—say, in one year from now.

- Make a decision today that you will form your own mastermind group. Even if it's just an informal group of like-minded friends, plan to meet with the express purpose of being of mutual benefit to each other.

- Determine what kind of attitude you would like to develop and foster within yourself. Think of people whose attitudes you admire and model yourself on what you find desirable in them. How do they deal with negative feedback and setbacks? How do they make the most of things that go right? Write down some constructive ideas in your journal and begin to practise them today.

We shall not cease from exploration
And the end of all our exploring
Will be to arrive where we started
And know the place for the first time.

—T. S. ELIOT

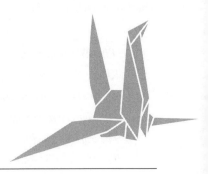

Epilogue — living with success

Before you tell your life what you intend to do with it, listen to
what it intends to do with you.

— PARKER J. PALMER

As I prepared to write this epilogue, something unusual happened. While working on which ideas to include, I got the feeling that coming to a 'conclusion' was something of a false move. After all, no-one has the final answer regarding what it means to be truly successful or knows all the ways of achieving success. Far from wishing to supply such an answer, in fact, the whole purpose of this book has been to encourage open-mindedness and flexibility. With this in mind, I decided to stop and take some time off from thinking about the book. For two whole weeks, I did nothing.

During these weeks, without any effort on my part, two poems found their way into my mind, and they wouldn't go away. When I awoke in the morning they tugged at me for attention and throughout the day I found myself being drawn to them like a magnet. I began to notice that, as a pair, the poems magically got to the core of what it truly means to live a deliberate life. And they perfectly articulate what I want to say to you as we part.

I came across the first poem in the writings of Parker J. Palmer. Written 2300 years ago by the Chinese philosopher Chuang Tzu, it tells the story of a master carver who was commissioned to craft a bell stand for the Prince of Lu. When the bell stand was finished, everyone who saw it marvelled at its beauty, and assumed that it must be the work of someone who was not of this world. But as the poet explains, the carver sees himself as 'only a workman'. As you read the story of Khing the woodcarver, let the words find their way to your heart.

The Woodcarver

Khing, the master carver, made a bell stand
Of precious wood. When it was finished,
All who saw it were astounded. They said it must be
The work of spirits.
The Prince of Lu said to the master carver:
'What is your secret?'

Khing replied: 'I am only a workman:
I have no secret. There is only this:
When I began to think about the work you commanded
I guarded my spirit, did not expend it
On trifles, that were not to the point.
I fasted in order to set
My heart at rest.
After three days fasting,
I had forgotten gain and success.
After five days
I had forgotten praise or criticism.
After seven days
I had forgotten my body
With all its limbs.

By this time all thought of your Highness
And of the court had faded away.
All that might distract me from the work
Had vanished.
I was collected in the single thought
Of the bell stand.

Then I went to the forest
To see the trees in their own natural state.
When the right tree appeared before my eyes,
The bell stand also appeared in it, clearly, beyond doubt.

All I had to do was to put forth my hand
and begin.

'If I had not met this particular tree
There would have been
No bell stand at all.

'What happened?
My own collected thought
Encountered the hidden potential in the wood;
From this live encounter came the work
Which you ascribe to the spirits.'

What I love about this poem is the idea that 'inner' work must precede 'outer' work. You will notice that the carver did not ascribe his success to any techniques or tools — for example, the use of certain chisels or mallets or particular methods of applying pressure to the wood. Instead, he described his own personal preparation and, in particular, the careful management of his own ego prior to his search for the perfect tree.

There is a lesson here for us as we seek to live more deliberate lives. Success is not so much a matter of 'doing' but of 'becoming', and of having the confidence to ask searching questions of ourselves. What do I truly value? What's enough? What am I passionate about? What makes me feel alive? What is life asking of me? Raising and addressing these kinds of provocative questions is the critical inner work, the 'work before the work', that is the gateway to finding your true authentic self. One of the key messages of this book that I would choose to emphasise, therefore, is the importance of asking yourself good questions. When you have a clear sense of what's really important to you and when, like the woodcarver, you have systematically let go of all the extraneous things barring your way, positive action is bound to follow.

A second theme running through the poem is self-discipline. It's no accident that the woodcarver fasted and 'collected' himself and was not in any way hurried in getting to the forest. He knew it would take time to prepare and he was willing to do whatever was necessary. In other words, he was not looking for a 'quick fix' but was happy to put the work in without seeing an immediate outcome. We would do well to adopt the same degree of patience in our own lives. Living deliberately is not a quick fix either, but requires self-discipline, consistency and attention to the small things as well as the big. I believe actress Cate Blanchett got it right when she said:

> Someone might have a germ of talent, but 90 per cent of success is discipline and how you practise it—what you do with it. Instinct won't carry you through the entire journey. It's what you do in the moments between inspirations that matters.

Indeed it is.

The second poem I want to share with you was written by Brendan Kennelly, an Irish writer and scholar who I had the privilege of meeting while I was in Ireland preparing to write this book. As I walked around Dublin City one bitterly cold day in November 2008, I by happenstance saw Brendan coming towards me. I had always been an admirer of his writing and here was my opportunity to meet the man himself and to tell him how much I liked his work. Despite the cold, we talked that day about writing, the creative process and about one of his poems in particular: 'Begin'. For me, this lovely little poem evokes the idea that no matter who we are, or what we are doing, we are always beginning.

Begin

Begin again to the carolling birds
to the sight of light at the window,
begin to the roar of morning traffic
all along Pembroke Road.
Every beginning is a promise
born in light and dying in dark
determination and exaltation of springtime
flowering the way to work.

Begin to the pageant of queuing girls
to the arrogant loneliness of swans in the canal
to bridges linking the past and future
to old friends passing though with us still.

Begin to the loneliness that cannot end
since it, perhaps, is what makes us begin,
begin to wonder at unknown faces,
at crying birds in the sudden rain
at branches stark in the willing sunlight
at seagulls foraging for bread
at couples sharing a sunny secret
alone together while making good.

Though we live in a world that dreams of ending
that always seems about to give in,
something, something that will not acknowledge conclusion
insists that we forever begin.

No matter what your circumstances, what you have achieved or what you are about to embark on, you're a beginner — all the time. I find tremendous hope and encouragement in the last line: 'something that will not acknowledge conclusion insists that we forever begin'. To live a deliberate life is to see everything you do as a beginning, as an opportunity to do better and to be more. If we live our lives from this perspective, all our successes and failures are truly learning experiences.

In closing, I would like to comment on a question that I am often asked: 'How can I keep the momentum of being deliberate going every day?' It's a good question because personal mastery and transformation is indeed a long-term process of development that requires perseverance. Here are my best recommendations:

- Carry your ULP, campaigns and goals with you.

- Make it an absolute priority to plan your upcoming week, every week.

- Take the DQ Quiz frequently and use the results you get to focus your attention on just one or two areas of improvement — don't try to do everything at once. Also, identify your key strengths and build on them.

- Form a mastermind group of like-minded friends who can assist you and vice versa.

- Teach someone what you are learning—teaching helps not only the student, but also the teacher.

- Read or listen to good books every day.

Here we are—we have come to the end. You now know how to be deliberate in both your professional and personal life. There are no limits to what you can be, do or have, except for the limits you put on yourself. You can live an extraordinary life. The key is to begin today, and then never, ever give up!

I dread success. To have succeeded is to have finished one's business on earth, like the male spider, who is killed by the female the moment he has succeeded in courtship. I like a state of continual becoming, with a goal in front and not behind.

— GEORGE BERNARD SHAW

Recommended reading

You are the same today as you'll be in five years except for two things:
the books you read and the people you meet.
— CHARLIE 'TREMENDOUS' JONES

Listed here are all the books I recommend as options to take you further in your lifelong journey of reading. You can also access this list on the website for this book www.artofdeliberatesuccess.com, where each book links through to a relevant website for further details. This allows you to easily read more about each book, possibly look at sample pages, check out reviews, view some author videos, and purchase the book if you want to. Many of these titles are available in ebook and audio format. To access the list on the website, you'll need to register using the access code provided in this book at the beginning of the DQ Quiz.

Success in general

Here is a list of general success titles to get you started in your reading. Remember to come back to these classics often, because every time you do, you'll learn something new:

- *50 Prosperity Classics, 50 Psychology Classics, 50 Self-Help Classics, 50 Spiritual Classics* and *50 Success Classics* — all by Tom Butler-Bowdon

    Together, these five volumes are a marvellous addition to any book collection. Butler-Bowdon not only identifies the key titles in all of these fields, but he also writes superbly about each author's most significant ideas and the influence they have had. Careful cross-referencing in each volume enables you to easily explore books of related interest. It's like having 250 classic books for the price of five!

- *The Success Principles* — Jack Canfield

  Canfield, perhaps better known as co-author of the *Chicken Soup for the Soul* series, presents 64 success principles based on his personal experience of building a $100 million business and on his extensive knowledge of success literature. I particularly like the audio version of this book, which is read by Canfield himself.

- *The 7 Habits of Highly Effective People* and *Everyday Greatness* — both by Stephen R. Covey

  The 7 Habits, which has now sold more than 20 million copies, is a seminal study that presents a principle-based approach to success. Covey's seven habits provide an integrated framework for living a life of integrity and contribution. *Everyday Greatness* is an inspiring book of true stories featuring people who have made a difference.

- *Outliers: The Story of Success* — Malcolm Gladwell

  This is one of those provocative books you'll either love or hate — there's no middle ground. Gladwell argues that success in any endeavour hinges upon certain critical 'historical events' in a person's life. It's worth a read, even if you don't agree with all of Gladwell's conclusions.

- *HBR's 10 Must Reads on Managing Yourself* — Harvard Business School

  A wonderful collection of classic articles reprinted from the pages of the *Harvard Business Review*. The collection includes Peter Drucker's excellent article 'Managing Oneself'.

- *The Five Secrets You Must Discover Before You Die* — John Izzo

  This book is based on Izzo's interviews with over 200 people, ranging in age from 60 to 106. Interviewees were selected on the grounds of having found 'happiness and meaning' in their lives and the book tells what they learned along the way. The five secrets are inspiring and within reach of us all.

- *Why People Fail*—Siimon Reynolds

  Reynolds, an Australian-based entrepreneur and speaker on high performance, identifies 16 obstacles to success and suggests ways of overcoming them. This book not only offers practical, intelligent advice, but is also a real page-turner.

- *Maximum Achievement*—Brian Tracy

  This was Tracy's first book and, in my opinion, his finest. It lays out a 'system' for success that emphasises the power of goal-setting. Tracy goes on to show how these ideas can be applied in the different aspects of your life, from work to personal relationships.

- *Life's Greatest Lessons: 20 Things That Matter*—Hal Urban

  In this inspiring little book, former school teacher and youth worker Hal Urban explores a range of ideas about what it means to live a successful life. With catchy chapter titles such as 'Goals are Dreams with Deadlines' and 'It's Okay to Fail—Everyone Else Has', this is an easy read that nonetheless contains a lot of wise reflection.

Decide: what's important

As you write, craft and finesse your ULP and campaigns, the books in this section will inspire you to make them great:

- *The Secret*—Rhonda Byrne

  Made famous by Oprah, this movie (available online at www.thesecret.tv) introduced millions to the Law of Attraction—that is, 'what you think about, you bring about'. Although widely criticised for its oversimplification of what it takes to be successful, *The Secret* presents a critical idea in a dramatic and engaging way. Try to look beyond the hype to discover the essential message.

- *The 8th Habit*—Stephen R. Covey

  An extensive companion volume to *The 7 Habits of Highly Effective People*. Covey's eighth habit—to 'Find Your Voice and Inspire Others to Find Theirs'—introduces a new dimension to the original seven-habit framework. The accompanying workbook is excellent.

- *The Shift: Taking Your Life from Ambition to Meaning*—Dr Wayne W. Dyer

  Developing an idea first proposed by Carl Jung—that as we get older, we step from the morning to the afternoon of our lives—Dyer argues that whereas the 'morning' of our lives is driven by the needs of our egos, the 'evening' and 'nighttime' is all about finding a sense of purpose. The book (and movie of the same name) beautifully illustrates this transition point in life.

- *Living Your Best Life*—Laura Berman Fortgang

  This book does a fine job of helping the reader identify his or her unique path in life. Fortgang introduces the simple yet powerful concept of the Life Blueprint, and encourages us to challenge ourselves with the right questions.

- *Finding True North*—Michael Henderson

  A practical step-by-step guide to clarifying and prioritising the most important things in your life. The workbook style format of this book makes it very usable.

- *Success: The Best of Napoleon Hill* and *Think and Grow Rich*—both by Napoleon Hill

  These classic books (*Think and Grow Rich* was originally published in 1937) report on Hill's interviews with 500 of the most affluent men and women of his time. Not only does Hill teach us about gaining great financial wealth, but he also sheds light on how successful people think and behave in all aspects of their lives. Hill's philosophies are as valid today as when they were first written.

- *Put Your Dream to the Test* and *My Dream Map*—both by John C. Maxwell

Together these two books invite you to answer 10 straightforward yet powerful questions in order to discover what is truly important in your life. *My Dream Map* is the companion workbook to *Put Your Dream to the Test*.

- *Goal Mapping: How to Turn Your Dreams into Realities*—Brian Mayne

  Goal mapping is a practical technique that helps you achieve any goal you wish. Arguing that most self-mastery books tend to be 'left-brained', Mayne combines left- and right-brain thinking by using imagery to appeal to the reader's creative and subconscious mind.

- *Goal-Free Living*—Stephen M. Shapiro

  This book takes a refreshingly different stance on goal-setting. Shapiro argues that if we focus too much on where we are going, we forget to enjoy where we are. By living for each moment, it's possible to have a successful life *and* follow your passions at the same time.

- *Flight Plan* and *Goals!*—both by Brian Tracy

  All Tracy's books are easy to read and very practical. *Flight Plan* uses the metaphor of piloting an aeroplane to help you create the life you want. *Goals!* provides 21 strategies to unleash the power of goal-setting and goal-management in your life.

Eliminate: focusing on the important

Many of us need help with simplification. Reading about what makes us want what we want is a major step on the lifelong journey of simplification:

- *The Power of Less*—Leo Babauta

  This small volume—how could it be anything else?—is a joy to read. It explores the notion that simplicity is best and goes on to demonstrate practical ways of simplifying all aspects of our lives, from the big picture to the small details.

- *The Clutter Cure*—Judi Culbertson

  Packed (but not cluttered!) with good ideas, this book is primarily about decluttering your home, but it applies equally well to the workplace. Culbertson helps us to understand our strong emotional ties to stuff and then goes on to show how we can overcome them—and feel great about it.

- *Affluenza: When Too Much is Never Enough*—Clive Hamilton

  According to Hamilton, the Western world is in the grip of a consumption binge unprecedented in human history. As we aspire to the lifestyles of the rich and famous, our rates of stress, depression and obesity are all up. As well as looking at the political challenges that lie ahead, Hamilton explains how we as individuals can make changes to achieve more balance in our lives.

- *On Desire: Why We Want What We Want*—William Irvine

  In this fascinating book, Irvine invites us to explore how our impulses, wants and needs influence our feelings and how we behave. Making reference to such diverse fields as science, philosophy, religion and contemporary literature, Irvine advances a new theory of how our desires evolve within us. He concludes with the observation that if we can convince ourselves to want what we already have, we can dramatically enhance our happiness.

- *Affluenza*—Oliver James

  Psychologist Oliver James shares Clive Hamilton's opinion that an epidemic of 'affluenza' is gripping the developed world. He observes that our need to 'keep up with the Joneses' is making us more prone to depression, anxiety and addiction than ever before. Taking a cross-cultural perspective, and drawing on a year-long world tour, James argues that we must begin to really look at our needs rather than our wants.

- *Enough: Breaking Free from the World of More*—John Naish

  For millions of years, humankind has operated on the principle that more is better. But now, thanks to technology of all kinds, many of us have more than we could ever use, enjoy or afford. Nash challenges us to consider the question 'What is enough?' It's a great question and masterfully explored in this provocative, easy-to-read book.

- *The Paradox of Choice: Why More Is Less*—Barry Schwartz

  This is one of my all-time favourite books. Beginning with the amusing story of the author setting out to buy a new pair of jeans, it makes the point that our world has become increasingly complex due to the overwhelming abundance of choice with which we are presented. Schwartz convincingly argues that reducing the choices we have available will lead to reduced stress and anxiety in our lives.

- *Enough Already!*—Peter Walsh

  The 'undisputed king of decluttering', Australian-born Walsh looks at ways of decluttering not just your 'stuff' but also your relationships, work, family, money and even your health. The book teaches one practical strategy that, once learned, can be applied to all these areas.

Language—your internal soundtrack

When you understand the power of language, you'll become awake to its awesome potential within our lives:

- *The Power*—Rhonda Byrne

  In the tradition of *The Secret*, this book examines how positive and negative thoughts influence how you feel and, therefore, the results you get in your life. Byrne has an interesting thesis regarding the different frequencies of certain kinds of thoughts, and argues that thoughts of gratitude in particular have the power to generate more positive energy.

- *The Gratitude Effect* and *Count Your Blessings*—both by John F. Demartini

  In these two books, Demartini—in common with Rhonda Byrne— shows how gratitude can influence all aspects of our lives. Drawing on his own experience of humble beginnings, Demartini illustrates how we can incorporate gratitude into everything that we do, no matter what our circumstances.

- *The Inner Game of Work*—Timothy Gallwey

  Based on his experience as a tennis coach and later as a business consultant, Gallwey challenges us to examine our fundamental motivations for going to work and to revolutionise our thinking about our working lives. His essential idea is that we need to carefully work on our inner thought patterns in order to unlock our full potential.

- *Creative Visualization* and *Developing Intuition*—both by Shakti Gawain

  Now a classic in its field, *Creative Visualization* shows how you can use mental imagery and affirmations to produce positive changes in your life. It is brimful of advice about creating the best environment for visualising, and offers practical strategies for overcoming likely problems and challenges as you develop your skills. *Developing Intuition* similarly focuses on the power of intuition, and suggests ways of sharpening this under-used faculty.

- *You Can Heal Your Life* and *Experience Your Good Now!*—both by Louise L. Hay

  In the 1980s Hay broke new ground with *You Can Heal Your Life* by encouraging readers to carefully replace their negative self-talk with helpful affirmations. Her most recent book, *Experience Your Good Now!* (2010), builds on her earlier work and extends the use of affirmations to such domains as critical thinking, work, money and prosperity, love and intimacy, and ageing. The latter book has an excellent accompanying CD.

Information—managing inward and outward flows

These days—with information available as never before—knowing about how you interact with information is something to be carefully studied:

- *The Mind Map Book*—Tony Buzan

  From the inventor of mind maps (one of the most useful information management tools I know of) comes a practical, full-colour book full of the best mind mapping techniques.

- *The Attention Economy*—Thomas H. Davenport and John C. Beck

  A fascinating look at how attention is fast becoming the newest scarce resource in professional organisations. Drawing on compelling research conducted at Accenture and Babson College, the authors present a way for organisations and their leaders to foster the attention of their staff, their customers and other key stakeholders.

- *How to Have Creative Ideas, Six Frames for Thinking About Information, Six Thinking Hats* and *Think—Before It's Too Late*—all by Edward de Bono

  A master of creative thinking, de Bono in his many books provides an extensive toolkit of techniques and strategies that can be used by individuals, groups or entire organisations. *How to Have Creative Ideas* tends to repeat and summarise his earlier findings and so offers a good place to start.

- *The 4-Hour Workweek*—Timothy Ferriss

  In this very popular book, Ferriss puts forward challenging ideas about how we work. He points out that communication technology is enabling many of us to work when we want, for whomever we want, and from anywhere we want.

- *The Personal Efficiency Program*—Kerry Gleeson

  Based on more than 20 years of research and practitioner feedback, Gleeson has produced a book that is packed with practical strategies for turbo-charging your productivity.

- *Information Design*—Robert Jacobson

  In this somewhat technical book, Jacobson has assembled 16 challenging essays dealing with the nature of information and some of its philosophical underpinnings.

- *Information Overload*—David Lewis

  This book reports on the famous Reuter's study of information overload among thousands of workers. Lewis offers a detailed exploration of the condition he calls IFS—information fatigue syndrome. He argues that IFS accounts for much of what we call 'stress' in the workplace.

- *The Age of Missing Information*—Bill McKibben

  McKibben has a most unusual way of looking at the world of information and the impact it can have on our lives. Upon executing a series of (sometimes very amusing) experiments involving intensive television-watching, the author concludes that less is indeed more. You'll never watch television—or the world—in the same way again.

- *The Age of Access*—Jeremy Rifkin

  Rifkin, who describes himself as a 'techno-critic', takes a fascinating look at how cyberspace is changing the rules of business, the marketplace and, indeed, the very structure of society. His key thesis is that we are moving from a world dominated by a philosophy of ownership to one based on access to information.

- *A Whack on the Side of the Head*—Roger von Oech

  This classic book on creativity is full of ideas for breaking through the constraints on your thinking. As well as being highly readable, it comes with a very useful deck of cards for getting your creative juices flowing.

- *Information Anxiety, Information Anxiety 2* and *Follow the Yellow Brick Road*—all by Richard Saul Wurman

  As you would expect from a guru on how to make information more accessible and, therefore, more usable, Wurman's books are beautifully presented and really interesting to read. *Information Anxiety 2* puts forward the idea that there has not been an information explosion, but rather an explosion of non-information, or stuff that simply doesn't inform. Following the publication of these and several other books, Wurman went on to found the TED (Technology, Entertainment, Design) conference series that can be accessed at www.TED.com.

Beliefs — guiding your behaviour

In your professional and personal life, it's your beliefs that determine what's possible and what's not. Put some of yours under the microscope by reading about the experiences of others:

- *The Answer* — John Assaraf and Murray Smith

  Coming from a business perspective, Assaraf and Smith supply tools and strategies for achieving financial independence and for building any organisation into a more profitable enterprise.

- *Happier* and *Being Happy* — both by Tal Ben-Shahar

  According to Ben-Shahar, the teacher of Harvard University's most popular and life-changing course, happiness is not as elusive as people think. He provides a set of principles you can apply to your daily life.

- *Virus of the Mind* — Richard Brodie

  Brodie, the creator of Microsoft Word and Bill Gates's personal assistant, is also one of the world's leading authorities on memetics — the study of culture's self-replicating aspects. In this book he explains how, if we are not careful, we can allow ourselves to be too influenced by the media, advertising companies and multinational corporations.

- *Excuses Begone!* — Wayne W. Dyer

  Based on Dyer's earlier book *Change Your Thoughts — Change Your Life*, which provides 81 essays on the Tao Te Ching, this book applies a seven-step 'Excuses Begone' paradigm to 18 of the most common excuses we use for not changing our beliefs and behaviours.

- *The Luck Factor* — Max Gunther

  First published in 1977, this classic tackles the question of why some people are luckier than others, and how you can become one of the lucky ones. According to Gunther, 'lucky' people have five traits in common. Well worth a read, this book will challenge your beliefs about your relative luckiness or unluckiness in life.

- *Question Your Thinking, Change the World*—Byron Katie

  This is a short collection of inspirational thoughts and passages on diverse themes like love and relationships, sickness and health, death and grieving, parenting, work and money, and self-realisation. If you want to learn more about Katie's hugely influential self-enquiry paradigm 'The Work', the introduction to this book gives an excellent summary of her key ideas.

- *Rich Dad, Poor Dad* and *Rich Dad, Poor Dad 2: The Cashflow Quadrant*—both by Robert Kiyosaki

  Together these two excellent books are designed to increase your Financial IQ by challenging some of your fundamental beliefs about money. Among the 'myths' uncovered are that you need to earn a high income to be rich, and that your house is an asset.

- *The Biology of Belief*—Bruce Lipton

  Former cell biologist turned popular author, Lipton makes the fascinating case that our beliefs and what we think can influence not only our behaviour but also our DNA.

- *The Four Agreements*—Don Miguel Ruiz

  In the tradition of the Toltec—people of Southern Mexico known as 'men and women of knowledge'—Ruiz reveals the source of self-limiting beliefs that rob us of joy and create needless suffering.

- *Happy for No Reason*—Marci Shimoff

  Drawing on extensive research, Shimoff suggests that each of us has a 'happiness set-point', the setting of which is largely self-determined and not dependent on our particular achievements or circumstances. This book will change how you think about happiness.

- *You Can Change Your Life Any Time you Want*—Robin Sieger

  In this collection of inspiring essays, Sieger invites us to question many of the common beliefs we take for granted.

- *The Millionaire Mind*—Thomas J. Stanley—and *The Millionaire Next Door*—Thomas J. Stanley and William D. Danko

  Together these two books present the findings of the authors' extensive empirical-based research into the habits and lifestyles of millionaires. Two conclusions are that many millionaires live surprisingly low-key lifestyles, and, less surprisingly, have well-developed habits of saving and investing.

- *The Art of Possibility*—Benjamin Zander and Rosamund Stone Zander

  Ben Zander is the conductor of the Boston Philharmonic Orchestra and his wife, Rosamund, is a highly successful coach and workshop leader. They have joined forces to put forward the idea that 'possibility thinking' can dramatically influence every aspect of our lives.

Energy—synchronising your body and mind

No matter what our ages or circumstances, we can all get better at managing our various energies. It makes sense to become a lifelong student of what you can do today, to ensure an even better tomorrow:

- *Ageless Body, Timeless Mind*—Deepak Chopra

  Drawing on both modern science and ancient wisdom, Chopra argues that ageing is more of a choice than people think. Using evidence from inspiring case studies, he shows how we can reshape the ageing process through a proper understanding of our minds and bodies.

- *Meditation: An In-Depth Guide*—Ian Gawler and Paul Bedson

  Gawler and Bedson, two leading Western meditation teachers, explain in fine detail how meditation works and how to practise it well. The book reports on many recent scientific studies into how meditation can enhance relaxation, improve wellbeing and increase performance in sport and in business.

- *The Miracle of Mindfulness*—Thich Nhat Hanh

  In this short and beautifully written book, we learn the art of mindfulness from the renowned Buddhist monk and peace activist Thich Nhat Hanh. With these skills, we can slow our lives down and begin to live in the moment.

- *How to Meditate*—Lawrence LeShan

  A simple and straightforward guide to learning the art of meditation.

- *The Power of Full Engagement*—Jim Loehr and Tony Schwartz

  This book proposes that in the modern world, it is our ability to manage energy, not time, that determines our success at work and in our personal lives. The authors apply their extensive experience helping high-performing athletes to reach their full potential to the demands of everyday life. They show that with careful personal energy management, everybody can become more fully engaged and mentally focused.

- *I Can Make You Thin*—Paul McKenna

  Encouraging us to fundamentally rethink our relationship with food, this book and accompanying CD presents an approach to health that rejects the diet mentality. McKenna shows how you can change your thoughts about yourself and your health in order to establish new eating habits that are sustainable over time.

- *Hurry Up and Meditate*—David Michie

  In this thought-provoking and very accessible book, Michie explains the nuts and bolts of meditation. In particular, his account of recent research into the benefits of meditation is excellent.

- *Inner Excellence*—Jim Murphy

  Applying sports psychology to the world of business and everyday life, Murphy provides a series of performance-enhancing exercises.

A key focus of this book is on helping you improve your mental toughness.

- *The Structure House Weight Loss Plan: Achieve Your Ideal Weight Through a New Relationship with Food*—Gerard Musante

  Based on the important idea that it is your *relationship* with food that determines your ability to reach your ideal weight, this book shows how boredom and stress levels are the main contributors to unhealthy eating habits, and provides practical strategies for taking control back.

- *Happiness: A Guide to Developing Life's Most Important Skill*— Matthieu Ricard

  Coming from a Buddhist perspective, Ricard proposes that happiness is not just an emotion, but also a skill that can be learned. A real strength of this book is the 20-minute exercises for managing your emotions.

Responsibility—accepting and taking ownership

Remember that the choices you make, make you. Why not become an expert in making good choices and in taking full ownership of the consequences of those choices? Check out the following:

- *Change Your Mind and Your Life will Follow*—Karen Casey

  One day Casey sought some professional help to change the behaviour of someone in her life. She learned, for the first time, that the only person she could change was herself. Organised around 12 simple steps, this book provides tools for changing your behaviour from the inside out.

- *Man's Search for Meaning*—Viktor E. Frankl

  Frankl spent the years between 1942 and 1945 in four Nazi death camps, where he was tortured and where his parents, brother and pregnant wife perished. Written from his own direct experience, the author argues that we cannot avoid suffering but we can choose how to cope with it. If you ever feel discouraged by your current situation, this book will put things in perspective for you.

- *The Dip*—Seth Godin

  Sometimes quitting is the right thing to do. But how do you know if quitting now is a mistake when perhaps a little more effort would bring success? This short book helps you answer this important question.

- *What Got You Here Won't Get You There*—Marshall Goldsmith

  No matter where you are in your career, the techniques you've used so far are unlikely to get you to the next level. Goldsmith challenges you to accept this truth and try something different.

- *Feel the Fear . . . and Do it Anyway*—Susan Jeffers

  Whatever you may fear—public speaking, changing jobs, making decisions or anything else—this classic book contains a toolbox of techniques to help you banish your worst demons.

- *The Difference Maker*—John C. Maxwell

  According to Maxwell, attitude is the factor that separates high-performing from low-performing people. He shows you how to overcome the five biggest attitude obstacles: discouragement, change, problems, fear and failure.

- *The Art of Confident Living*—Bryan Robinson

  Based on scientific research into human brain chemistry, this book shows you how to excavate the 'confident self' that dwells deep within. Robinson's art of confidence is subdivided into 10 easy practices.

- *You Are Your Choices*—Alexandra Stoddard

  In this delightful collection of 50 short essays, Stoddard offers simple steps for taking charge of your life. With essay titles such as 'Live from the inside out', 'Stop complaining', 'Intuition is your guiding light' and 'Understand the law of cause and effect', this book is an inspiring guide to making better choices.

- *Choices that Change Lives*—Hal Urban

  Our lives are the result of our choices and the most important choices we make determine our character traits. Urban examines 15 of the most positive traits (for example, humility, patience, empathy and courage) and teaches that it is never too late to cultivate them.

Action—getting work done

We can all get better at getting things done. Don't put off reading the many great books on the subject:

- *Getting Things Done, How to Make it All Work* and *Ready for Anything*—all by David Allen

  These practical books encourage a way of thinking and working that will help you to be more clear-headed, relaxed and organised in your daily life. Structured into an overall framework called GTD (Getting Things Done), all three are packed with useful strategies to help you on your way.

- *The Art of Effortless Living*—Ingrid Bacci

  According to Bacci the most productive, creative and healthiest individuals do less and achieve more.

- *Execution: The Discipline of Getting Things Done*—Larry Bossidy and Ram Charan

  Action—or 'execution', as these authors call it—is integral to the success of all organisations. Through multiple case studies, this book makes the case that execution is everybody's job—including the most senior and strategically focused executives.

- *Finding Flow*—Mihaly Csikszentmihalyi

  Professor of psychology Csikszentmihalyi, who is as well known for his baffling surname (pronounced 'chick-sent-me-high') as he is for his pioneering work on concentration and motivation, has written a fascinating book on living fully in the here and now.

- *Mindfulness@Work*—Daniel Goleman and Jon Kabat-Zinn

  This helpful audiobook introduces the concept of mindfulness and is based on research conducted at the Massachusetts Institute of Technology. It takes the form of an engaging conversation between the authors.

- *You Are Here*—Thich Nhat Hanh

  Coming from an Eastern perspective, the Buddhist monk Thich Nhat Hanh explores the power of mindfulness to transform every aspect of our lives. *You Are Here* teaches practices and techniques for cultivating present-moment awareness in our everyday lives.

- *In Praise of Slow*—Carl Honoré

  Honoré offers compelling evidence that slowing our lives down leads to a more rewarding and productive lifestyle.

- *End Procrastination Now!*—William Knaus

  In this accessible and practical book, Knaus explores the psychological and emotional triggers for putting off until tomorrow what should be done today. He offers some very helpful hints and strategies.

- *The 80/20 Principle*—Richard Koch

  With a modern-day take on the old Pareto law—20 per cent of the effort produces 80 per cent of the results—this book offers many examples of the principle in action as well as strategies that can be applied in your professional and personal life.

- *Find Your Focus Zone*—Lucy Jo Palladino

  Palladino believes that in order to perform at your best you have to actively manage your focus zone—something she associates specifically with adrenaline. Too much adrenaline and you're overstimulated; too little and you're sluggish. This book teaches you how to get in the zone and stay there.

- *The Procrastination Equation*—Piers Steel

  In perhaps the most comprehensive account of procrastination ever written, Steel has produced a truly humorous and valuable book on a problem that is affecting more and more people.

- *A New Earth, The Power of Now, Practicing The Power of Now* and *Stillness Speaks*—all by Eckhart Tolle

  In *The Power of Now*, Tolle extols the virtues of living in the present moment. His other books extend this basic concept and offer strategies for applying it to our everyday lives. Many people find *The Power of Now* a difficult read, but relate much better to *A New Earth*. The latter was featured by Oprah in her Book Club (her interview with the author can be downloaded from Oprah.com).

- *Eat That Frog!*—Brian Tracy

  Tracy provides 21 brilliant strategies for dealing with procrastination and getting more done every day. It's a book I have recommended to many people over the years.

Time—achieving your priorities

Time, and your relationship with it, determines what you do, and the results you get. Make reading about time one of your highest priorities:

- *Getting Things Done: The ABCs of Time Management*—Edwin C. Bliss

  Although old, this classic work gives some excellent practical advice. It can be read in a sitting.

- *First Things First*—Stephen R. Covey, A. Roger Merrill and Rebecca R. Merrill

  Building on the third habit from *The 7 Habits of Highly Effective People*, the authors of this book introduce what they call the 'Fourth Generation of Time Management'. Emphasising effectiveness rather than efficiency, they do an excellent job of explaining the Time

Matrix and its application to our professional and personal lives. I also highly recommend the audio version of this book.

- *Do It Tomorrow and Other Secrets of Time Management*—Mark Forster

  Forster provides some great time-management advice in this very readable book. His central idea reverses the usual adage: we are to try, if at all possible, to 'do things tomorrow' so as to stay focused on what is important today.

- *Taking Control of Your Time*—Harvard Business School

  Part of the Harvard Business School's Results-Driven Manager Series, this motivating collection of short articles includes such titles as 'Be Sure You're Spending Your Time in the Right Places', 'How to Make Every Meeting Matter' and 'Pump Up Your Volume'.

- *Time Management*—Harvard Business School

  A handy book of tools and techniques to help managers make the best use of their limited time. The book is supported by a helpful website from which templates can be downloaded.

- *Freedom from Tyranny of the Urgent*—Charles E. Hummel

  Coming from a Christian perspective, Hummel invites us to look on time in a new way by focusing our attention on things that are *not* urgent.

- *Ten Thoughts about Time*—Bodil Jonsson

  Part philosophy, part history, this best-selling book—translated from Swedish into more than 10 languages—invites modern readers to re-examine their relationship with time. It's a challenging yet enjoyable read.

- *The Secret Pulse of Time*—Stefan Klein

  This book asks—and answers—fundamental questions about time: Why does time fly when we are happy? Why do minutes pass slowly when we are waiting impatiently? Approaching everyday experiences from a scientific perspective, Klein takes us on a fascinating journey.

- *How to Get Control of Your Time and Your Life*—Alan Lakein

  Almost 40 years old, this classic book on time management is full of wisdom.

- *Cut to the Chase*—Stuart R. Levine

  Levine, the former CEO of Dale Carnegie & Associates, offers 100 tips for staying focused on what you value most.

- *Time Management*—Marc Mancini

  Another worthwhile book on time management that identifies 'tips and traps'. It's a quick read, so even if you only pick up one good idea it's worth the investment!

- *Leave the Office Earlier* and *Find More Time*—both by Laura Stack

  Both these books offer sound advice about how to 'find' more time each day. The first book is aimed at your professional life, while the second one is targeted at your home and personal life.

- *Time Power*—Brian Tracy

  Introducing Tracy's 'system' of time management, this easy-to-read book is packed with great advice and time-saving strategies.

- *The Time Paradox*—Philip Zimbardo and John Boyd

  Drawing on extensive research undertaken at Stanford University, Zimbardo and Boyd claim that each of us has a unique relationship with time that influences every aspect of our lives. To help you learn about your unique time perspective, the book contains a 56-question quiz.

Evaluate—managing your overall performance

Be careful what you measure because that's what you'll attract into your life. By reading about the lives of others and what they have achieved, you'll choose your measures carefully and deliberately:

- *Go Put Your Strengths to Work* and *StandOut*—both by Marcus Buckingham

  According to Buckingham, people who are more successful focus on building up their strengths rather than dwelling on their weaknesses. The *Go Put Your Strengths to Work* book takes you on a six-step, six-week journey towards making your assets work for you. The *StandOut* book features a strengths self-assessment tool (with online support) based on work with thousands of high-performing individuals.

- *Never Too Late to be Great*—Tom Butler-Bowdon

  Based on the idea of 'thinking long', this book debunks the myth of 'overnight success' by recounting that many of the most successful people in history achieved their greatness later in life. It's an inspirational book that can put everything into perspective for you.

- *Talent is Overrated*—Geoff Colvin

  What makes some people world-class performers? Colvin argues that it is not simply raw talent that makes the difference, but enduring and repetitive practice in the order of 10 000 hours of effort.

- *On Measuring Corporate Performance*—Harvard Business School

  This groundbreaking collection contains influential articles on performance evaluation by Robert Kaplan, David Norton and Robert Eccles.

- *Harvard Business Review on Work Life Balance* and *On Managing Your Career*—both by Harvard Business Press

  Together these two books provide many strategies for getting the most out of your professional and personal life.

- *Talent is Never Enough*—John C. Maxwell

  Everyone has talents. That's a given. But how do you take the talents you already have and put them to best use? In this book, Maxwell has identified 13 choices that will enable you to become what he calls a 'Talent-Plus Person'. With inspirational stories from the lives of people such as Charles Dickens and sporting legends, this book is both motivational and informative.

- *Ben Franklin Autobiography for Modern Times*—adapted by Blaine McCormick

  Published in 2006, exactly 300 years after Franklin's birth, this beautifully illustrated edition comes with an insightful commentary on each chapter by McCormick. It's by far the best edition of Franklin's autobiography I have encountered.

- *Drive*—Daniel H. Pink

  What is it that really motivates people to do what they do? Shedding new light on what drives us, Pink reveals that the secret to high performance is a combination of three factors: the deeply human need to direct our own lives, the desire to learn and create new things, and the need to constantly do better.

- *StrengthsFinder 2.0*—Tom Rath

  Drawing on research conducted over several decades by the Gallup organisation, Rath helps you to isolate your five greatest strengths and to act on them.

- *The Element: How Finding Your Passion Changes Everything*— Ken Robinson

  In this inspiring book, Robinson reminds us to follow our passion no matter what others might say, or how we have lived our lives up to now. Rich with stories about people who have found themselves working in their 'element'—many of whom took some time (sometimes decades) to identify their passion—the book offers encouragement to us all.

- *Bounce: The Myth of Talent and the Power of Practice*—Matthew Syed

  Full of wonderful examples from the world of sport, this book debunks many of the myths we have about achieving extraordinary success and the role played by 'talent'.

  Education's purpose is to replace an empty mind with an open one.
  —MALCOLM FORBES

My story

God, grant me the serenity to accept the things I cannot change, courage to change the things I can, and wisdom to know the difference.

— REINHOLD NIEBUHR

If you're like me, you will be interested in the background and life experiences of the author of the book you are reading. You may be asking the following questions about me. What kind of a person is he, where did he come from, what shaped him, and what gives him the moral authority to put out a book that people will buy and spend their time reading? And, perhaps more importantly, does he actually practise what he is teaching? What kind of an impact has this advice made in his life?

My mother and father met and married when they were both 20. Growing up in the countryside of West Cork in southern Ireland, they both were people of the land. My father came from a family of eight children, while my mother had one natural brother and also a step-brother. While my parents were of the land, their families did not *own* land and they mostly earned their income from labouring and manual work for local farmers. Although a bright boy, my father left school when he was 13 to work locally and to help provide for his younger siblings. My mother had a couple more years of education, but left school early to take up a job as a receptionist in a doctor's surgery.

When my mother and father met they had 'not a penny to their names'. Soon after they married, they decided to move to the city of Cork, about 32 kilometres from their home. There, they rented a small house and tried to build a life for themselves. My father was lucky to get a job driving a truck for a livestock merchant and this allowed my mother to give up her work — as was the tradition for young brides at the time in Ireland.

I was born in August 1963, exactly a year after my mother and father were married. Some of my earliest memories are sitting in the cabin of the livestock truck with my dad as he transported cattle, sheep and pigs throughout Ireland. It was a difficult life for my father with long hours away from home and little pay. I can still remember the sparseness of our house and the joy of occasional little treats such as a lollipop, or, if I was really lucky, a bar of chocolate.

By the time I was two, my parents had saved enough money for a deposit to buy a small house of their own. For the next few years, they struggled with mortgage repayments, which meant that my father had to work extra hours and be away from home even more. I can still remember the excitement I felt when my father came home from what felt like weeks away. As a young boy, then, I had a very simple existence. Unlike other families on our street, we had no books or other luxuries in our house, and it wasn't until years later that we had a television. This meant that my focus was pretty much on the immediate living environment and I hardly knew that a world existed beyond the end of our street.

When I was three my sister Margaret was born, and then four years later came my second sister, Maura. When Maura was 10 months old, an event happened that would change our lives forever. One day she had a high temperature and my mother took her to the local doctor, who told her that it was probably the flu and not to worry. That night, Maura had a seizure and was taken to the emergency department of our local hospital. I can still recall the state of panic in our house that night as my mother and father frantically tried to revive the baby by putting her in a cold bath of water. Despite all their efforts, Maura did not respond and continued to shake.

After a few days in hospital, it emerged that Maura did not have flu, but had in fact contracted meningitis — a disease which would leave her with permanent brain damage. In the months that followed, visiting my sister in hospital was part of our daily routine. It was not clear how long she had to live or what the implications of the brain damage would be. The months have turned into years and Maura, following several major operations, has been able to live within the constraints of her abilities. These events were to have an enormous impact on our family life together, and in particular on my mother. Whenever I think of what true love means, I always think of my mother and how she selflessly gave herself to the full-time care of my sister.

When I was 10, an event happened that was to lift us out of poverty and allow us all to live life in a different way. My father, who had by now been driving trucks for more than a decade, got an opportunity to apply for a managerial job in the company he worked for. I can remember a friend of my father's coming to our house and 'coaching' him before he went for the interview. At that point, my father had no qualifications, no management experience and, I would imagine, little confidence that he would get the job. In any event, his friend encouraged him, and gave him the most important gift of all: hope. My dad got the job. As well as a much better salary, my father was given a new house, which came as part of the 'manager' package, and we moved to a town 24 kilometres east of Cork City. My father was very enthusiastic about his new role, putting in new systems and ways of working and eventually staying with the same company for almost 45 years until his retirement.

For me, the move to a new town did not have too many consequences other than arriving at a new school and making some new friends. Life in our new house was good, we were eating better food, and there was not the same financial pressure in our lives.

When I was 13, I got a job pumping gas in the Esso (Exxon) petrol station that was right across the road from our house. As it turned out, this part-time job was to introduce me to the world of business and it also taught me many valuable life lessons. Unlike modern service stations, where customers fill their own cars with fuel, this station was serviced. It was my job to talk with the customer, dispense the fuel, take the money, and do other jobs like checking oil and water, and pumping tyres. My enduring memory of this job was working in the winter cold with my hands numb from the cold fuel running through the nozzle of the pump. I did this job most weekends until I graduated from university when I was 20.

Despite the cold, my years at the service station were some of the most enjoyable of my life. Part of the attraction of the job was that the boss happened to own a speedboat and was an enthusiastic water-skier. As an employee of the station, I was an automatic member of the waterskiing 'club', which meant that we would take any opportunity to go for a 'burn' in the boat. With all this practice, I turned into a pretty good water-skier; I was especially good at competitive slalom, which involves navigating buoys at 58 kilometres per hour with a progressively shortening rope. For a time, my friends and I became fanatical water-skiers, spending more time on the water than attending to our school work or upcoming examinations.

At school, I was not motivated. The only subject I really enjoyed was Mechanical Drawing, which I excelled in. I loved the precision of it and being able to draw objects by mentally flipping them around and looking at them from different angles. English and languages were my worst subjects. Thinking about this now, this does not surprise me, as my exposure to books and writing up to that time was non-existent. I cannot remember ever reading a complete book while I was at school. When I was 16 my formal schooling came to an end. Because of my interests elsewhere on the water, my school grades were only just adequate to get me into university. At the time, I debated with myself whether or not to go at all.

A pivotal point in my life came one day on the forecourt of the service station. One of my customers—a professor as it happens, but I did not know this at the time—was talking with me about my future. I was telling him about my poor school grades and that I was just not sure if further education was for me. He stared me in the eye and said, 'David, if you want to go beyond pumping fuel for the rest of your life, getting a good education is your passport to the future. And, you have unlimited potential'. With that, he firmly placed his hand on my shoulder, and I knew what my decision about university would be. For days after that encounter, I remember thinking about how exciting it was to have 'unlimited potential'. This man had belief in me—and I am forever grateful.

The university I attended was about 100 kilometres from where we lived. I lived in accommodation local to the university and returned home at the weekends to work and also get some waterskiing in if the weather was good. The first couple of years of my four-year business degree were difficult. I felt that I had a lot of catch-up work to do and tasks such as essay writing were difficult for me and consumed much of my time. All the while, I kept thinking of my 'unlimited potential' and just put the hours in.

One of the courses I took as a required part of my degree was Introductory Computing. This course involved learning the skill of writing computer programs and using mainframe computers in the technology centre to test them out. While many of my classmates struggled with this course, I found it really easy. In no time, I was developing the reputation of 'computer whiz-kid' and my network of friends began to extend every day as I helped struggling classmates with their projects! I don't know whether it was my early experiences with mechanical drawing or my seemingly innate ability to think about and flip objects in abstract space, but I was able to write computer programs in my head which, when tested, would work every time. Finally, I had found something that I was really good at. And it felt good.

At the start of my third year of university, it was a Sunday morning I recall, I was watching a re-run of a 1973 BBC program *Use Your Head* while eating breakfast. I didn't normally watch television at this time, but perhaps one of my flatmates had forgotten to turn it off before they went out. In any case, I was amused by the presenter—Tony Buzan—because of his colourful shirt and the ridiculous length of his collar. It just so happened that this episode of *Use Your Head* was introducing the idea of mind mapping as a way of organising information in a visual way. I was instantly drawn to the idea of mind mapping and knew right away that I could make tremendous use of this mental tool. As I learned more about the technique, I began to use it everywhere: at lectures, reading textbooks, preparing for essays, studying for exams, writing exams, and even for writing computer programs.

About the same time as learning about mind mapping, I saw a notice introducing meditation—transcendental meditation (TM)—for students. As I learned to meditate, I realised the importance of stillness in one's daily life and how 'tapping into' that stillness can make all the difference to both the quality and quantity of what can be achieved.

I believe it was learning mind mapping and meditation that provided me with the mental toolkit I had been lacking all my life. From this point on, my university grades soared and I even finished first place in my graduating class.

At the time I graduated—1984—the Irish economy was severely depressed. Unemployment was at 16 per cent, personal tax rates were more than 50 per cent, and home loan interest rates were so high that few people could afford to get started in their own home. While jobs were difficult to get, I did succeed in getting an interview for the position of junior computer programmer in a local factory where we lived in Cork. Following the interview, the IT manager of the company gave me a tour of the factory and showed me the computer room where the programming staff worked. During the tour, I had the sense that I did not want to work in that environment and hoped that I would not be offered the job.

By the time I arrived home, I was greeted by my mother who was full of excitement. A telegram (no email back then) had arrived informing me that I was successful in the interview and that I was to start the following week in my first full-time job. My heart sank as I explained to my parents that I would not be taking the role because it just did not 'feel right' and that I believed that I was destined for greater things. I remember my mother being very upset and angry with me at the time.

For the next five months I was to remain unemployed, without income, and living at home. And then before Christmas, a job was advertised in the newspaper that I was determined to get. The role was Trainee Management Consultant with PricewaterhouseCoopers (PwC) based in Dublin. PwC was (and still is) one of the most prestigious employers in Europe and I knew that being selected for the role would put me on a career path without limits. In preparation for the upcoming interviews, I recall putting myself into a state of mind that actually had me believing, without doubt, that the job was mine. On Christmas Eve 1984, I had a phone call welcoming me to the team at PwC. At that point, I was convinced by the power of positive thinking.

Over the next several years, I had a most productive and enjoyable time working on a wide range of consulting assignments throughout Europe. As well as a huge variety of interesting work, PwC offered superb training and professional development in all aspects of the consulting business.

While at PwC, I decided to study part-time for a master's degree in business and management strategy. This study, combined with a demanding consulting career that often involved travel, was to really push me both physically and mentally. Starting the day at 4 am became the norm as I juggled the competing demands of my life. I recall being in a state of total exhaustion as I submitted my completed master's dissertation to my supervisor in July of 1987. I had stretched myself well beyond what I had once considered to be the limits of my capabilities.

About four years into my work with PwC a strange sense of boredom came over me. I began to feel that my life was just a series of repetitious days and that these days were turning into months and years. I knew that

I wanted to do something more exciting, but I didn't know what that might be. And then one day I was invited to give a lecture at the university where I had completed my MA on the topic of my dissertation. As I had never formally given a lecture before, I prepared well in advance but, despite this, I remember the feeling of utter fear—my knees were literally knocking—as I waited outside the lecture room before my talk. During the lecture I developed more and more confidence and, as the feeling of fear left me, I began to enjoy the experience very much. On the way home after that lecture I was emotionally charged and I knew that I wanted to develop a career as an academic and public speaker.

In the summer of 1988, I accepted a job as lecturer in information systems and computing at Victoria University of Wellington in New Zealand. At the time, the university was eagerly recruiting junior staff and my PwC consulting experience was just what they were looking for. When I look back on it now, giving up my career with PwC—I was now a consultant—for an uncertain future at a small university on the other side of the world was a big decision. Nevertheless, I remember how excited I felt when the aircraft touched down at Wellington airport. This was a totally new start for me and literally the first day of the rest of my life.

Within a few months at Victoria University, I realised that it was critical for me to start working on a PhD. A PhD would allow me to be successful as an academic and would also be invaluable if I wanted to return to a career in management consulting. Unlike PhD education in the US, where students undertake coursework and a dissertation, getting a doctorate in New Zealand involved little coursework, but a much more significant piece of research work called a thesis. This thesis would likely take me five years to complete as a part-time student—so I needed to make sure that I chose a thesis topic that would hold genuine interest for me.

After several months of exploring potential topics, I eventually decided to study the information management habits of chief executive officers (CEOs). My thesis was entitled, 'Unravelling the Mind of the CEO: An Information Management Study of 10 CEOs'. I became fascinated by how different CEOs handled information and how this, in turn, would influence how they made decisions and, indeed, their impact on their organisations. A key part of this research was working closely with each CEO over a two-week period to observe firsthand how they worked with information of all kinds.

During this period of research, a theme started to emerge that was to intrigue me for many years. I noticed that those people who seemed the most productive and effective also seemed the least busy. Somehow, the most effective CEOs were able to pay attention to things that really mattered and were able to direct their energy in a very focused way. By contrast, the CEOs who were the most hurried and busy were noticeably more stressed, less productive and less effective as leaders.

My thirtieth birthday was a significant day for me. On that day, not only did I complete my PhD, but I also asked Carmel Whiteford to be my wife. The following year, we were married in Wellington on a beautiful day in May.

In the years that followed my PhD research, I rose to the position of Head of Department within the Business School. All the while, I continued to maintain a strong personal interest in the patterns and behaviours of successful people and continued to undertake research and give seminars on this topic.

In 2000, Carmel and I, and our then two-year-old daughter, Sinéad, decided to live in Ireland so that we could be near my parents and family for a number of years. In Ireland, I continued to be involved in education and was eventually appointed to the position of Executive Dean of a Dublin Business School for a number of years.

I often think back on the unlikely journey I made from the forecourt of a service station to being a business school dean responsible for the welfare of thousands of students. The professor all those years ago was right—you truly have unlimited potential if you remain focused and continue to work hard.

When we returned to New Zealand in 2007, I decided that I now wanted to work for myself and, in particular, to have the freedom to teach and coach people to become more successful in their lives. While my earlier research was focused on the behaviour of successful CEOs, I began to see that these patterns and themes could be applied equally to everybody, irrespective of their life situation.

The result of this decision was the development of my Art of Deliberate Success® workshop and one-on-one coaching program. Since 2008, I have worked intensively with small groups of people to help them find new, better ways of thinking and working. I have had the privilege of assisting 860 people to live lives of greater meaning and significance.

They have also assisted me: my ideas have evolved considerably as I have learned from people from all walks of life.

The book you are holding is the culmination of that evolutionary process. It is my attempt to capture the essence of the workshop and coaching program, so that you too may learn these ideas and put them into practice in your own life. I wish you every success.

Acknowledgements and gratitude

Hillary Clinton once said, 'it takes a village' (in her book of the same name). And in the case of me writing this book, this is certainly true. Over the years numerous people have helped me become the person I am, and I have accrued many debts. Some of you know who you are, while many others may not and—even though we may have had only a fleeting encounter—you all have nonetheless influenced me or my thinking in a profound way. I'm glad to have the opportunity to thank you here.

First, I am indebted to the clients of my workshop and coaching program. On the last count, 860 people had come along to the workshops, participated, and been brave enough to test the ideas and then come back in our follow-up coaching sessions to discuss what you experienced. Each of you has added to my store of knowledge, and the ideas I now have about living a successful life have been significantly enriched by your collective insights.

None of these workshops would have happened without the support of corporate, government and not-for-profit clients who recognised that helping their staff with their 'personal mastery' is one of the best investments an organisation can make. I salute the many HR professionals, training managers and business unit managers who I have had the privilege of serving over the years.

Our network of Business Partners and Resellers play a key role in marketing, selling and promoting the Art of Deliberate Success® workshop and coaching program. I love working with you folks because you make our job so much easier by doing what you do best, allowing us to concentrate on delivering value to clients and our program content. In particular, I want to acknowledge the work and dedication of the following:

- Cindy Bradley, Jan de Zoete, Lisa Hosker, Darilyn Kane, Rawinia Lange, Rachel Lee, Darren Levy, Michael Moka, Kevin Morris, Ivan Moss, Emma Sullivan and Clarisse Sy from the Auckland University Business School

- Hannah Gee, Sue Hope, Digby Scott, Jamie Scott, Dan Tohill and Chrissy Webb of InspireLeaders and the Inspire Group

- Jen Bailey, Keri Bloomfield, Emily Byrne, Kelsi Doscher, Beverley Main and Louise Roberts of the Human Resource Institute of New Zealand

- Jeff Ashford, Sarah Cooper, Stephen Cummings, Sally Davenport, John Davies, Arun Elias, Louise Kotze, Paul McDonald, Tania McGowan, Maciu Raivoka, Susan Simpson, Natalie Stevens, Linda Walker and Keryn Weir of Victoria University of Wellington.

A book like this represents a lifetime of work and learning. For me, its publication marks an important junction because it contains so much of my personal energy—not only from the past four years of intensive research and writing, but also since I first became fascinated by the idea of personal and professional success 24 years ago. I feel the book will allow us to reach a new and much larger audience and I am hugely excited about the possibilities ahead.

Having said that, I am nonetheless aware that some of what I have done is to take certain pre-existing ideas and arrange them in a way that I hope is logical, appealing and of practical value. As I was writing, I often brought to mind these words of Isaac Newton: 'If I have seen farther than others, it is because I was standing on the shoulder of giants'. And now I want to pay homage to some of the 'giants' who have influenced me.

As you have no doubt guessed, I am an avid reader. My library contains thousands of books and audio programs that have shaped my thinking in so many ways that it's now impossible for me to trace the origin of many of my thoughts. Looking at my bookcases now, I can see titles from Stephen Covey, Brian Tracy, John Maxwell, Michael Henderson, Tony Buzan, Edward de Bono, Richard Carlson, Tom Butler-Bowdon, Jack Canfield, Jim Rohn, the Dalai Lama, Dale Carnegie, Eckhart Tolle, Wayne Dyer, Napoleon Hill, Nhat Hanh Thich, Daniel Goleman, Jim Collins, Robert Pirsig, Cheryl Richardson, Byron Katie, James Allen, Martin Seligman, Jon

Kabat-Zinn, Henry David Thoreau, Anthony Robbins, Charles Handy and Marci Shimoff. To these authors, among many others (many of whom are mentioned in my recommended reading), I owe an immense debt of gratitude.

Twenty-four years ago I had the good fortune to meet a remarkable man who changed my life and has since become one of my closest friends. His name is Dr Ivan Jackson. Ivan was the professor in charge of the section within the business school that I joined as a young academic and the supervisor of my PhD program. What makes Ivan remarkable is not so much what he says or what he does (he lives on the edge!), but the great questions he asks. Thank you, Ivan, for coming into my life at just the right time, and for teaching me so much.

In company with Ivan, Dr Blake Ives and Dr Sid Huff were hugely helpful in the early days of my research. Blake helped me to frame a super dissertation topic and to develop a research methodology that proved to be a fascinating 'way in' to the lives of chief executive officers. Sid — one of the smartest people I know, and a master executive development teacher — invited me to spend a sabbatical year at the University of Western Ontario's Richard Ivey School of Business, where he introduced me to the art of case-study writing and teaching.

When I look back on the 24-year evolution of this book, there is one week in the summer of 2002 that stands out in my mind. That's the week I went to the UK to attend FranklinCovey's 7 Habits of Highly Effective People 'Train-the-Trainer' certification course. It was delivered by Dominic Johnson who was, at the time, FranklinCovey's most experienced facilitator. During the course, Dominic really challenged my thinking about how I saw myself, and helped me to see that my self-image profoundly influenced my teaching approach. Following this life-changing experience, I began to alter my 'style' and this enabled me to become a much more effective seminar and workshop leader. Thank you, Dom, for telling the truth as you saw it — it has really helped me to help others.

Following my 7 Habits certification, I had the opportunity to work as an associate facilitator with FranklinCovey in Europe and to meet some amazing people. One of these was the late Stephen Covey himself — one of the most inspiring yet humble people I have ever met. I also met Paula Weir, herself a wonderful facilitator, who continues to be one of my most valued colleagues.

As I mention several times in the course of this book, nearly all successful people have a 'mastermind' group of trusted people who advise and guide them. In my case, I have benefited from the friendship and wisdom of some wonderful people who are passionate about what we are doing. As college friends, John Shiel and I always knew we wanted to do something significant with our lives. John, who is my business adviser, strategist and lifelong friend, has been instrumental in helping me come up with a distinctive 'business model' that has really allowed us to grow. Digby Scott, CEO of InspireLeaders, is one of the most creative and well-read people I know. Every time I chat with Digby, I come away with something new to think about. Thanks, mate! Gerard Whiteford has always challenged my thinking and has introduced me to some wonderful authors and resources that have helped me to think more broadly about what it means to be really successful. Thank you, Gerard, for your friendship and your wisdom. The author and corporate anthropologist Michael Henderson has played a critical role in assisting me to navigate the complexities of the publication process and in introducing me to the right people. Michael, as we discussed, I am looking forward to 'paying-it-forward' when I have the opportunity to help someone else as you have helped me.

Along the way, this book has also benefited enormously from the ideas of Fergus Barry, Jason Brennan, Diane Edwards, Brendan Foley, Jamie Ford, Carolina Gartner, Chrissy Lyons, Hamish More, Tony McCombs, Matt Murray, Denis Orme, James Peoples, Anna Sage, Peter Smailes and Jann Watt.

In preparing the book for publication, I have been helped by numerous people who have demonstrated a professionalism and a commitment to the project well beyond the call of duty. In particular, I want to thank:

- Britta Christiansen, Michelle Dalley, Frances McDonald and Averil Maher, our 'master' coaches and trainers who do an outstanding job with the in-house corporate Art of Deliberate Success® programs.

- Richard Edge, James Barnsley, Hayden O'Toole and the team at PlasticStudio for our branding and website design and for building the online DQ Quiz toolkit and resources. You guys rock!

- Theo Doucas and Chris Naziris from The Trademark Zone for doing a marvellous job of protecting our worldwide IP rights.

- Dr Victoria Coldham-Fussell, my personal editor. Your eagle eye and attention to detail are awesome. Thanks for a wonderful job.

- My assistants over the years, especially Niamh Farrell, who was instrumental in helping me to find the 'mental space' that enabled me to concentrate on this project.

- The Wiley Australia publishing team, who have been fantastic. Kristen Hammond, the senior commissioning editor saw the possibilities for the book and has been a wonderful professional throughout. Alice Berry as senior editor helped with printing schedules and overall administration along with Elizabeth Whiley. Charlotte Duff as copy editor not only brought consistency to the end product, but was also instrumental in improving the readability of the final text. Keira de Hoog took care of seeking all the permissions and legal matters. Gretta Blackwood as marketing manager made sure the book got the right profile and Katie Elliott worked on the publicity. And the overall project has been ably managed by Dani Karvess, who ensured all the elements came together at the end.

I also greatly appreciate the keen interest taken in the book by my good friends Michelle Barber, Angela and Terry Cole and, of course, my golfing buddies Steve, John and Pat.

Finally and foremost, I thank my family who have always believed in me. My mum and dad, David and Mary Keane, are my greatest fans and I thank them for their love and support. My sister Margaret Rohan, her husband, Phil, and their son, Vincent, have been so generous every time we visit them. And, of course, although restricted in what she can do, my 'special' sister Maura Keane has always inspired me to be the very best that I can be. You give me wings so I can fly, Maura.

My wife of 18 years, Carmel, and our teenage daughter, Sinéad, are the very centre of my life. Carmel has been a tower of strength behind me, my best friend, and the one I have chosen to be my life partner. I love you, Carmel. Sinéad, our beautiful daughter, is our pride and joy and we love you very much. Thank you for putting up with your dad—especially when he foolishly tries to give you advice!

Index

Bring the power of real success to your organisation with the Art of Deliberate Success® Workshop and Coaching Program

Positive and profound changes result when your employees, managers, members and students experience the Art of Deliberate Success® workshop and coaching program.

Quite simply, the program teaches you how to achieve greater success in your professional and personal life, and its effectiveness has been proven time and time again by thousands of inspired participants. A highly interactive approach ensures that everybody leaves with practical ideas they can start putting into action right away. It's also a powerful way for your teams to bond together and to define what 'real' success means for them both individually and collectively.

Two weeks following the workshop, every participant receives a one-hour private coaching session with a qualified Art of Deliberate Success® coach. This can be done over the phone or in a face-to-face meeting. The purpose of the coaching is to review what has been learned, to customise ideas to particular circumstances, and to chart an action plan for the future.

All participants are given access to secure online resources such as the DQ Quiz®, workshop templates and guides, and regularly updated recommended reading lists and website links. These resources, along with membership of the program's alumni community and discussion forum, ensure that learning continues well after the workshop has ended.

The Art of Deliberate Success® workshop and coaching program is ideal for:

- employees and team groups of all kinds
- new hires, first time supervisors, new managers and emerging talent
- participants of management development and leadership programs
- small-business owners, sales professionals, health professionals and other specialists
- managers, professionals and specialist staff
- government employees, non-profit employees and managers
- professional body and trade association memberships
- business school students, MBAs and professional qualifications.

We also certify trainers to deliver the workshop and coaching program in-house. If you are interested in learning more about what we offer, contact us directly or call one of our authorised resellers in your area.

www.artofdeliberatesuccess.com

Have Dr David Keane speak at
your next event

David Keane is available for keynote presentations and half-day masterclasses. He is a frequent speaker at company meetings, trade shows, conferences and events around the world.

David knows that sitting through a boring or off-topic speech is utterly painful. So he keeps things a bit edgy. His style is very engaging and he likes to have the audience 'doing stuff' rather than passively listening. He rarely uses slide presentations, preferring instead to get his message across with memorable stories and the creative use of movie clips to engage the audience at an emotional level.

Over the years, he has addressed many thousands of people in all kinds of settings. For example, he has delivered: keynote addresses to CEOs and business executives; conference talks for HR and other professionals; inspiring and motivational talks to people from all walks of life. He has even spoken to teens and to graduating students.

Before he speaks, he works hard to understand the exact needs of your audience and then creates a talk that is custom designed for your group. Audiences rate him in the top 5 per cent of speakers.

Success Symposium

Every year, Dr Keane presents the latest thinking on achieving professional and personal success to audiences around the world. The symposium—which also features two other experts—is delivered in a high-impact 3-hour session. The symposium tour begins in March each year.

For further information about speaking arrangements and symposium cities and dates, visit us at...

www.drdavidkeane.com

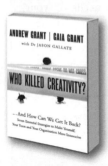